The Arts and Crafts of
Napoleonic and American

PRISONERS
of WAR

1756-1816

VUE D'UNE PRISON FLOTANTE EN RIVIÈRE DE PORTS-MOUTH

Maurier. Vue d'une Prison Flotante en Rivière de Portsmouth.

Opposite. View of Portchester Castle from the creek. Unknown artist.

The Arts and Crafts of
Napoleonic and American

PRISONERS
of WAR

1756-1816

Clive L. Lloyd

ANTIQUE COLLECTORS' CLUB

ISBN 978-1-85149-529-0

British Library Cataloguing-in-Publication Data
A catalogue record for this book is available from the British Library

Printed in China
for the Antique Collectors' Club Ltd., Woodbridge, Suffolk

THE ANTIQUE COLLECTORS' CLUB

Formed in 1966, the Antique Collectors' Club is now a world-renowned publisher of top quality books for the collector. It also publishes the only independently-run monthly antiques magazine, *Antique Collecting*, which rose quickly from humble beginnings to a network of worldwide subscribers.

The magazine, whose motto is For Collectors–By Collectors–About Collecting, is aimed at collectors interested in widening their knowledge of antiques both by increasing their awareness of quality and by discussion of the factors influencing prices.

Subscription to Antique Collecting is open to anyone interested in antiques and subscribers receive ten issues a year. Well-illustrated articles deal with practical aspects of collecting and provide numerous tips on prices, features of value, investment potential, fakes and forgeries. Offers of related books at special reduced prices are also available only to subscribers.

In response to the enormous demand for information on 'what to pay', ACC introduced in 1968 the famous price guide series. The first title, *The Price Guide to Antique Furniture* (since renamed *British Antique Furniture: Price Guide and Reasons for Values*), is still in constant demand. Since those pioneering days, ACC has gone from strength to strength, publishing many of today's standard works of reference on all things antique and collectable, from *Tiaras* to *20th Century Ceramic Designers in Britain*.

Not only has ACC continued to cater strongly for its original audience, it has also branched out to produce excellent titles on many subjects including art reference, architecture, garden design, gardens, and textiles. All ACC's publications are available through bookshops worldwide and a catalogue is available free of charge from the addresses below.

For further information please contact:

ANTIQUE COLLECTORS' CLUB

www.antiquecollectorsclub.com

Sandy Lane, Old Martlesham
Woodbridge, Suffolk IP12 4SD, UK
Tel: 01394 389950 Fax: 01394 389999
Email: info@antique-acc.com
or
Eastworks, 116 Pleasant Street - Suite 18,
Easthampton, MA 01027, USA
Tel: 413 529 0861 Fax: 413 529 0862
Email: info@antiquecc.com

This book is dedicated
to the memory of
Clive L. Lloyd

1920 – 2004

Contents

Overleaf. *A.C. Cooke. Plait Merchants trading with the French Prisoners of War at Norman Cross.*

Examples of Prisoner of War Bone Work.

Chapter One

Introduction and Authenticity

After many years of search and research, thrills and disappointments, it is often difficult for even the most serious and dedicated collector, to recall the circumstances which led to his interest in his chosen subject. In my case, I clearly remember my first encounter with an artefact which turned me into a collector of 'prisoner of war work' and set me on the long rewarding road of collecting, research and investigatory travel, which culminated in the creation and publication of this book.

IT IS APPROPRIATE THAT THE ABOVE HEADING should introduce this volume, as the artefact referred to was a tiny prisoner of war ship model.

Many years ago, with very little money and while browsing among the stalls of Portobello Road, with their hotch-potch offerings of junk, bric-a-brac, and the occasional treasure, I spotted a beautiful little model of a man-of-war, in almost perfect condition and made from what, in my ignorance, I thought must be ivory.

After half an hour of enjoyable bargaining, though by now completely broke, I departed with my prize. Only months later did I learn, from an old retired museum curator, that the material used in its construction was bone, not ivory, and that the little vessel may have been the work of a Frenchman taken captive by the British during the Napoleonic Wars.

Somehow it was not enough to possess my treasured find, I had to know more about it. I needed to learn something of its probable history. Was it really possible that a prisoner of war nearly a century and a half before, may have enjoyed conditions of confinement – and access to appropriate tools – which enabled him to produce such a wonder of delicate craftsmanship? As a designer, and something of a model-maker myself, I greatly doubted it. I knew that Italian prisoners held in Britain during the Second World War had made very good cigarette lighters and similar odds and ends – but this was a very different kettle of fish!

Local libraries could provide me with next to no information. Contemporary writers had been, understandably, more occupied with events at the seat of war, than with our enemy captives safely pent up in depots and prison ships, or under open imprisonment in the parole towns of Britain. The military actions and sea battles themselves, were recorded in such detail that they could be reconstructed like the moves in remembered games of chess – or re-enacted in now popular war games. Yet of the soldiers and sailors who fought in them, little was said. Furthermore, if the conditions and everyday life of many hundreds of thousands – millions in fact – were barely touched upon other than as numbers, how much less was generally known of the comparatively few who were unlucky – or lucky – enough to fall into enemy hands?

Thus began my thirty-year spare-time devotion to acquiring knowledge in a neglected and almost forgotten field of history – the prisoner of war – from the Seven Years' War to Napoleon's downfall in 1815. Knowledge was gained only by rummaging through the public records offices of England, Scotland and Wales and the archives of county towns; wandering round more than a hundred towns and villages where paroled captured officers were detained; visiting the sites of prison depots great and small, and the ports and rivers where the dreaded hulks had been moored and gathering artefacts, relics and other relevant information.

Over those years, during which I assembled what may well be the largest private collection of its kind, my research proved doubly rewarding. Valuable as it was in its own right, the revelation of where prisoners had been confined, made collecting relatively easy. Objects which would now qualify for inclusion in the catalogues of top auction houses could still be found in the vicinities of the old prisons, at prices way below what their obvious quality should have commanded. There were then few collectors of prisoner of war work as such; some who specialised in ship models included prisoner of war examples in their collections – sometimes without suspecting their provenance – as I have good reason to believe. I discovered such items as Noah's Arks and automata in second-hand and toy shops; bone games boxes, ship models and straw marquetry in salerooms and junk-shops near the old prison towns. However, those exciting days – alas for the present-day seeker! – are long gone.

It is surprising that so few British museums, located in or near those towns, have preserved worthwhile mementoes of those wartime days, Peterborough Museum being the great and outstanding exception. It cannot be because of a scarcity of possible exhibits; for prisoner of war work in most of its many aspects, has never been rare. Many thousands of examples have survived to this day; though in recent years, most have disappeared into private collections, at home or abroad. Could it be that the paucity of contemporary museum interest in the arts and crafts of our unwilling guests, was the result of nearly three-quarters of a century of almost constant warfare with France, (not to mention periods of hostility with most of the rest of Europe and America!), and that this country was sick of war, and needed no reminders of it? Or perhaps the sheer abundance of prisoner artefacts which issued forth from the prison markets over so many years, made even the most beautiful of them something of a commonplace.

Some museums of today possess examples of prisoner of war work, obtained either through purchase, donation or bequest; some amounting to quite large collections. However, sadly, in many cases, these treasures are stowed away in basements and storerooms, often divorced from their descriptive labels of provenance. On a recent trip to America, I was thrilled to track down more than twenty bone ship models in a New York museum. The porter who brought them up from the cellars for my inspection confided in me that, to his certain knowledge, it must have been at least twenty-five years since anyone had asked to see them!

I was delighted to note that each was complete with its identifying numbered label. I could not wait to discover whether any of them bore evidence of American prisoner of war origin – for we know that Yankee model-makers were busily engaged in that craft in English depots as early as the War of Independence, and again, in Dartmoor, during the War of 1812. This would indeed have been a great discovery although imagine, then, my disappointment when the curator informed me that the particular ledger to which the numbers referred, had long been irretrievably lost.

The almost unbelievable artistry and craftsmanship which went into the production of the finest examples of prisoner of war artefacts, and the generally high standard of work which came out of the markets; the magical effects achieved by the laying down of tiny slivers of split straw at different angles onto wooden boxes, or the delicate carving and intricate rigging of a superb bone model are wonders that may well inspire the oft-asked question, 'Why only *French* prisoner of war work? What about the British or, for that matter, the American?' It cannot be imagined that *all* Frenchmen, at that or any other time, were naturally gifted and skilled in a wide range of crafts; whilst other men, by national characteristic, were clumsy, idle and ham-fisted. A number of facts contribute to what is really a simple answer.

First, there was the difference in the basic make up of the respective armies and navies

Left. **Wood and Bone Watch Stand** *constructed in the form of a Grandfather clock. Right.* **Bone Watch Stand**. *See also pages 109 and 112.*

of Britain and its foes. Our rank-and-file forces were generally made up of soldiers and sailors mostly of low class and poor education: their numbers maintained by men unwillingly impressed into service and of insufficient importance, wealth or influence to save themselves from the attentions of the press-gangs. There was, however, a call-up into the Militia Regiments, which served only in this country as an internal defence force. This was in theory compulsory for men of all positions between certain ages; but, as it was quite legal for the better-off to purchase substitutes to take their places in the ranks, the Militia was also largely made up of the unskilled and men of lower class.

Napoleon, on the other hand, had introduced conscription, and the men who served in the French army and navy came from every level of society and a multiplicity of trades and professions. Of these we took a disproportionate number of captives – the ratio varying over the years from five to ten 'Frenchmen' to every British prisoner taken. Therefore, the captives in the prison yards of our depots, in the parole towns and on board the hulks, would have represented a cross-section of continental life and talents. Also, of course, they were not all 'French' as more than a dozen nationalities had been absorbed into Napoleon's armies and navies, through alliances or capture.

The second, and perhaps more important, explanation for the existence of continental work in such bewildering variety, quantity and quality – against the almost non-existence of evidence of similar industry on the part of the British prisoners – was that the latter were deprived of the means of vending anything which they may have manufactured; whilst the former had every encouragement to spend his otherwise idle hours profitably.

The most enlightened of all prison of war privileges was the depot market. This was a strictly British inspiration, which was worth a thousand extra guards or sentinals. With its advantages to both captive and local trader, this privilege was a powerful weapon which commanded a great deal of respect from both sides of the wall. Without it, especially at times when we had fewer soldiers, militia and guards than would have been needed to quell a general uprising of prisoners, there would have been a very different tale to tell!

Napoleon, who had walled fortress towns in which to confine his comparatively few British captives, never copied this bit of English administrative wisdom, and allowed no prisoner to produce articles of any kind, for sale to the French public. He did, however, allow his British prisoners to work, under guard, outside their prisons on public works; but even this 'privilege' was primarily in the interests of France, 'as the French male labour market was exhausted by the serious depletion due to conscription of the adult male population'. Even if we had introduced conscription and our captured craftsmen rivalled their continental counterparts, it is doubtful that many would have indulged their talents without a facility for their profitable disposal.

A newspaper article on prisoner of war work, of a few years ago, was headed 'Boredom into Beauty'; but it is probable that, in the absence of a market, the French industrialists, too, would have been more likely to adapt their inventive talents to the planning of escape attempts, or combated their boredom by making life more of a hell for their keepers and Agents.

During the wars, Britain shipped hundreds of thousands of prisoners of war into this country: more than 130,000 during the Seven Years' War alone. Thousands more arrived during the War of Independence, and it is estimated that from the beginning to the end of the Napoleonic Wars another 200,000 were added to our mixed bag of foreign captives. Between the resumption of war in 1803 and the abdication of Bonaparte eleven years later, 122,440 prisoners of all nations were confined under one or the other of our prison systems: the greatest number at one time being 72,000, in 1814; and the lowest 25,646.

These huge numbers of captives were distributed between the fifteen or more land prisons: Millbay, Forton, Stapleton, Winchester, Yarmouth, Shrewsbury, Roscrow, Kergilliack, Pembroke and Edinburgh Castle; the great depots of Norman Cross, Sissinghurst Castle, Portchester Castle, Dartmoor, Liverpool, Perth, Greenlaw and Valleyfield at Penicuik as well as many make-do accommodations where prisoners were temporarily interned at times of extraordinary influx. And, of course, many less-fortunate thousands were sent to the hulks. Officers and 'gentlemen', if they were willing to sign their *parole d'honneur*, were paroled to one of the one hundred and twenty or so *cautionnements,* parole towns or villages.

Those who found themselves in a prison ashore, were the luckier ones – that is, if any prisoner may be called lucky – for in each of the depots there was more opportunity to find a rewarding way of employing the long and depressing days, months and perhaps years, of captivity, than would be possible on a crowded prison ship.

As the following chapters will illustrate, the standard of everyday war-prison life experienced by the individual, depended almost entirely on his own character and ability to adapt. This was not dictated by education or class. Some, known as the *indifférents*, accepted their fate and made the best of it, avoiding trouble and existing – as *was* possible – on bare Government rations. Some were crushed by the misfortune of their capture and drifted into despondency and idleness; Then there were the gamblers and the down-and-outs and, as we shall see, the two terms were almost inevitably synonymous.

The British Government's wise encouragement to make some use of their captivity, created an atmosphere of creative activity which could not be found in any of the places where our own prisoners were incarcerated. A number of prisoners who had heard dreadful stories of the fate of the captive who fell into British hands, recorded their surprise on first entering the depot inner yards. There they found themselves in the midst of an organised cosmopolitan mini-world of hustling. bustling humanity, from beggar to

Four Bone Calvary Models, *two contained in straw marquetry cases. See also pages 62-63 and 124-125.*

baron; every type of man who might be found in the free world – the greatest difference being that their world was, almost exclusively, masculine.

The American, Josiah Cobb, told of his wandering, and wondering, through the Dartmoor yards; of the small stalls and shops and craftsmen busily working at artefacts which would later be offered for sale to the main market visitors.

The stories of the individual depots (see *A History of Napoleonic and American Prisoners of War 1756-1816 – Hulk, Depot and Parole*, Chapters 12–13) have made it clear that just about any man could have found some form of employment. Fatigue parties would have raked in a few pence, and carpenters, sawyers, masons and labourers would have been kept busy as depots and barracks were always in need of maintenance and repair – and there were even occasions when prisoner of war labour was employed in the building of additional depot accommodation. Jobs such as cooks, bakers, barbers, tailors, lamplighters and hospital staff were essential and sought after. Broke-parole surgeons and prisoners with any sort of medical knowledge were always welcome inmates, as were nurses, though most of the latter would have been loblolly boys. Teachers of fencing, dancing, boxing, mathematics and languages; actors, musicians, stall-holders and buskers, and a hundred other enterprises – including coiners and forgers of passports and bank-notes – all of which could add to their small allowances and improve their meagre rations. However, the work of the most talented can be celebrated today by the surprisingly wide scope and quantity of the little masterpieces which have survived as long as two hundred years – and still continue to elicit wonder and admiration.

Close scrutiny can evoke many questions such as where they obtained their tools and their raw materials – questions dealt with in appropriate chapters. As to the source of their raw materials, but the second can be answered in part in three words – 'they wasted nothing' and they had, in over-abundance, that blessing to the industrious, and curse to the idle – 'time'. Every scrap of wood, bone, metal, string, wire, cloth, nails, glass – in fact anything which might have potential for conversion into a saleable something, was valued by the creative craftsmen, who turned debris into desirable artefacts. For example, a large picture of the Portsmouth hulks in my collection, was painted by Ambroise Louis Garneray, on a joined canvas of two pieces of mis-matched sailcloth. There is a also record of bones thought unsuitable for model-making, being crushed into a powder and boiled for use by the professional pastry-makers as shortening.

The ingenuity with which they fashioned next to nothing into something worthwhile – and often beautiful – would today have earned them the title of 'Masters of Recycling'. There is, however, some evidence which suggests that a few were guilty of 'recycling' before the material had outlived its original purpose!

There is a story of Dartmoor counterfeiters stealing lead from the depot roof, for use in the coining of dud English shillings. Woodcarvers on the ex-Spanish Chatham hulk, *Bahama*, made fine cedar snuff-boxes and razor-cases from the fabric of their floating prison and a contemporary writer tells us of other opportunists. When the first consignment of prisoners were sent to the newly built depot at Perth, in 1812, they were transported by frigate and landed at Dundee. On their march to Perth, they were lodged in the church of Inchture, and during the night 'they found means to extract the brass nails, and to purloin the green cloth from the pulpit and seats, with every other thing they could lay their hands on'. Perhaps if those light fingers which lifted anything liftable, were later employed in transforming their ill-gotten raw material into something of beauty, their sacrilege might have been somewhat mitigated!

Authenticity.

The most frequently posed enquiry to anyone professing to be knowledgeable on the subject is how can a collector be certain that a piece of prisoner of war work is in fact made by a prisoner. The simple answer is that, without an irrefutable provenance or proof of its whereabouts since the day of its creation, 'You can't!' The shock of that reply can be softened a little in a number of reassuring ways. Just as a painting may be attributed to a certain period, artist or school, by the apparent age of its canvas, style, technique and subject matter, a similar approach can be applied to prisoner of war work – in both cases much depending upon the experience and 'gut-feeling' of the person making the judgement!

It cannot be doubted that many local civilians who possessed a jack-knife, a saw and a file, plus a little talent, would have been capable of producing the less challenging artefacts, such as teetotums[1], apple-corers, pipe-tampers or the like. Some may well have seen an article offered for sale in a depot market and thought that they could make it just as well, then gone away and achieved that boast. It is, however, likely that these attempts would have been only 'one-off' efforts, for they could never have competed price-wise with *Les Laborieux,* who did not have to pay for the roof over their heads or have to worry where their next meal was coming from – simple though it may have been.

The same applies to the 'classics' of prisoner of war work, the straw marquetry, the ship models, guillotines and automata, etc. There was no lack of British craftsmen and skilled model-makers – as a visit to the National Maritime Museum will show – but in the past it would have been unprofitable for them to produce 'fake' prisoner of war work. To have made, say, a 74-gun ship-of-the-line, with fine carved stern and figurehead, retractable guns and hair rigging, would not have been a financially sound venture.

There is another interesting category of work which, although strictly speaking and date-wise falls outside the period of our study, nevertheless might be welcomed into any collection – 'ex-prisoner of war work'. It cannot be imagined that men who had spent periods of captivity varying from a few months to ten or twelve years, during which time

Bone Ship Model in a Straw Marquetry Case*. See also page 95.*

they had learned or perfected a profitable art or craft, would have all downed tools when the peace bells chimed. We know that a fair number of continentals did not return to Europe when released in 1814/15. Some had married English girls, whilst others, staunch Bonapartists, were uncertain of the welcome they could expect in a new Bourbon France. It is possible that any prisoner of war work collection could include the odd 'ex-prisoner of war' example, as the following few disparate examples might suggest:

> The huge bone ship model in the Watermen's Hall in London, which is reputed to be the largest of its kind in the world, was made by ex-prisoners of war in 1825.

Louis Garneray, who as a lad escaped from the artistic career planned for him by his father, to follow an adventurous life at sea, painted during most of his captive years on the Portsmouth hulks. He did not go back to sea after the war, but on his return to France became painter to the Duc d'Angoulême in 1817.

> The great model of the Norman Cross Depot which was preserved in the Musée de l'Armée in Paris for many years was made by ex-prisoner of war M. Foulley, when he returned home in 1815.

So much for authentication. Perhaps of more importance to the collector, should be the privilege and pleasure of handling and studying a thing of beauty, whether or not it has the added romance of a background history of war, captivity and fortitude. If one day, in some mysterious way, a gadget could tell us whether an article is of actual prisoner of war manufacture or not, either way the treasure itself is no less beautiful.

---

1. Teetotum – child's four-sided spinning top. Any top spun with the fingers.

Chapter Two

The Depot Markets

REGULATIONS FOR ALL WAR PRISONS Article 9:
'All Dealers (excepting such as Trade in Articles not proper to be admitted into Prison) are to be allowed to remain at the principal Gate of the Prison from six o'clock in the morning until three in the Afternoon, to dispose of Merchandize to the Prisoners; but any of the Prisoners who shall be detected in attempting to introduce into the Prison Spirituous Liquors, or other improper Articles, or receiving or delivering any Letter, shall be punished for the Abuse of this Indulgence, in such manner as the Commissioners may direct.'

NAPOLEON ONCE DESCRIBED ENGLAND as 'a nation of shopkeepers'. His description was not intended as a compliment, but the prisoners captured from France and her allies had good reason to be thankful for the shopkeeper mentality which inspired that most admirable of prisoner of war privileges – the prison markets. Napoleon also opined that, 'Ability is of little account without opportunity'; and without the opportunity to profitably dispose of their wares, only the most dedicated men of ability among the prisoners would have spent their time in producing the little works of art and craft which adorn this volume. Without the market, which provided an outlet for their industry, and was the source of the small luxuries made possible by its rewards, the ranks of the trouble-makers, escapees and delinquents would doubtless have been greatly added to.

Most surviving prints and engravings of the old prisoner of war depots present a

Above. Arthur David McCormick. Prisoners of War trading at Portchester Castle.

chilling aspect of bleak remoteness; the high walls providing a forbidding screen which preserved the mysteries within from the gaze of the local inhabitants – as effectively as it would appear to shut off the outside world from its foreign inmates. In this they present a false picture. Over the years many thousands of the inmates of these closed prisons would have come into contact with large numbers of British civilians, through the commercial intercourse of the prison markets. Admittedly, the prisoners to be met with would have been, in the main, the privileged representatives of their fellows, who were delegated to buy and sell on their behalf. Direct knowledge of the main body of prisoner population would have been limited to what could be observed through the railings and grilles which separated the inner yards from the trading area. The dealing and bargaining and friendly familiarity of the market place would ensure that few basic facts of prisoner of war life were secret from the local countryfolk or the country at large.

Every prisoner of war establishment, and even the hulks, had recourse to some sort of two-way trading facility. The great depots had markets which would have compared in colour, variety and sometimes in size, with those of their local towns and villages. Captives on the hulks, on the other hand, depended on the daily bum-boats, which arrived with all manner of produce, and on members of the ship's company who sold prisoner of war work ashore in return for a rake-off, or carried out commissions (not always lawful!) on behalf of individual prisoners.

The market areas were usually located between the inner and outer walls of the prisons, often in the secured yard within the main entrance. In the case of smaller depots the buying and selling was carried on through grilles in the prison wall or at the prison gate. A Scottish observer described such transactions at Edinburgh Castle in the early 1800s: 'There was just room between the bars of the palisade for them to hand through their exquisite work, and receive in return the modest prices which they charged'.

There were other prisons where trading possibilities fell between the dealing 'through the grilles' facility and the busy two-way markets of such great depots as Perth, Dartmoor and Norman Cross. In the 1780s, the market day ar Stapleton Prison, near Bristol, opened in the morning at ten o'clock and closed at three in the afternoon. It was typically situated 'between the inner and outer walls, just inside the great main gate, within sight of the porter's lodge', but only the local traders were allowed into the yard. At that time this comparatively small depot housed a thousand or more Spanish sailors, a very few Dutch and some French and, as it had first opened its gates as recently as the first year of the decade, the authorities might well have doubted its untried security.

There was usually a sound reason behind what may at first appear petty prohibitions. The inadmissibility of some religious literature – John Wesley's translations of tracts into Spanish, French and Dutch being a case in point – is explained and justifiably excused by an order which warned that 'intrigues, enticements, or force may not be used to oblige any prisoner to change his religion'.[1] Although the Spanish at Stapleton were cut off from a buying public, there is, nevertheless, evidence that they had already got down to work!

> 'The country people might sell anything they chose, provided that they did not smuggle spirits, letters, or tools for escape. The prisoners paid for their purchases out of the small grant from their own Government, a penny a day for sailors and boys, and twopence for bosuns and mates. In return they sold or exchanged the models and toys they had manufactured.[2]

It may well be that some enterprising country dealers in most of the markets may have acted as retailers of prisoner of war work in their villages and towns.

From the early hours of the morning on two or three days of each week – and in some cases, every day except Sunday – the British dealers and suppliers from the neighbouring towns and villages made their way to the depots to set up shop in the market precinct. The approach roads to such great prisoner of war establishments as Dartmoor, Perth, Norman Cross, Greenlaw and Valleyfield, became veritable caravan routes, crowded with every type of transport and bundle-carrying hawker and vendor. The long train included the carriers of chickens and live-stock, brewers' drays and fish trucks, wagons and handcarts laden with all manner of merchandise and provisions. Then there were the Devon countrywomen mounted on their donkeys and each one driving before her a dozen or more panniered pack animals, loaded with the produce of the local farms and smallholdings – all headed prisonward.

Many of the market stall-holders were women – some of them great characters whom we shall meet later. At the end of the day's trading, they often had quite long homeward journeys to face, and if the trail to farm or village led over Dartmoor, the prospect could be daunting. It is said that the superstitious among them packed up early, untethered their donkeys from the market railings and timed their departure 'so as to clear the pixie-haunted moor before dark; and from the upper windows of the prison one might watch them winding the distant mule tracks sinuously like torpid snakes'.

Tobacco, coffee, tea and clothing were always in particular demand and the lure of easy selling to so many literally captive customers brought dealers from far and wide. With no alternative shopping facilities at hand, it might be assumed that the prisoners would have been at the mercy of the hucksters and that, in what was to a great extent a seller's market, the prices of such 'necessities' as tobacco, coffee and tea would have rocketed sky-high and that take-it-or-leave-it would have been the order of the day. It is therefore pleasant to record that the markets were controlled by a strict set of fair-trading rules and regulations, designed to protect both prisoner and native from the unscrupulous on either side. There are stories of prisoner swindles practised on gullible visitors to the market-places, and no doubt there were crooked officials and traders who sometimes bent the rules against the prisoners, but in general the system worked well.

The price of all produce brought into the depots was pegged to that pertaining in the principal market town of the district. It was one of the many duties of each appointed Agent for Prisoners of War to see to it that his depot was kept informed of the current rate on all incoming merchandise for that day. Before the traders were allowed to enter the market they were checked in by official market clerks who, chalk in hand, weighed their merchandise and marked each bale, sack and crate with the maximum asking price. No doubt this could only have been strictly applied to farm produce, beer, tobacco and provisions where the current prices were easily ascertainable; for to have covered the thousand and one items which we know were put on display, from 'gold' watches to second-hand clothing, would have been a mammoth task – and the market would never have got under way.

This was an admirable procedure and, where the Agent was conscientious and the clerks uncorrupted, the prisoner-shopper was well protected. I have encountered few complaints in the memoirs of ex-prisoners – although the French General Pillet, who for good reason was sent to the prison ship *Brunswick* at Chatham, and whose hatred of everything English taints his every memory, says that the vendors on the Medway's floating equivalent of the depot markets – the two bum-boats which came alongside with tea, sugar, candles, tobacco, butter and potatoes – demanded prices one-third higher than those obtainable on shore.

Once past the check-points, the unloading began and no time was lost in setting up the goods for sale, for only when everything was ready were the privileged prisoner vendor/purchasers allowed into the square. Most of the local traders put up trestle tables or market stalls on which to display their wares, or hawked their goods on trays or trolleys throughout the markets; but some of the regulars were concessionaires of stalls and booths, properly built and permanently sited. These took on the appearance of established shops, with painted fascia-boards, owners' names and advertising blurbs. That such fixed stalls and established shops were a feature of the trading areas of the war prisons, is confirmed by the catalogue of the auction at Norman Cross which followed the demolition of the Depot in 1816, when the pebbled paving, the market fence and the material of the stalls and shops, realised a highest bid of twenty pounds.

When all was set up, the sound of a bugle or the clanging of the market bell was the signal for the guards to admit the waiting prisoners from the adjoining yards. It also announced that everything was ready for the commencement of another day's commercial battle between the nations. Chalk-marked prices or not, there must have been some competition between rival British vendors, and it cannot be imagined that the continentals would have been happy buyers or sellers without a good deal of haggling and chaffering, of bargaining and bartering – where the quality of the local produce, the strength of the beer and the soundness of fruit and vegetables, would be unfavourably compared with the perfections of the prisoner-made articles offered for sale or exchange.

However, all this would have been more in the nature of good-humoured marketmanship than serious bickering; for each was conscious of the importance of the other to his own well-being. What was misfortune to the prisoner of war, was a godsend to our countryfolk – albeit the god was Mars – presenting as it did undreamed of possibilities for trade in areas where, in peacetime, there was little demand for their produce. As our countrymen imprisoned in France, and enjoying no such privilege, knew only too well, the life of a prisoner of war confined in a depot without a market or some other means of selling and buying, could be miserable indeed.

Just as the merchandise which came in from the outside world was subject to strict rules of admissibility, so were the manufactures from the other side of the wall. The regulations regarding the former, mentions 'articles not proper to be admitted into the Prison' and likewise, there were items of prisoner of war work which it was considered 'not proper' to allow out from it. Restrictions were imposed in cases where, either because of price-cutting or superior quality, or both, the prisoner-made article came into serious competition with the products of our local craftsmen and cottage industries. The chief among these was the straw hat and bonnet making, which was banned from an early date and, from 1806 onwards, the straw plait from which these millinery confections were made. This ban was nation-wide, designed to prevent loss of revenue on these taxable items and for the protection of the local workers in straw whose livelihood depended on the craft. Yet the trade was so lucrative – both to the prisoner and the merchants on the outside who encouraged them – that this was the most disregarded of all interdicts. The historian of the Norman Cross Depot, Dr Thomas Walker, was acquainted with a very old lady, still living at the beginning of this century, who remembered the Peterborough children following one particular market-woman through the streets and chanting:

'Wind and storm, hail or snow,
To the Barracks she will go.'

It was rumoured that she did not earn this little rhyme because of her assiduity to legitimate market business, but because it was supposed that she smuggled straw into

Norman Cross prison depot and brought out finished straw plait, hidden under her clothing.

Apart from such general prohibitions there were many local restrictions. These usually resulted from complaints put forward by tradesmen and craftsmen in the neighbourhood, who felt, with some justice, that it was unfair that foreign captives – who were being kept at the expense of their taxes – should be in a position to undersell them.

Although there was never any deliberate plan on the part of the authorities to deprive prisoners of any legitimate method of adding to their petty cash or even, as some did, accumulating small fortunes, it is not surprising to find that where the interests of prisoners and locals clashed, the Transport Board usually came down heavily on the side of our own countrymen.

The records of local prohibitions are fascinating in their variety and provide an interesting insight into the resourcefulness and industry with which many of the captives set about the task of bettering their lot. In 1807, for example, an enterprising group of prisoners at Millbay offered to undertake the manufacture of worsted gloves for one of the British regiments. The offer was turned down, not only for the sake of the women knitters in the district, but because of the not unreasonable fear that all the Government-issue blankets would soon disappear into the new 'factory', to reappear soon after as handwear for our troops.

Then there was the thread-lace making at Portchester Castle, which enjoyed great success until the tools and equipment were broken up by Government order. Similarly, the prisoner-built theatre in that same castle, which staged productions of such excellence as to arouse the envy of the local theatre managers who, it was said, engineered one of the meanest of restrictions – its closure to the visiting public – though there may well have been more understandable reasons. At Penryn, the activities of the French pastry-makers and confectioners were halted after complaints from the Cornish traders in those lines; but on a recent visit to Scotland I sampled a prisoner of war confection still on sale to this day – 'Jethart Snails' – said to be based on a recipe first introduced by a French officer paroled to the Border town of Jedburgh in 1811. Paroled doctors and surgeons at Welshpool came under fire for injecting private people and inoculating them against smallpox. Boot and shoe making was forbidden to parolees at Portsmouth, because they were undercutting the wholesalers in the area – and many other examples could be cited.

Any sympathy which might be aroused on behalf of those enterprising captives whose bright ideas came to nought, has to be tempered with the realisation that many of the people whose crafts were being protected lived on the borderline of poverty at the best of times, whilst the prisoners need never starve whilst protected by a subsistence allowance, even if prohibitions did leave him unemployed. It is also the duty of any government to protect its revenues and its peoples.

There was one general prohibition which was aimed at the protection of the morals, rather than the pockets, of our countryfolk – a letter to the French Government from the Transport Office in 1800, informed them that:

> 'The Prisoners at all the Depots in this Country, are at full Liberty to exercise their Industry within the Prisons, in manufacturing and selling any Articles they may think proper, excepting Hats, which could affect the Revenue in Opposition to the Laws; Obscene Toys and Drawings, and Articles made either from their Clothing or the Prison Stores.'

The improper artwork referred to was no new branch of prisoner of war industry. In

1798, only a year after Norman Cross opened its gates for the first time, the Agent received an instruction from the Board:

> 'Obscene figures and indecent toys and all such indecent representations tending to disseminate Lewdness and Immorality exposed for sale or prepared for that purpose are to be instantly destroyed.'

However, a brisk undercover traffic in pornography, much of which could be described as lewdly amusing and 'soft' by today's standards, rather than obscene, continued on and off in most depots throughout the wars. It was regarded with real or pretended horror by the authorities at that time – although it is to be doubted that many of our country people would have been irredeemably corrupted by these curiosities.

That the illicit business was still going strong years later, is shown by a letter received by the Home Secretary, Lord Liverpool, in 1807, requesting that magistrates should help in stopping the prison market trade in prohibited articles, particularly the selling of suggestive artefacts, 'to the great injury of the morals of the rising generation'.

Dr T. J. Walker would have preferred to leave this aspect of prisoner of war work out of his history of Norman Cross Depot. Writing in 1913, he said:

> 'One would gladly pass over another illegal traffic which was with difficulty suppressed. To the disgrace of those British purchasers whose depraved tastes made it worth the while of the prisoners to expend their ingenuity on the production of obscene pictures and carvings, it must be mentioned that an illicit, secret trade in such articles was carried on at Norman Cross'.

It would appear that the Transport Board had received a number of complaints from some indignant locals about trafficking in what Walker called 'this vicious manufacture', and swiftly took action. On the 18th December, 1808, the prison market was completely closed down, to the great distress of both pornographers and innocent prisoners alike. The Order which brought about the shut-down acknowledged that the 'innocent were to suffer with the guilty' but added:

> 'If they connive at such scandalous proceedings they themselves can no longer be considered free from blame, but if they give the names of those who make the toys and drawings the market will again be opened.'

The names came to light through intercepted mail, and the ringleader, a prisoner with the nickname Black Jimmy, his gang and their English accomplice, a Corporal Hayes were caught red-handed with a collection of their curiosa offerings. Black Jimmy and his partners in erotica were sent to a Chatham prison ship, most probably the *mauvaise sujets* hulk, *Sampson*.

Despite the restrictions which applied to all prisons and the many others which affected only certain areas, there still remained a wide scope of opportunity for the ability and something-from-nothing ingenuity of the talented and industrious among the prisoners. The truth of this was fully on display on every market day. Only the most incurious of people living within reasonable distance of a depot would have neglected to visit the prison market, at least occasionally, during the long war-time years of its existence. Once inside the gates, the visitor would find as lively a scene of bustling activity, of buying and selling and shouting of wares, as could be found on market day in his own town or village square. He could not fail to be fascinated by the ingenuity and variety of prisoner of war work displayed on the stalls and stands ranged round the periphery of the market. Little marvels in bone, straw, wood, hair and what have you, each piece carefully labelled in accordance with the strict 'trades description' regulation – with the maker's name and his asking price. As these were only lightly attached, few prisoner-craftmen's tags have survived – the Peterborough Museum collection includes no more than half a dozen.

For the visitors' amusement and entertainment, there were prisoner puppeteers and Punch and Judy shows; the buskers who wandered through the market, playing the fiddle, flute or flageolet, in the hope of reward in the form of small change; and 'numerous groups of jugglers, tumblers and musicians, all of whom followed their various callings, if not invariably with skill, always with most praiseworthy perseverance.'

The first-time visitor, who may have imagined that he was about to see poor prisoners selling their work and buying small quantities of little luxuries with the proceeds, would have been in for a surprise. What he was most likely to see, to his amazement, would be certain prisoner-customers buying goods in great variety and in quantity not measured by the ounce or pound but often by the hundredweight. This merchandise was then carted into the inner prison yards by sack, crate and barrow-load. The onlooker could not, of course, know that these shoppers were of two distinct types: those who were buying on behalf of groups and messes of their fellows, and others who were wholesalers – no doubt including a few representatives of the unpleasant 'broker' fraternity – who bought stock for resale on their own pitches in the inner markets.

If, along with his feelings of amazement, fascination and amusement, the visitor found room for some compassion for the unfortunate situation of these men, and admiration for their enterprise, then so much to his credit – but he had also to beware. He would, for instance, be most unwise to carelessly give change for a bank note at the request of even the most honest-looking prisoner – particularly if he were a Frenchman – and he could not be accused of unfair mistrust, or extravagant caution, if he bit hard on any silver offered in change after having made a purchase. Forgery and coining were arts and sciences at which the French prisoners excelled and practised in just about every place of confinement in the land – undeterred by the truly terrible punishment meted out to the detected and convicted. The innocent and too-trusting recipient of their false notes or coins was also in great danger. If found in possession of, or 'uttering' (trying to pass), the forgeries, he might well find himself on a transport vessel bound for Botany Bay, or even end his days on the gallows. The following newspaper article is but typical of what was going on wherever there were prisoners of war, at least during the Napoleonic Wars:

The Perth Courier. 19th September, 1813

'We are sorry to learn that the forgery of notes of various banks is carried on by the prisoners at the depot, and that they find means to throw them into circulation by the assistance of profligate people who frequent the market.

'The eagerness of the prisoners to obtain cash is very great, and as they retain all they can procure, they have drained the place almost entirely of silver.'

'Last week a woman coming from the Market at the Depot was searched by order of Captain Moriarty, when there was found upon her person pieces of base money in imitation of Bank Tokens (of which the prisoners are suspected of being the fabricators), to the amount of £5. 17s.

'After undergoing examination, the woman was committed to gaol.'

The markets were the easiest outlet for forged notes and false coins. No matter how often warnings and reward notices were posted up, nothing could stop the profitable but dangerous trade. The market inspectors whose job it was to scrutinise all paper money coming into or leaving the prisons were occasionally successful in detecting fraud; but unsuspecting dupes and willing accomplices among the market visitors were responsible for the distribution of the penman's art, to the tune of many thousands of pounds.

The meeting-ground of the trading area was a natural attraction for the worst as well as the best of both captive and market visitor alike. It was there that the makers of forbidden products met and contracted with the shady local dealers – and where the hatchers of escape plots purchased outside help. It has to be admitted that, in these dealings, our own country-men show up in a worse light than their foreign associates. Without the profit-inspired encouragement of the handlers of their illegal merchandise, it would have been pointless for the prisoners to have put themselves at risk by ignoring Government prohibitions. The unparoled prisoner of war who made good his escape can be as much admired as his bribed British accomplice can be condemned.

The market guards had always to be on the alert for escape attempts by prisoners in disguise. The second-hand clothing stalls did a roaring trade, for the first ambition of any captive with cash was to get out of his sulphur-coloured TOTO suit and blue-striped shirt as soon as possible, and the fashions in the inner prison yards ranged from complete nudity of the unsuccessful gamblers and ne'er-do-wells, to the laces and ruffles of 'Les Lords'. However, such variety of costume could hardly have been permitted outside the walls and grills of the closed yards of the depots. Even the most vigilant of guards would have found his task impossible, had he not been able to spot a prisoner by his garb in the crowded main market place. There must certainly have been a regulation which dictated the type and colour of clothing to be worn by inmates who were granted the privilege of the market and allowed to mix with the public – though so far I have been unable to trace a definite order to that effect.[3]

Second-hand English military and naval uniforms were, for obvious reasons, particularly in demand and many a successful escape was accomplished by their purchasers. The Agent at Dartmoor once took possession of a number of uniforms which had been brought up from Plymouth and sold in the depot market. He meticulously informed the prisoners concerned that, whilst they could not retain them at that time, he acknowledged that, as they had legally purchased them, they were the rightful owners and that the uniforms would be returned to them when the war was over!

There were, of course, the blacksheep of the markets, the pickpockets and petty pilferers and 'gold-watch' tricksters, always to be found in such crowded gatherings; but no doubt the bulk of the market transactions were carried out with a feeling of fair dealing between honest buyers and sellers. There is evidence, too, that the prisoners who wisely appreciated the advantages of this contact with the outside world, did their best to protect the privilege – and therefore the public – by punishing their crooked brethren, after trial in one of their own internal rough courts of justice.

The markets were visited by people of all classes and mentalities. Some to gloat over the side-show of unfortunate captives, others with a natural, and intelligent, interest in first-hand contact with foreigners who had been our enemies for so long. Then there were others who brought in their damaged treasures and broken knick-knacks, for restoration by one or the other of a dozen or more specialist craftsmen to be found in the square. It can be believed that many of those who purchased from the captives would have been motivated by feelings of charity, as much as by a desire to possess a souvenir or their appreciation of the labour and craftsmanship involved in the production of the finest of their works.

Robert Louis Stevenson began his unfinished book, *St Ives*, with a description of a prison market,[4] seen through the eyes of his hero:

'We had but one interest in common; each of us who had any skill in his Fingers passed the hours of his captivity in the making of little toys and *articles of Paris*; and the prison was daily visited at certain hours by a concourse of people of the country, come to exalt our distress, or – it is more tolerant to suppose – their own vicarious triumph. Some moved among us with a decency of shame or sympathy. Others were the most offensive of personages in the world, gaped at us as if we had been baboons, sought to evangelise us to their rustic, northern religion, as though we had been savages, or tortured us with intelligence of disasters to the arms of France. Good, bad, and indifferent, there was one alleviation to the annoyance of these visitors; for it was the practice of almost all to purchase some specimen of our rude handiwork. This led, among the prisoners, to a strong spirit of competition. Some were neat of hand, and (the genius of the French being always distinguished) could place upon sale little miracles of dexterity and taste.

'Some had a more engaging appearance; fine features were found to do well as fine merchandise, and an air of youth in particular (as it appealed to the sentiment of pity in our visitors) to be a source of profit. Others again enjoyed some acquaintance with the language, and were able to recommend the more agreeably to the purchasers such trifles as they had to sell.'

When Stapleton Prison reopened its doors in 1793, and the first thousand French prisoners arrived, the market was once again closed to British visitors, this time on the orders of Viscount Bateman, the colonel in charge of security. Lord Bateman, who found the French 'tractable, cheerful and orderly', did not issue his decree in the interests of security but to protect the finer feelings of the prisoners themselves: 'Humanity even to our enemies should prevent their being exhibited to an idle mob, like wild beasts at a fair'. Although the more sensitive of the captives may have appreciated his tender consideration, it is to be doubted that the industrious makers of models and trinkets would have applauded his protective spirit.

Gawkers and embarrassing starers there may have been, but the easy going atmosphere of the marketplace, 'which gave scope for the exchange of Jean Crapaud's manufacture for Nancy's eggs, or Joan's milk or home-baked loaf' was sure to break down barriers between theoretical enemies and result in friendly relationships – and even romances. 'Engaging appearance' and 'fine features' sometimes won for their possessors something valued far above financial or romantic gain – their freedom. Our fictional friend, St Ives, escaped and eventually married a girl he had met in the market-place of his Scottish prison, and his tale is no stranger than dozens of similar but true stories.

A young Dartmoor market-girl was smitten by the good looks and charm of a sixteen year old prisoner of war, and helped in his escape by providing him with one of her dresses. The night of his getaway was foul, the hail and storm so obscuring his vision that he did not see the sentry-box below him, as he jumped from the wall and landed on top of it. He must have thought the game was up, and waited for the challenge, but when none came he made his way across the Moor, disguised as a girl. Next morning the sentry described the storm which had kept him snug inside his shelter and said that, at one time, the force of the wind had been so great that it almost overturned his box. The dress was later found by the roadside at Moretonhampstead.

The famous French escape-artist, Louis Vanhille also got out of Dartmoor Depot via the daily market. His disguise was also supplied by a local girl. On each of her visits the girl, Mary Ellis, brought Louis an article of clothing – clod-hopper boots, brown worsted stockings, a countryman's wide-brimmed hat and all that was needed for him to pass through the gates, convincingly got up as a local potato merchant.

Traitorous, misguided, love-struck, over-sympathetic, or just plain stupid, call them what we will, there were many 'Mary Ellises' all over the country; willing to risk loss of reputation and punishment in the dangerous role of escape assistant. It is too much to hope that the feelings of these girls would always be reciprocated in the hearts of their captive boyfriends. Most, but not all, of these freedom-hungry men were more infatuated with their dreams of home than with our womenfolk. Whilst they could not but have felt gratitude towards these gullible girls, the majority took heed of yet another of their Emperor's maxims – 'The only Victory over Love is Flight' – and left their loves behind. What follows, however, is a market story of escape and elopement which tells of two people who found a happy ending.

After the abortive French 'invasion' of Fishguard, in 1797, some five hundred of the captives were quartered in the Golden Tower Prison, near Pembroke, where discipline was slack, security poor and the buildings entirely unsuited to the purpose. Some quickly settled down to produce the usual prisoner of war handicrafts for sale in the small market, and were always on the lookout for raw materials from which to make their little artefacts. In this they were helped by some of the girls who were employed in menial tasks about the prison, and who, quite openly and legitimately, brought in odds and ends of bone, wood. and other materials.

Two of these Welsh lasses soon fell in love with young French captives and, 'not having the law of Nations or the high policy of Europe before their eyes', determined to help their lovers escape. As the idea grew it was extended to include all the men in that part of the prison – about one hundred men in all. However lax the discipline, it was impossible for the girls to bring in shovels and spades, but an ingenious alternative was found. Each day they carried with them the shin bones of oxen and horses and passed them off as working materials for the bone carvers. These were quickly converted into tunnelling tools and a burrowing operation was started, some of the excavated earth being scattered about the prison yards and some taken away by the girls in their covered pails. When a sixty-foot long passage had been dug under the prison, it only remained for the girls to keep watch until a suitable vessel came into the nearby harbour, tip off the prisoners and the escape would be on.

One dark night, thirty of the absconders and the two young women made their way to the harbour and boarded a sloop, only to find that the tide was against them and the coaster aground. However, their luck did not desert them for long. As though Fate had decreed that one more act should be added to the Fishguard fiasco, a small pleasure yacht was at hand – a craft which belonged to Lord Cawdor, the British hero of the 'invasion' and the captor of the now fleeing men – who, it must be said, were putting up a better show on leaving England than they had on entering it. After the crew of the sloop had been securely bound hand and foot and the navigational instruments, charts, water casks and provisions transferred to the yacht, the thirty men and two girls set sail for France.

Next day there was a great commotion in the town. A prominent local figure, Dr Mansell, had notices posted up all over Pembrokeshire, which offered a reward of £500 (a huge figure at that time) for the return of the girls, dead or alive; but by that time the runaways were well out to sea. Off Linney Head they met up with a coasting brig carrying corn, which they boarded, forcing the crew below decks and battening down the hatches. Having no further use for Lord Cawdor's yacht they cast it adrift and when, a few days later, its stern and other wreckage was washed up on the Pembrokeshire coast, the hunt was called off and the 'wanted' posters taken down, it being piously supposed that 'the vengeance of Heaven had overtaken the traitors.' The traitors meanwhile had safely reached St Malo, where they married their French admirers – what stories they must have had to tell their grandchildren. It is surprising to learn that during the short peace which followed the Treaty of Amiens, one of the couples returned to Wales and opened a public house in Merthyr Tydfil. With the recommencement of hostilities in 1803, they hurried back to France and there, for us, the story ends.

Prisoners of war were never allowed to take the privilege of the market completely for granted. From time to time they were given ungentle reminders that this valuable concession, freely given by a benevolent government, could just as easily be taken away. The 'Indulgence', as it was termed in official orders, was a powerful disciplinary weapon in the hands of the authorities, and one which they did not hesitate to use when occasion demanded. Trouble in prisons both afloat or on shore was often settled at the first threat of withdrawal of all trading facilities. The bum-boats, which catered for the wants of both prison hulks and naval and merchant vessels returning to harbour, provided the seaboard traders with a lucrative income. The American prisoner, Josiah Cobb, who with his fellow captives was brought to England on the British sloop-of-war *Pheasant*, at the end of January, 1815, was amazed at the great number of small boats which surrounded her as she anchored some three miles off the Plymouth shore. Many were crowded with the 'wives' of the returning Jack Tars, but others were bumboats 'loaded to their gunwales with eatables and gew-gaws of every description, to entice the hard-earned money from the pockets of the sailors. Many of these boats were occupied by those who were prepared to trade: long-bearded Jews, woolly-mouthed Christians, blarney-primed Irish, burly-bellied English and skip-jack grinning Frenchmen[5], were all eager to show off the good qualities of their merchandise, and depreciate that of their neighbour, each with an earnestness, dialect, and grimace peculiar to himself.'

The sending away of the market boats from a prison ship's side was an effective method of suppressing disorder aboard the hulks. Several days without extra food and such important luxuries as tobacco, coffee and candles was a severe punishment, inflicted on the innocent and trouble-maker alike; and the former were often as effective as extra guards in seeing that order was quickly restored.

The complete closure of a shore depot market was a very drastic measure, resorted to only when all other threats had failed. It was used in cases of general misdemeanour and as a means of enlisting the aid of the well-behaved majority in stamping out particular prison vices. Thus, in 1813, Captain Cosgrove at Dartmoor included the threat of market closure in his praiseworthy efforts to halt the activities of the vicious 'brokers', who dealt in the rations and clothes of their fellow prisoners and did far more damage to their health and bodies than the Norman Cross pornographers could have ever done to their minds or morals. However, the markets never stayed closed for long. For apart from the appeals from the honest buyers and manufacturers among the captives, there would have been as great an outcry from the local tradespeople. Most of these suppliers depended almost entirely on the captive foreign patronage, and it is probably not too outrageous to suggest that there may have been at least some prison officials who were not disinterested in an early reopening. After the escape of twenty-eight prisoners from the depot at Perth, in September 1813, the market was closed for only one day. It was more usual to deny access to the representatives of the inmates of any part of a prison where trouble was brewing at the time, but without closing it to all. This selective punishment was frequently, and rather unpleasantly, employed as a means of forcing the occupants of a particular block to reveal the names of wanted men. Unfair and un-British as this may seem, it should be remembered that, in most depots, prisoners outnumbered the guards by more than ten to one, and unchecked trouble could spread like wildfire.

The 'Indulgence' of the market was denied to one group of prisoners of war even before they had had a chance to offend. These were the first five hundred Americans transferred from the hulks to Dartmoor Depot during the War of 1812. Their reputation as wild trouble-makers had reached the prison ahead of them and had created such consternation in the official breast that they were put into the *caserne* reserved for the very worst class of French down-and-out, and were not trusted to mix with the visiting public. This meant that they had no inspiration to employ their time in any sort of worthwhile manner, as they would have had no outlet for the product of their industry – and the fact that they could only obtain the important extras from the markets at inflated prices, through French middlemen, did nothing to soothe their rebellious spirit. The nine months following their arrival, in April, 1813, during which time many more Americans were transferred from the prison ships, was a time of trouble, resentment and complaint; but the New Year saw a change for the better. In December, Captain Shortland had taken over from Captain Cotgrave, as Agent for the prisoners of war at Dartmoor, and much of the discrimination against the Americans went with the retiring Agent.

It says much for the farsightedness of Shortland, tough disciplinarian though he was, that once the market was opened to the Americans, all but the most incorrigible amongst them settled down; most employing at least some of their time in worthwhile and profitable occupations. Soon the stalls in the outer market were displaying American, as well as French, ship models, straw-work boxes and carvings in bone and wood. Much of this work was in imitation or in the manner of the articles made by the continental craftsmen and already proven 'best-seller'market lines. It is probable that many collections of 'French' prisoner of war work contain anonymous examples from American hands. On a recent visit to New York, I was able to examine a very well-made bone ship model, an example of American prisoner of war work at the Museum of the New York Historical Society, which, but for its provenance, would doubtless have carried the label 'French'

It should not be inferred from the above that the American craftsmen were mere copyists of the French. Naturally they would have taken advantage of the French technical know-how and knowledge of whatever was popular at that time in the early nineteenth century – knowledge gained from 'market research' over their many long years of war and captivity. Memoirs and records reveal that American prisoners of war had been busily turning out artefacts for sale to the public – without continental inspiration – from as long ago as the eighteenth century, when confined in British prisons during the War of American Independence. Young Andrew Sherburne, who was a captive in the Old Mill prison at Plymouth for a number of months from January, 1782, observed the various ways in which the industrious among fellow captives employed their talents:

'Mr. Bodge, of Portsmouth [N.H.], was an artist in making punch ladles, of apple tree wood, I believe he made some which were sold for nearly half a guinea, wooden spoons, busks [corset stiffeners], and knitting sheaths, were very curiously wrought. Capt James Brown, of Kittery, taught navigation: and employed his leisure hours in manufacturing nets for drying glue[!?]. Ship-building was the most extensive business which was carried on. An old Mr Hudson, was indefatigable in building sloops, and schooners; and would generally have some in hand, he generally supplied the boys, whose curiosity led them to take a peep at the yankees. The old gentleman would sell them from a penny, to two or three shillings. There were sloops of war, frigates, two deckers, and even three deckers built or manufactured there. A Mr John Deadman, of Salim, exceeded all others in this business, he built one which was not a foot in length, which I think he sold for four guineas; he built a three decker, and rigged her completely, which, (if I do not mistake,) he sold for twenty guineas. She was between three and four feet in length, she showed three tier of guns, had her anchors on her bows, and her cable bent; by pulling gently on one of the cables, the parts [ports?] on one deck would fly open, by pulling on another, the guns would all run out of the ports: the same process would have the same effect on the other decks. My impression is, that he was twenty-two months in building her.'

Yet earlier, in June, 1777, another young American, nineteen years old Charles Herbert, was delivered into that same prison, where he was to stay until March, 1779. During that long period of incarceration he made the best of his often uncomfortable lot, and took full advantage of the privilege which allowed him to use his skills and to buy and sell. It was said of him that he could turn his hand to almost any task and 'He could be carpenter, carver, shoemaker, merchant, could make boxes, sell tobacco (which he bought with the money he made from his craftsmanship and retailed within the prison), or labor in any way to make a shift, and to prevent starvation.' However, the piece of prisoner of war work which preserves his name is the secret diary which he kept, at great risk of punishment and in spite of the scarcity of writing materials, on an almost unbroken daily basis. It was written under the most difficult of conditions; in the cable tier of the British man of war which brought him to England; the hold of a prison ship or the smallpox ward of a prison hospital; at night in the heat or bitter cold of the Old Mill prison, by the light of a marrow bone or a valued stump of candle.

Early in 1814, the United States Government granted an allowance of tuppence ha'penny per day to each man, intended for the purchase of soap, tobacco, coffee and tea. This little windfall, added to the newly acquired opportunity to profitably employ themselves, made all the difference to the American way of prison life. It is true that the gaming tables would have claimed more than their fair share of this new-found wealth, but the Dartmoor market people also benefited greatly from this additional purchasing power.

The British traders on the Moor were doubly lucky; they were still in business for a full year after all the other depot markets had put up their shutters – for the American prisoners of war were the last to be released. By May, 1814, the war was, it seemed, over and the signing of the Treaty of Paris came as a liquidation order to countless small businesses, which had sprung up and prospered in the vicinity of the depots. Just as the joy of many of the released continentals must have been marred by the downfall of their beloved Emperor, so must the celebrations of the British victory have been spoiled for the country traders and market suppliers, as they watched prosperity disappearing with their departing foreign customers – for most, never to return.

It is impossible to do more than indicate the value of the merchandise which passed through the depot markets, or the magnitude of the loss to the merchants. Some idea of the business calamity which hit both the small cottage workers and smallholders, and the contractors who supplied the daily rations is indicated by an article in *The Times* for the 14th August, 1814, which stated that 'about £300,000 a year is spent by the Government in Stilton, Yaxley, Peterborough and the neighbourhood in the necessary provision of stores to Norman Cross Depot alone.' Something like two tons of meat each day was delivered to that one depot, and an interesting entry in the books of the Oundle Brewery at Peterborough recorded that, during the year 1799, no fewer than 4,449 thirty-six gallon barrels of beer had been delivered to the barracks of the regiments quartered there. For a few weeks after the Peace the depot markets were busier than ever. There was a great rush on the clothing merchants, a short-lived sellers-market in boots, shoes, hats, baggage and all the odds and ends and necessities required for the homeward journey. Afterwards, the markets died.

But Dartmoor lived on for some time yet, and there are still a few more tales to tell. With most of the French and their allies gone, the Americans had Dartmoor almost entirely to themselves. The Depot on the Moor was now the centre for all the prisoners of war in the land, its population ever increasing, as drafts came in from Stapleton and the Chatham hulks. By the end of the year, more than five thousand Americans were concentrated at Dartmoor – and *'Hail, Columbia'* replaced the *'Marseillaise'* in the noisy prison yards.

The American memoirist, Benjamin Waterhouse, 'The Young Man of Massachusetts', who arrived at Princetown in October, 1814, found that 'a man with some money in his pocket might live pretty well through the day in Dartmoor Prison, there being shops and stalls where every little article could be obtained, [these were the prisoner-run businesses in the inner yards and which the public would never have seen] but added to this we had a good and constant market, and the bread and meat supplied by the Government was not bad.'

After his imprisonment on the hulks, the exchange of the bumboats for a real market, and personal contact with the local inhabitants through its traders and visitors, made prison life much more bearable for Waterhouse. He found, however, the West Country dialect difficult for an American to follow, being particularly confused by their quaint use of the second person singular:

> 'The language and phraseology of these market people are very rude. When puffing off the qualities of their goods, when they talk very fast, we can hardly understand them. They do not speak near so good English as our common market people in America. The best of them use the pronoun he in a singular manner – as can he pay me? For can you pay me? [obviously, 'e' or 'he' for 'you' was their dialect form of 'ye'] I am fully of the opinion with those who say that the American people, taken collectively, speak the English language with more purity than Britons, taken collectively.
>
> 'Every man or boy of every part of the United States would be promptly understood by men of letters in London; but every man and boy of Old England would not be promptly understood by the lettered man in the capital towns of America. Is it not the Bible that has preserved the purity of our language in America?'

After reading the above, we must pity the many French captives who, over the years, would have learned the English language from these market countryfolk – and afterwards spoken West Country-English with a French accent!

The social life and conditions of the prison yard must have been much the same for the American and the Frenchmen, but the very different temperament of the 'Sons of Liberty' made it impossible for them to adapt so readily to prison life. On a number of occasions during the now almost completely American occupation of Dartmoor, the market was closed down for days at a time, as punishment for escape attempts and general defiance; each day of closure was an acutely painful experience which hit the British stall-holders in the pocket and the prisoners in their stomachs. Conscious that the heyday of dependable trading with captive customers was nearing its end, the market people valued every dealing day left to them and, according to more than one ex-prisoner, made the best of it by marking up their goods, and charging over the odds.

The 'Young Man' tells us that the market was filled with all manner of vegetables and other food stuffs, piles of broad cloth, boxes of hats, boots, shoes and second-hand clothing. He added that women who ran their businesses in the market were as sharp as the Jews who came up from Plymouth with their watches, seals, trinkets and dirty books, and that they were harder to deal with, 'for a sailor cannot beat them down as he can one of these thieving Israelites. Milk is cheap, only 4d. a gallon, but they know how to water it down'.

His journal records that, in February, 1815, the market was completely shut down for six days in consequence of a number of wooden stanchions being stolen from Prison No.6. However, the old market dames, 'conceiving that the Captain [Shortland] encroached on their copy-hold, would not quietly submit to it. They told him that as the men were going away soon, it was cruel to curtail their traffic. We always believed that these market women, and the shop and stall keepers, and the Jews, purchased in some way or other the unequal traffic between them and us.' Be that as it may, Shortland could not resist the commercial interest, so that he, 'like good Mr Jefferson, listened to the clamour of the merchants, and raised the embargo.'

Prices were increasing alarmingly and the discontent which now kept pace with the inflation did not stop at grumblings and complaint. The criminal element among the Americans, the tough, trouble-seeking mob known as the 'Rough Alleys', took advantage of the situation. A number of them got into the main market and, under the pretence of indignation, tore down and looted some of the shops and stalls. Again using the justification of profiteering, they also plundered the little shopkeepers in their own inner prison yards; whose prices were, understandably, regulated to make a profit on what they had had to pay in the main depot market. Some of the victims of these gangs of robbers were put right out of business, their entire stocks disappearing in a matter of minutes.

The Committees formed by the Americans to maintain order in the Dartmoor Depot, did their best to calm things down and preserve the privileges of trading; they 'never rested, or allowed the culprits to rest, until we saw the cat laid well upon their backs.' But the gangs continued to plague the market people with their tricks and petty pilfering. They were particularly hard on the German Jewish merchants who traded in cloth – sometimes playing the childish trick of persuading them to cut up a whole bale of cloth into lengths and then walking off.

A favourite thieving technique was by 'the hook and line' method. One or two of their number, respectably dressed enough to gain admittance to the main market – for most of these roughs were filthy, verminous and half-naked – would approach a stall and one would fix a hook into a pair of shoes, a hat, or whatever took his fancy. He would then give the signal to his accomplices in the inner prison yard and the loot would be whisked through or over the gratings. Handkerchiefs, stockings, bunches of carrots, the occasional chicken and anything light enough for the line, were played and landed, sometimes over distances of forty or fifty feet. Of course, only inexperienced traders were selected as victims; the old hands were aware of most market tricks. Whenever these petty thieves, who caused so much trouble for their unoffending fellow captives, were caught, they were brought before a court set up in one of the inner prisons, by a Committee of Americans and, after trial, sentenced to a public flogging.

The acknowledged leaders of the 'Rough Alleys' at that time were two villains who had so distinguished themselves in the fields of lawlessness and vice that they were known as Sodom and Gomorrah. One was of German extraction and the other was fluent in so many languages that he could have come from anywhere. These two had been tried for stealing a dozen times, but had always managed to lay the blame elsewhere; but 'The Green Hand' witnessed an occasion when they were not so lucky and has left us the story of their humiliating and amusing punishment:

One market day, early in 1815, a trader set out his wares close to the railings which separated the prison proper from the market, and was soon engaged in what he thought was genuine dealing with a group of reasonably attired 'Rough Alleys' in the adjoining yard. Suddenly a hand shot out through the railings and snatched his watch from its chain and the thieves made off. This bit of daylight robbery was deplored by all decent American inmates and a search and inquiries were made throughout the Dartmoor prisons. Sodom and Gomorrah were the prime suspects and after two days of investigation they were brought to trial. They were found guilty and the Committee came up with a Mikado-like sentence which made the punishment fit the crime. As they had offended against the market, the square was to be the scene of their chastisement. With hands tied behind their backs, they were to be handed over to the market women who were to deal with them as they saw fit.

Criers were sent throughout the prison yards and round the market to announce the sentence – and to acquaint the women with the fact that these were the leaders and, if they had old scores to pay off, now was their opportunity. 'For all those, who, at any time, has lost ought, by pilferings of these or their companions, to now come forward, take their due, or forever hold their peace or complaints – whatever ye do unto these two, ye do to the whole gang, for these two are their chiefs.'

The women needed no second invitation and after Sodom and Gomorrah had been handed over by an escort of prisoners, and their shirts had been stripped and twisted over their heads by women experienced in rabbit-skinning, they were hauled over a bench and held down by a couple of women as tough and as strong as themselves. Soon their bare backs were being lambasted with riding whips, shoes, bunches of celery and anything else that came to hand. One over-enthusiastic fishwife laid in with a gander which she had grabbed by the neck from a nearby stall and was doing well until, to use her own words, 'Dom the twaddling baste, it slupped off the handle', and hit a neighbouring flogger hard across the breast. The row which ensued saved Sodom and Gomorrah from further beating, but if a beating with a gander was less painful than the cat-o'-nine-tails, the humiliation and the blow to their macho pride must have been sorely remembered for many a long day.

The gander-wielding Dartmoor fishwife was a notorious market character. She had seen as much war service as any of her patrons; had served in India and had been 'kicked out of the army in Spain for her unblushing immoralities'. It is a pity that not more of her recollections were noted down; for she often boasted a youthful acquaintanceship with the Duke of Wellington, 'before he know'd a hawk from a handsaw in a military way, for I put him in the way to be a general, a real general.'

The roughs would afterwards have given a wide berth to this fearsome old virago, with her six-weeks' growth of unclipped beard and peakless dragoon forage cap, great fisherman's boots and jacket, as she watched over her stock of seafood. Yet not all the Devon market women were old or unattractive harridans. There was lovely young Agnes, the vegetable girl, who was a veritable 'Miss Dartmoor, 1815.' Neat and feminine in her fresh-starched fancy aprons, high pattens protecting her feet from the mud. She was always sure of willing hands to help unload her donkeys as soon as she entered the trading area. Rival vegetable sellers had to wait until she had sold out before they had a hope of anything like brisk trade. Agnes won the hearts of all the prisoners who came into the market, but she finally chose one of their keepers, a drum-major of the Dartmoor garrison, when her market days were over.

On the 14th March 1815, the *Favourite* reached England bearing the ratified Treaty of Ghent, and it seemed that the days of the market were really numbered. The square was filled with every sort of merchandise in a last mad rush to rake in as much money as possible before the Americans left; but there was nothing of a clearance sale about all this, for five and a half thousand prisoners were still in the depot and prices were as high as ever.

The American Charles Andrews tells of one trader who thought he saw an opportunity to make an easy three pounds on the way to the market. He was about eight miles out on the road to the depot when he saw a lone figure on Peak Hill, and jumped to the conclusion that it must be an escaping American Prisoner. The man he had detained was, in fact, a Roborough farmer with a sense of humour, who had less sympathy for a bounty-hunter than he had for an escaping American prisoner. He agreed to go quietly, but said he had no intention of walking back into captivity. Relieved that no resistance had been offered, the trader paid half a guinea to a wagoner from Dousland Barn and, with the prisoner sitting in the back and singing 'Yankee Doodle', they made their way to Dartmoor. On arrival the farmer was immediately recognised by the turnkeys and it was the trader who was locked in the guard house. Several hours later he was released, after agreeing to pay the farmer five pounds compensation for wrongful arrest; but his troubles did not end there. From then on he was boycotted by all Americans and never sold another thing in the marketplace.

Now that the war was over, the prisoners naturally anticipated immediate release, but the arrangements were long drawn-out and weeks went by before the first cartel ship was ready to sail. By the beginning of April, frustration and uncertainty had made the never-docile Americans even more troublesome and hard to handle. Rumours of an uprising, spread by market people supposedly in the know, sent many Dartmoor families scurrying to the comparative safety of Plymouth and Tavistock. The restless temper of these men, and the nervousness and blunders of Captain Shortland and his staff, culminated in the bloody and tragic events which took place in the market square on the 6th April, 1815 – long remembered with bitterness in America as the 'Dartmoor Massacre' (see *A History of Napoleonic and American Prisoners of War – Hulk, Depot and Parole*, Chapter 19).

The last of the American prisoners did not leave Dartmoor until late July, and the intervening three months were the most miserable in the depot's history. The waiting was bad enough, but want was added to worry and depression, now that the United States Government's allowances had ceased. The extra food and the craved-for chew of tobacco was now beyond the pockets of many, and as their funds ran out the market began to break up. The shops shut up, the stalls were bare and only a few tenacious pedlars hung on. Pretty Agnes went off with her drum-major and her colourful associates no longer found it profitable to make the long journeys across the Moor.

There was a flutter of renewed business at the beginning of July, when 4,000 Frenchmen, captured on the battlefields of Waterloo, were marched up from Plymouth. However, once Napoleon Bonaparte – our most famous prisoner of war – had been safely lodged at St Helena, they, too, were homeward bound.

On the 10th February, 1816, the last prisoner of war passed out through the gates of Dartmoor, and the market square, which for seven long years had been the busy, noisy centre of the prisoners' world – and the font of the locals' livelihood – was given up to silence and the weeds.

---

1. Admiralty Papers FP/24, Mar 24.

2. D.Vinter. B.&G. Arch. Soc. Vol. 75.

3. A contemporary watercolour by the British Captain Durrant, of the Portchester Castle market shows prisoner-traders dressed uniformly in blue or grey.

4. Edinburgh Castle.

5. If Josiah Cobb was not mistaken, it is surprising to learn that French traders were back in business on this side of the Channel, so soon after the temporary peace.

Chapter Three

The Inner Markets

'There to the left is a new beginner to shop-keeping, who has but just laid in his goods, consisting of a pound of butter, a plug of tobacco, half a dozen pipes, as many skeins of thread, a paper of needles, and eight or ten rows of pins. He already shows the future merchant, by the multiplicity of his designs in exhibiting his scanty stock, so as to make it appear as large and attractive as his neighbour's of longer standing across the way, who is now sneering at his rival, for hoping to entice the secure custom from his well-established stall, by adding a crumb of butter of a pea's size to the top of the usual penny'sworth lump.'   *A Green Hand's First Cruise* by a Yonker.

THE PRISONERS WHO WERE GRANTED THE PRIVILEGE of direct contact with the local dealers and the visiting public were but a small percentage of the whole at any one time. To have admitted five or six thousand captives into the market area would have been madness, even had space allowed. For most, this fascinating glimpse of freedom, of British civilians and their womenfolk, of shops and stalls piled high with desirable merchandise and the whole colourful activity of the market-place, could only have been taken through grilles and palings which enclosed the trading areas. The principal market of any depot, with its constant supply of fresh country produce and all manner of non-issue commodities, was, in fact, a miniature Covent Garden, where captive wholesalers purchased stock for resale in their shops within the inner markets.

The great depots were divided into numbered prison blocks or *casernes*, each with its own courtyard or airing ground, and there each held its own interior market, where prisoner dealt with prisoner. The inner markets were often even more colourful than the parent market, and collectively they were larger and even wider in their scope. Prisoners from more than a dozen nations rubbed shoulders in these micro-worlds; Frenchmen in abundance, and Dutchmen, Italians, Danes, Norwegians and Swedes; Russians, Poles, Germans, even a few Chinamen and Malays, made up the motley throng of sellers, buyers, browsers and envious hard-up window-shoppers. The Americans came in three varieties of colour: mainly white, many black and the occasional 'redskin'.

The French were the organisers of the social life of the prison yards and the business brains behind most enterprises – both legal and illicit. Theirs were the coffee-houses, the cook-shops and the stalls and shops which traded in everything saleable and in demand. Theirs, too, the most booming of all prison enterprises, where stock-in-trade was no more than a persuasive manner and an unrelenting heart; where overheads were low and profits sky-high – the gamesters with their Alagalitie, Rouge-et-noir and Kaka tables, roulette wheels and Vingt-et-un schools, which dotted the prison yards – and, of course, the ubiquitous billiards table, one of the Frenchman's most efficient fleecing instruments.

The businesses ranged in size and importance from the hawkers' trays of odds and ends to well-established grocers, greengrocers and second-hand clothing companies. Bespoke and alteration tailors, cobblers and laundrymen; vendors of crockery, eating utensils and tools; cooks, carpenters and the exponents of every imaginable craft; all set up their stalls, stands and booths in these busy squares.

In a much smaller way of business, but with no less enterprise, there were merchants and vendors on the crowded hulks at Portsmouth, Chatham and elsewhere. A lasting impression on the mind of the prisoner-painter, Louis Garneray, on the day of his arrival on the prison ship *Prothée* at Portsmouth, was of pedlars who wandered round the dimly-lit gun-deck, crying: 'What can I sell you? What'll you buy?' Some of the many improvident and hungry men would trade in parts of their ragged clothing to one of these pedlars, then spend a few pence with another who dished up portions of a messy stew, the ingredients of which were best not enquired into. There were tobacco-sellers on every hulk, and on the *Prothée* there was one who produced under his own label, and, when not peddling, could be found 'working on a foetid mass which he claimed was tobacco, and actually sold as such, though it cannot have contained a trace of the fragrant weed'.

Another tobacconist had a small stall on the *Bahama* hulk at Chatham. He was a popular privateersman, named Mathieu, who sometimes gave credit, but on one occasion refused a soldier who already had too much marked up on the slate. The soldier was desperate and made a sudden grab at the packs laid out on the stall; but Matthieu was quicker, drew a knife and seriously wounded him. The stallholder was tried by a court of his fellows and was released after paying compensation to the man who tried to rob him.[1]

These hulk enterprises were pathetically small, but the depot markets were often bigger and more important than the local civilian market-places – few villages had populations of six or seven thousand customers with nowhere else to shop! Dealers and traders who could cater for the inner and outer needs of their captive customers were always sure of selling their goods. Food and tobacco came first on the list in importance, each helping in its way to compensate when Government rations failed to satisfy. Next came clothing, to protect against the chill of the winter months, and to replace the hated TOTO garb.

The well-breeched prisoner could 'eat out' in style in his own, and perhaps on occasion, one of the neighbouring prison yards. With every trade and profession represented among the thousands of conscripted soldiers and sailors in the larger depots, good chefs were not hard to find. The choicest foodstuffs could be ordered from suppliers in the main market, and those who could so indulge themselves, probably dined on far better fare than was available in the village inns beyond the walls.

For the many, there were the pastry sellers and the vendors of tidbits and little luxuries; but busiest of all, the booths which dished up cheap and nourishing stews. Some of the beef, pork and other ingredients being Government issue – bought from the rations of gamblers needing a stake. Everything obtainable in the outer market was on sale at a slightly higher price here in the inner. Here, too, the *Les Capitalists* collected together the works of *Les Laborieux*, for sale next day to the visiting public – and the dealers in prohibited straw-plait and the money-lenders carried on their shadier transactions.

Competition was keen. The stalls and shops were made bright with signboards and placards, painted up with blurbs and puffs extolling the virtues of the merchandise and the honesty of the proprietors. Everywhere the vendors were shouting their wares. These inner markets were as noisy as they were picturesque; the barkers doing their utmost to make themselves heard above the din of the musicians, the calls of the croupiers and the polyglot hubhub of the crowd. It is to our loss that there was no 'Garneray of the Depots', and that photography came along just too late to record those colourful scenes. However, the rare little journals of Josiah Cobb, Waterhouse, Herbert and, to a lesser extent, their fellow American Charles Andrews and some of the less-bitter French, are illustrated with word-pictures as vivid as any canvas. A few contemporary British writers also recorded their first-hand impressions of certain depots. There was George Borrow who left his picturesque description of Norman Cross Depot – and his scurrilous criticism of the 'straw-plait hunts' – in the third chapter of 'Lavengro'[2]. Also, William Chambers, writer and the publisher of *Chambers' Journal* painted his word-picture of Valleyfield Depot, one of the three prisoner of war depots at Penicuik, Scotland, ten miles or so from Edinburgh. He was a young lad when his father took him on a Sunday morning stroll which led them to the prison, where, from a high vantage point they had a bird's-eye view into the prison yards. The memory of that visit was still fresh in his mind when years later he recorded it in his 'Journal':

> 'Here on a level space in the depth of a valley, was a group of barracks, surrounded by tall palisades, for the accommodation of some hundreds of prisoners, who, night and day, were strictly watched by armed sentries, ready to fire on them in the event of an outbreak. The day on which we happened to make our visit was a Sunday, and the scene presented was accordingly the more startling. Standing in the churchyard on the brink of the hollow, all the immediate surroundings betokened the solemnity of a Scottish Sabbath. The shops in the village were shut. From the church was heard the voice of the preacher. Looking down from the height on the hive of beings, there was not among them a vestige of the ordinary calm of Sunday – only dimanche! [the French Sunday]. Dressed in coarse woollen clothing of a yellow colour, and most of them wearing red or blue cloth caps, or party-coloured cowls, the prisoners were engaged in a variety of amusements and occupations. Prominently, in forming the centre of attraction, were a considerable number ranked up in two rows, joyously dancing to the sound of a fiddle, which was briskly played by a man who stood on the top of a barrel. Others were superintending cookery in big pots over open fires, which were fanned by the flapping of cocked hats. Others were fencing with sticks amidst a circle of eager onlookers. A few men were seated meditatively on benches, perhaps thinking of far-distant homes, or the fortune of war, which had brought them into this painful predicament. In twos and threes, some were walking apart to and fro, and I conjecture they were of a slightly superior class. Near one corner was a booth – a rickety concern of boards – seemingly a kind of restaurant, with the pretentious inscription, 'CAFÉ DE PARIS', over the door, and a small tricolor flag was fluttering from a slender pole on the roof. To complete the picture, imagine several of the prisoners, no doubt the more ingenious among them, stationed at small wickets opening with hinges in the tall palisades, offering for sale articles, such as snuff-boxes of bone, that they have been allowed to manufacture, and the money got by which sales produced them a few luxuries.'[3]

Chambers' account reveals that at least some Sunday trading took place in some depot markets on the day when the main markets were closed. T. J. Walker quoted one isolated near-contemporary mention of a Sunday market at Norman Cross: '…French prisoners who were confined here during the late war, and employed themselves in making bone toys, and straw boxes, and many other small articles, to which people of all descriptions were admitted on Sundays, when more than £200 a day has been laid out in purchasing their labours of the preceding week'.[4]

Another interesting memoir tells of a Penicuik prison market where the prisoners collectively 'sold at times £2,000 worth of goods in a week'. A local historian, J. L. Black, wrote: 'a weekly market was held in the Square and civilians were allowed to enter and examine their work', but he went on to mention a surprising way in which the prisoner craftsmen disposed of their wares, other than through either inner or outer prison market. Wives or women companions, who in a few cases had accompanied their menfolk into captivity at Penicuik, journeyed into Edinburgh to offer 'the knick-knacks made by their husbands to likely buyers'.[5]

The Americans at Dartmoor were not granted the same privileges as the French until March, 1814, and once allowed to fraternise with the continental captives, they, too, began to set themselves up in little businesses in the Depot yards. Charles Andrews, with, for him, a rare touch of humour, tells us that they now considered they had achieved their country's aims for which they had fought – 'Free Trade and Sailors' Rights' – and all but the laziest and the deadbeat engaged in the production of a profitable something or other.

The 18th March saw the opening of the first American rival to the French-owned coffee houses at Dartmoor. The proud Yankee entrepreneur, all ready for business, took his stand between two large tin boilers, each bubbling over a charcoal fire. One boiler was marked 'TEAY', the other 'KOFY', and the beverages were sold by the pint. One can imagine his satisfaction as his first customers rolled up, attracted by the steam, the aroma and the painted sign above his booth, which announced:-

AT HAP'URTH A POINT
HOT TEAY SOLD HEAER
HOT KOFY AT DUBBLE THE FUST
IF LESS, IN A WEAK, BY HOKA, WE FEAR
WE SHOULD FALE,
SO DAM'ME - NO TRUST

The price was inviting, but considering the high cost of ingredients at the time – coffee at 2s.3d. a pound and molasses at £3.10s. a hundredweight, it is to be doubted that the quality would have lured many French patrons from their usual haunts. However, the colour was approximately right and the beverage hot, so when the coffee was running out and he topped up the pots with 'teay', it was said that few customers were any the wiser.

This was not the first time an American had set up a coffee house in a prison market yard. Some Yankee privateers had shown similar enterprise during the War of Independence, more than thirty years earlier, in the Old Mill Prison near Plymouth. Andrew Sherburne noted in his 'Memoirs' that, in 1782:

'Some of the Kittery people had sailed in privateers from France [their ally], and had some money with them when they were taken. There were individuals who would furnish themselves with a kettle, a few pounds of coffee, and a small quantity of fuel, (bones were carefully collected for fuel) and make coffee and sell it for half a penny a pint, and if they could realize the gain of three or four pence, or even but one penny a day, it was an inducement to continue the business.'

When the 'Greenhand' took his first stroll through the Dartmoor yards and markets, the atmosphere was wholly French. Gambling booths and gaming tables everywhere, but also every description of industry and craft. The skilled model-makers fashioning ships in bone or wood, delicate and ingenious toys and beautifully made caskets and boxes in finely-fretted bone, or of wood intricately inlaid with straw parquetry and marquetry. Then there were the schools of fencing and dancing, the theatrical companies and music societies. All this may sound like pure imagination, but we have a great deal of evidence of the wonderful works of art and craft that were created in such unlikely surroundings. As to the rest, the workshops, schools, clubs, the gambling, etc., it must be remembered that some of the greater depots housed anything from five to seven thousand men – some confined for many years – who were not obliged to carry out any official tasks, and had to decide according to their own ability, pride and energy whether they employed their captivity usefully or allowed it to destroy them. We should also remind ourselves that, unlike our own soldiers and sailors who were recruited in a very different way, French conscription brought captive members of just about every trade and profession into our depots, hulks and parole towns.

Within a few weeks of the establishment of the 'Kofy-house', the atmosphere began to change. The war was over for the French prisoners and the Americans began a take-over of the markets and yards. The many thousands of continental prisoners were repatriated over the following two months, in drafts of a few hundreds at a time; and as the names of the French proprietors were called, eager American buyers were waiting to snap up their stalls, booths, shops and stock-in-trade at bargain prices. Under new management, many of these businesses would have changed in little but their name-boards and sales-talk. The vegetable and general provision booths would have been much the same as before, but chewing tobacco was more in evidence, beer more in demand, and greater risks taken in the smuggling in of hard liquor – through the agency of corrupt guards or bribed visitors to the main market square.

Perhaps the most noticeable change was in the preparation of food, the new aromas from its cooking, and the new sounds and cries of the market. The ragout booth now sold a plainer mess, made up of much the same ingredients, but minus the herbs and spices. And the pâtisserie pedlar was replaced by the American vendor of piping-hot fish-cakes, concocted from a mixture of more mashed potato than cod, but flavoured with onions and fried to a mouth-watering golden-brown. His customers hardly needed encouraging to dig deep for their pennies; but still he cried:

> **'Hot plumgudgeons!**
> Who'll but buy nice hot large
> **Hot plumgudgeons, for a penny a-piece?**
> Just now smoking from the frying-pan,
> warranted to cure all diseases, and a never
> failing remedy for that very unpleasant, as
> well as ungenteel complaint about the region
> of the stomach, most commonly felt after some
> hours of fasting vulgarly called **HUNGER!**
> Come buy my large, fine lot,
> Crisping, nice and smoking hot,
> **Plumgudgeons for a penny.**
> **Be quick, I have not many!.**
> They've double the worth of fish,
> To say nothing of the dish,
> The potatoes and the fat,
> Onions, pepper and all that.
>
> At once now don't you all,
> For Plumgudgeons so fast call,
> But give time for me to see
> If you all pay, who've bought of me.
> **Oh-Ho! My Plumgudgeons, Hot!**
> **Crisping! nice and smoking hot!'**

Josiah Cobb noted down a number of the market cries and described the colourful and enterprising pedlars who shouted them. There is the negro who boasts, with some justice, that his fritters are twice the size of rival offerings. So they are, though he uses no more material, having mastered the art of blowing up the batter so that they look enormous. Neither can his competitors outdo him as a shouter and puffer of his wares. He has hinged his tongue with a spring in some fashion, the better to trill as he sings out:

> **'Fr-r-r-r-r-r-r-ritters**
> **lighter dan a 'punge,**
> **Bigger dan are nobodies -**
> **de pan so clean what fry 'um,**
> **a man can shabe heself in,**
> **or see he purty face**
> **dout tearing it to tatters**
> **tur-r-r-rit tur-r-r-i-t**
> **frit -ter-r-r-r-r fr-r-r-i-t.'**

Then there was Frank Dolphin, hawker and second-hand clothing merchant. Frank, who acted as an agent for anyone with garments for sale, cut a comical figure; hats of all descriptions stacked high upon his head, like baskets on the heads of old time Billingsgate porters. His body was completely hidden under layer upon layer of commissioned garments; stockings and caps hanging from his waistcoat buttons, breeches and trousers round his neck, he moved through the yard like a walking wardrobe. Frank Dolphin's ready wit bent the truth to endow each garment with a make-believe provenance, each stain or tear became a selling-point rather than a fault – every hole the trace of a bullet fired in some famous action, each rent the mark of an enemy sabre. In the fashion of the prison criers, Frank often told his lies in rhyme; but on the day early in 1815, when Cobb saw him in the Dartmoor yards, he was spinning a hat on the end of a cane and shouting:-

'Now buy the hat, that once was shot, while on the head of him who took, and killed outright, a bloody Turk, without himself once being hurt! Now here it twirls upon the cane that once belonged to him so great at Trafalgar's almighty fight, which can be had for a shilling, with a bond and security (as far as hard promises go) that the ferule is of solid silver and alone worth eighteen pence, at half the price that old metal is selling at!

'Or if the hat or cane don't suit, try a cap that was worn at the Battle of the Nile, by one so close in the fight as to have its knap carried away by the enemy's shot, till it was left in the threadbare state you see it! Had I the impudence of some in the trade, I might say it had a charm against danger, but I scorn to say what I have not the authority to prove!'

The 'Greenhand's Dartmoor wanderings revealed to him many strange sights; from boxing booths to 'a library association, opposite, who let out their books (mostly odd volumes) at ha'porth per week'. But most enterprises were concerned with food or were set up to make the money with which to purchase it. He noted that four men who were industriously employed beating beef bones to a powder, between stones, were a firm who have undertaken this mode of making something beyond their rations, and a fair return they receive for their labour. As dry as these bones, which are gathered from the cookhouse, appear, after being reduced to a powder and boiled, a palatable, sweet, unctuous marrow is extracted, which is far richer as a shortening for pastry, and any other culinary purpose, than either butter or lard. It readily commands a shilling per pound, and is bought up with avidity by all who know its worth'.

Rather than a mere statement of numbers, a better idea of the size of the jostling mass of captive humanity which crowded these prison yards, can be visualised from a description of a visit to just one *caserne's* official depot kitchen – which displayed the notice over its door: 'NO LOITERERS ALLOWED HERE!':

'Let us just take a peep inside the cook-house… but our visit must be brief, for cooks like not to be troubled, as every one knows, for they are the best natured people on earth when off duty, and the worst when on. The three by the window, are busily engaged weighing off the bread for the next serving out, under the direction of the fourth, who is the head of the establishment. All are prisoners, who obtain the situation through interest alone with the committee of the prisons [the internal prisoner-Committee which laid down rules of conduct and punished offenders]; and they receive for their labour, the skimmings and slush of the kettles [plus a Government payment of 3d. a day]; but woe to their backs, if they are caught skimming too close; as, for the offence, expulsion follows conviction instanter; and if their crime be of a very heinous nature, they are tried before the committee, found guilty, and are punished by whipping with the cat.'

At least one member of the Committee was always present during the preparation of the food as there were so many tricks possible in the handling of such great quantities of raw material. Cobb continued:

> 'Now the cooks have gone through with the bread, the cooks begin with the meat for the day's dinner, and are weighing it off in parcels for each mess, with the nicety of gold dust, to be again subdivided and weighed to the different members of the messes, when they receive it. You can see that we form an expensive family for his majesty to feed, by yonder pile of bread of more than four hundred loaves, weighing four and a half pounds each; with these two copper boilers, each capable of holding more than one large sized bullock, a cart load of turnips and cabbages, and two or three bushels of barley, the whole mass to be multiplied by five, the number of prisons occupied; and this to be provided every day.'

He was, of course, talking of just the Dartmoor Depot alone, and at a time when the depot was not fully occupied. Over so many years of war, with so many depots and hulks crammed full with captives, 'his majesty' certainly did have an expensive family to feed! Benjamin Waterhouse's 'Journal' also mentions the cooks and their skimming:

> 'To be a cook is the most disagreeable and dangerous office at this depot. They are always suspected, watched and hated, from an apprehension that they defraud the prisoner of his just allowance. One was flogged the other day for skimming the fat off the soup. The grand Vizier's office at Constantinople, is not more dangerous than a cook's at this prison, where are collected four or five thousand hungry sons of liberty. The prisoners take it upon themselves to punish these pot-skimmers in their own way. We have in this collection of prisoners, a gang of hard-fisted fellows, who call themselves "THE ROUGH ALLIES". They have assumed to themselves the office of accuser, judge and executioner.'

The 'Rough-Alley-justice' mentioned, should not be confused with that dispensed by the legitimate prisoner-elected Committees which did their best to control depot and prison ship life to the benefit of captive and captor alike.

Like Josiah Cobb and Benjamin Waterhouse, Charles Andrews recalled the great upsurge in the American spirit once they had the liberty of the markets. The gates between the *casernes* being now opened:

> '…we traded with the French. We could buy potatoes at six-pence a score, butter at one and six-pence per pound; and as for meat, that was out of the question altogether. Every man began to use all the economy he could, which we perceived the French did. Some went to work for the French at making straw hats [strictly against Customs restrictions, as these were dutiable and therefore a fraud on the Revenue], at which they could earn one penny per day. Others were employed in making list shoes, some in the manufactory of hair bracelets, necklaces, &c.; while a great number employed themselves in working the bones we got out of the beef, in imitation of the French, who were very ingenious.'

To depend on the daily ration was, to a degree, to go hungry; and the 'Greenhand', as hard-up as the majority of his fellow prisoners, soon realised that he must find employment to augment his diet by purchases from the market. Untalented in any art or craft which might earn him an honest penny, 'Greenhand' entered an enterprise very close to the dangerous edge of gambling. He went into business with a teacher of navigation known as the Doctor, and between them bought out the proprietor of a Wheel of Fortune table who had gone bankrupt. Just about the only way this could have happened, would have been by staking his profits on more risky games of chance, such as the vingt-et-un or rouge-et-noir tables! The purchase was only possible because the price was moderate and they were allowed liberal credit; and to raise the capital to buy the opening stock – a dozen tuppenny loaves from the local bakers in the main market – the 'Greenhand' sold his best pair of stockings for a shilling and the Doctor sold some clothing for a similar amount.

The Wheel of Fortune was a large brightly painted circle, divided into sections like an outsized version of the modern dart-board, laid flat on a table. Each division bore either a number or a decorative symbol or device and there was a painted arrow pivoted at its centre. A number of cards, each corresponding with a section of the table were shuffled and the proprietor dealt five cards to the player who had just paid his halfpenny. The player then spun the arrow, and if it stopped at a point on the circle which echoed one of his cards, he won a tuppenny loaf from the pile of wheaten loaves, the savoury aroma of which had attracted him to the stand. By the end of the day they had lost only four loaves from their baker's dozen, and soon they were able to settle the debt with their bankrupt creditor.

A great deal of money was in constant circulation throughout the inner markets. Prize money paid to the hundreds of American sailors who had been serving in the British Navy until the United States declared war in 1812 brought many thousands of pounds into the prisons. Earnings from the sale of 'prisoner of war work' country-wide, over so many years, cannot even be guessed at. Some prisoners made smaller but useful wages in semi-official employment about the depots – a barber, for instance, could earn himself threepence a day. Many 'broke-paroles', privateer officers and officers who had refused to pledge their word in the first place, were often men of private means. For the last few years, all Americans received the US allowance of tuppence-ha'penny in addition to their prisoner of war allowance, so everyone but the 'Rough Alleys' and their continental equivalents, the 'raffalès' and the 'romans' would have had a copper or two to spend.

Benjamin Frederick Browne, another Dartmoor Yankee, also wrote an account of a stroll round the inner market food shops, similar to that of the 'Greenhand'. In the same way as Josiah Cobb preserved many of the barkers' cries, Benjamin Browne added to the interest by noting some of the recipes and manufacture of their offerings. In his 'Yarn of a Yankee Privateer', he says that any who had money could live well enough in Dartmoor; that there were prisoner-run cook-shops and stalls of every kind, from some dignified by the name of 'taverns' down to the humble coffee shops and wandering vendors of snacks. The taverns boasted meats roasted and boiled, stewed and fried; and pastries, cakes, fruits, beer, wine and liquors were all on offer. The cries heralding 'Hot Plum-gudgeon.' competed with 'Hot Fresco', 'Lobscouse nice and hot', 'Burgoo, lovely burgoo' and a dozen other mysterious concoctions. Browne rightly assumed that most outsiders would never have heard of many of these 'dainties' as they were 'not to be found in any cook's oracle':

Plumgudgeon was a compound of salt fish and potatoes, or rather of potatoes and fish; for the fish was like a grain of wheat in a bushel of chaff; you might search all day until you found it. This mass was formed into obtuse pointed cones, about as large as a tea-saucer, and fried in a little, very little, butter. Each plumgudgeon sold for a penny, and made a very decent mess for breakfast.

Fresco was a stew, made of the marrow and fat of bones, boiled out, with a few small pieces of meat and some potatoes, and thickened with barley, water being the predominant ingredient. When well and cleanly made, it was not unpalatable, and a pint might be bought for two pence.

Lobscouse was a thicker stew, made with a larger proportion of meat, part of which had been salted; it sold at about double the price of Fresco.

Burgoo [also known to seamen and Americans as 'hasty-pudding'] was an oatmeal porridge, dished up with butter and molasses, or 'trickle' as it was called in Dartmoor.

The Kofy sold had seldom seen a coffee bean, and an enterprising prison-market coffee-merchant needed little capital to set up in business; just a kettle and a few tin pots. The main ingredient was burnt crusts of bread or burnt peas. It may not sound an inviting beverage, but it was in great demand. More prisoners were in the tea and coffee business than any other, and when the doors were opened each morning the fires of coffee-merchants all round the yards were already blazing under steaming kettles and cans.

Soon after his arrival in the Depot, Benjamin Browne set himself up as a market trader in the Dartmoor grocery business. With a mess-mate he opened up their first venture in the retail trade, obtaining their first stock on credit from a Tavistock grocer who sold in the prison outer market. Like other similar enterprises, he sold 'glasses of rum, pipes, ha'penny-worths of tobacco, butter, snuff, tea, coffee, trickle &c.', always willing to cut a candle, halve a glass of rum or sell a single chew of tobacco. He described with pride his prospering little shop. Alongside the ha'penny plugs of tobacco, 'redolent of the aromatic perfumes of the land of hominy and hoe-cakes – of double-shuffle and kite foot… you might have seen the odiferous herb of China, or the aromatic berry from the sunny isles of slavery and sugar-canes.'

Alas, Benjamin's pride was soon followed by a fall. After their first stock was sold at a good profit, and the settlement date with the Tavistock trader arrived, he found that his mess-mate partner, who was also the book-keeper, had lost all their cash – probably to the French sharps and gamesters or to alcohol.

The relative wealth of the potential customer could usually be spotted by their manner of dress – from tailor-made broadcloth to the ill-fitting yellow kersey; but their purchases at the food stalls and cook-shops were just as good a guide. Most added to their rations by making group purchases for a mess of six men – each man taking his turn as 'cook of the mess'. By so doing, they could live quite well – each tuppence-ha'penny meant a couple of pounds of mixed vegetables, or an ounce and a half of coffee – but 'hot plumgudgeons' or 'golden fritters' would have been only an occasional treat for most.

At the upper end of the scale were those who could afford to patronise the restauranteurs who catered for the better-off and the owners of the gaming tables. For years the French had developed top-table eating for the lucky few, to a degree which was positively indecent in a prison world where so many barely survived. The sight and smell of tables laid out with dainties, sucking pig, geese, ducks, and fish with sauces, sirloin and beef hot from the oven (all of this is recorded), must have been a torture to the penniless and hungry – where, over the years, some of the most desperate had dined on dog, horse and rat.

The professional gamblers were the most extravagant patrons of these banqueting houses of the yards. We read of the laden tables at one of these eating places where 'the three men now sitting down to a good dinner at three shillings a head won heavily at the faro table overnight, and knowing not what tomorrow may bring forth at their trade, are banking some of their capital where it cannot be staked at the turn of a card.'

For a year the American markets in the five prison yards prospered and grew. There were occasional setbacks when supplies were cut off through closures of the main market, as a general punishment, or when storm or snow daunted the suppliers from braving the Moor. On those occasions the cost of living shot up alarmingly; the price of bread, meat and coal increased by as much as four hundred percent. However, all in all, the steadying and beneficial influence of these centres of trade and entertainment cannot be over estimated. Without them, five and a half thousand Americans would have been well nigh uncontrollable.

Charles Andrews estimated that by the end of the American occupation of Dartmoor, there were between sixty and eighty little businesses in each of the five prison yards. Their very existence depended on the supply from the other side of the inner wall and now, in the Spring of 1815, as the country traders began to drift away, and fewer and fewer market women led their donkey-trains across the Moor, the inner markets, too, began to slow down towards a standstill. Without an outlet for their works the craftsmen put aside their tools, and as existing stocks ran out, many of the shopkeepers began to go out of business. It was a time of great confusion and distress for both proprietors and customers; the shops which retailed small articles such as tobacco, thread, soap, coffee, sugar etc., had been a great advantage to their owners and as great an accommodation to every prisoner.

News of the ratification of the Treaty of Ghent and the end of that avoidable war between Britain and America, was greeted on both sides with flag-waving, cheers and patriotic song:

> 'All was now joy, congratulations, good humour, life and jollity. None supposed that we should be in prison a week longer, judging from the promptness with which the French were removed, when Bonaparte first abdicated, the whole eighty thousand being on their way home within ten days[!] after peace between England and France was promulgated abroad'.

The whole of Dartmoor was a scene of rejoicing and to cap it all the prisoners had only two days to wait before the aggregated 'tuppence- ha'pennies' were due to be distributed. The per diem allowance was not, of course, doled out daily. Each man received 6s.8d. every thirty-second day and, for reasons of office efficiency and to avoid handling the huge quantities of specie involved if the thousands of prisoners were individually paid their 6s.8d, a representative from each six-man mess was handed two One Pound notes, which he cashed either in the market or through one of the market 'brokers'.

The two days passed and pay-day dawned but no money came into the depot. At first there was no panic – until they heard from the Agent for the American Prisoners of War in England, the inefficient, neglectful and heartless Reuben Beasley. He informed them that he had halted the allowance and no money would be forthcoming as his orders had been to pay them 'during the war'. Nothing had been said about distribution of funds 'after the war', and he would have to await new orders from the American Government before he took any action on their behalf!

Joy turned to rage, Reuben Beasley was hanged and burned in effigy in the market yard, and thus began the long unhappy wait for their final release, made desperate by the one man whose job it was to deal with their problems and complaints. (See *A History of Napoleonic and American Prisoners of War 1756-1816 – Hulk, Depot and Parole*, Chapter 19.)

The excitement which had greeted news of the peace – and an expectation of the almost immediate appearance of cartel ships – was followed by a period of miserable uncertainty, trouble and hardship for the prisoners awaiting drafts to freedom. The Government ration was sufficient to ensure their survival, but it was not enough to satisfy the appetites of men grown used to those extras which their markets and their small allowance had afforded. Waterhouse wrote of hungry prisoners 'seen to traverse the alleys, backwards and forwards, with gnawing stomach and haggard look,' and that 'the comparative size of the pieces of beef and bread is watched with a keen jealous eye, lest one should have more than the other.'

The months which followed the peace were even more miserable than their wartime captivity when they had no idea of the length of their 'sentence'. Reuben Beasley's neglect had left them comparatively penniless, they felt abandoned by their government and on the 6th April there occurred the darkest blot in Dartmoor's history – the infamous 'Dartmoor Massacre' (see *A History of Napoleonic and American Prisoners of War 1756-1816 – Hulk, Depot and Parole*, Chapter 19, Part 2).

The loss of the food shops was bad enough, but as nothing compared with the closure of the tobacco booths. It may be that deprivation of almost every other comfort made tobacco of such importance to almost every seaman of that day. If necessity made it a toss-up between a meal or a chew of tobacco, the latter would almost always win. 'Joss the Tiger', a messmate of 'Greenhand', opined that: 'if it was not for tobacco, one half of impressed seamen in the British Navy would drown themselves in a week.' And a shipmate, Nimble Billy, was in a constant state of distress brought on by chew-plug deprivation. Each morning he would divide his issued bread in two, trading in one half to a stall-keeper in return for a morsel of chewing-tobacco, and making do with the other half over the next twenty-four hours; saying that if he must starve to death, he would rather it be for want of bread than for tobacco.

Thus, the sailor addicted to tobacco was really hard hit. At first it was only the price which was so depressing – the price at Plymouth had risen sky-high to nine shillings and sixpence a pound – and a penny could buy only a single small chew; but soon even at that price it was unobtainable. The real addicts became truly desperate, would barter their food ration for even the smallest plug. He would then first bind it with thread, 'do a day on it', leave it a day to dry out and, on the next day, smoke it. When their last quid had been chewed to tastelessness, the craving grew so intense that they would chew on anything – tarred rope, a piece of hard wood, a strip of old shoe leather, or the lining of a pocket which had once held tobacco.

A number of them became ill, some seriously, and were taken into the depot hospital, with swollen and protruding tongues. A few died – according to the Dartmoor surgeon, from no other cause than sudden deprivation of the weed. However, considering that they, like Nimble Billy, had probably put tobacco before food, lack of nourishment may have been a more important contribution to their demise.

The non-smoking or non-chewing reader may find all this hard to credit therefore, by way of a conclusion to this story and the importance of the markets in making available to prisoners of war some of the little 'luxuries', which were, in truth, 'necessities', I append this letter. Written by a free British sailor of the period, it makes more believable the extent to which a craving for tobacco could obsess the mind of a captive, living in uncertainty and discomfort.

Dear Brother-Tom-march 24, 1813

> This cums hopein to find you in good health as it leaves me save ankord here yesterday at 4 P.M. arter a pleasant voyage tolerable short and few squalls. Dear tom- hopes to find poor old father stout, am quite out of pigtail [chewing tobacco] Sights of pigtail at Gravesend but unfortinly not fit for a dog to chor. Dear Tom - Captains boy will bring you this and put pigtail in his pocket when bort. Best in London at the black boy in 7 diles, where go, acks for best pigtail, pound of pigtail will do, and am short of shirts.
> dear Tom- as for shirts only took 2 whereof 1 is quite wored out, and tuther most, but dont forget the pigtail as I ant had nere a quid to chor never sins Thursday. Dear tom- as for the shirts your size will do, only longer. I likes um long, get one at present, best at tower Hill and cheap, but be particler to go to 7 diles for the pigtail at the black boy, and dear Tom - acks for a pound of best pigtail and let it be good. Captains boy will put the pigtail in his pocket, he likes pigtail so ty it up. Dear Tom- shall be up about Monday there or thereabouts. not so perticler for the shirt as the present one can be washed, but dont forget the pigtail without fail so am
>
> Your loving brother T.P.
> P.S. - Dont forget pigtail.

---

1. *Memoirs.* Baron de Bonnefoux.

2. See Chapter 4, page 84.

3. 'Early Recollections': *Chambers' Journal.* No 600.

4. *Cosby's Complete Gazette.* 1818.

5. Ian MacDougall: *The Prisoners at Penicuik.*

Chapter Four

The Straw Workers,
Plaiters and
Marquetry Artists

IN NO OTHER BRANCH OF ARTISTRY or craftsmanship did the prisoner of war show such industry as in his working of straw. The ingenuity and skill with which he manipulated this simple and easily obtained raw material sometimes brought him comparative wealth – and sometimes brought him up sharply and painfully against the laws of Great Britain.

In the hands of the most highly skilled prisoner artist-craftsmen, this by-product of the harvest was employed to produce artefacts of such delicate beauty and quality that many are treasured to this day, in private collections and museums in many parts of the world. This chapter, however, tells of those captives who practised the straw-worker's art at a much lower level – the production of straw plait – and a surprising story it is, of smuggling, tax-evasion, imprisonment and floggings.

There were several districts in France and Italy where the production of straw plait for the hat and bonnet-making industry had been carried on for centuries, and it would seem that, in every depot or prison ship, there were prisoners of war who had at least some basic knowledge of the craft. Men with experience of the straw trade as civilians before the war, quickly grasped the opportunity to make a profitable use of their captive time, and were soon recruiting and training suitable hands from amongst their fellow prisoners. It is not so surprising that, quite apart from the professionals, many captives should have proved to be skilful plaiters, particularly if they had been sailors for any length of time. The knotting, whipping and splicing of ropes and twines could be as complicated and demanding of digital skill as any plaiting in straw. Most seamen were self-sufficient in many ways, including the ability to make their own clothes and headwear, and carry out repairs when necessary.

Captain Boteler of H.M.S. *Antelope* described how his crew set about fitting themselves out in 1815[1]:

> 'They were [each] issued with twelve yards of duck [heavy cotton or linen fabric], thread and needles and a black silk handkerchief. A brass nail was driven in the deck at three or six yards as a guide for measuring, and before the retreat was drummed, "Hear the news fore and aft! By next muster day every one will be expected in frock and trousers"'.

(Left) **Roll-Top Strawwork Chest.** *Fitted with a drop-front and roll-top that conceal numerous tiny drawers and compartments. Hinged upper lid for access to two lidded sections. Strawwork overlay throughout the interior and exterior surfaces.* 13 x 13 x 9 in.

Dome-Top Strawwork Chest.
Fitted with a decorated drop-front that conceals three drawers with bone pulls. Hinged lid for access to four compartments with lids decorated with geometric 'star' designs. Interior and exterior completely overlaid with strawwork of various designs. 10¼ x 7½ x 7½ in.

Roll-Top Strawwork Chest. Fitted with a drop-front and roll-top that conceal numerous drawers, compartments and mirrors. Behind the roll-top is a bone carved figure of a Roman. Hinged dome-top for access to two lidded compartments. Strawwork overlay throughout the interior and exterior surfaces.
15½ x 13¾ x 9½ in.

The crew then dashed to the galley fire to char sticks or pieces of wood with which to mark their patterns out in dots as a guide, before getting down to the work of cutting and tailoring. Those who doubted their skill as garment-makers employed the more expert, paying for their suits with cash or sacrificing their rum ration for a period. Captain Boteler also mentioned their dexterity in making things from straw: 'The same thing with straw hats. Every bum-boat was expected to bring off a bundle of peculiar grass, and soon you will see the men at work at their sennet [plaited straw] and in a very short time, with first rate hats.'

Dome-Top Strawwork Chest. *Fitted with a drop-front that conceals small drawers with bone pulls. Hinged lid revealing an upper section with numerous lidded compartments. Interior and exterior completely overlaid with strawwork of various designs. 9½ x 10¼ x 7 in.*

Roll-Top Strawwork Chest. *Fitted with numerous drawers, compartments and a hinged lid. Bone handles for the drawers and roll-top. Strawwork overlay throughout the interior and exterior surfaces.* 11½ x 10 x 6¼ in.

As with most other money-making prisoner of war industries, from model-making in bone or wood to gambling, there were business-wise men and entrepreneurs among the captives who took the straw trade firmly in hand and developed it far beyond the bounds of a pocket-money-making enterprise. These men were the *armateurs*, capitalist employers and organisers, who bought in the straw, divided it amongst the prisoner-plaiters, then set them to work on a piece-work basis. The finished plait was paid for at the rate of three sous per *brasse* – a length of just under six feet. Some of the more adept workers would make as many as twelve *brasses* a day and, with workers like these, the employer, himself, would soon be in a very big way of business. It is said that some of these 'straw capitalists' at Millbay Prison, Plymouth, amassed fortunes of between thirty

Roll-Top Strawwork Chest. *Fitted with a drop-front and roll-top that conceal numerous drawers, compartments and mirrors. Hinged upper lid for access to two compartments that have lids decorated with geometric 'star' designs. Strawwork overlay throughout all exterior and interior surfaces.* 13 x 11½ x 8½ in.

Strawwork Box. Hinged lid with a building, surrounded by numerous designs on the outside, and a scene from Aesop's fable 'The Fox and the Raven' on the underside. Interior divided into two lidded compartments decorated in floral and border designs. An exceptional example of the art of straw marquetry. 5 x 11½ x 8½ in.

Straw Marquetry Box. *Superb example with the front and sides decorated with Napoleon's coat of arms and masonic compasses. Inner lid has décor of a building, horses, coach, etc. Inside divided into four sections with decorated lids depicting navigating instruments, musical instruments, Nelson memorial and fruit in a basket. Lower side drawer lined with a Middle Eastern scene. 4 x 12 x 9 in.*

Strawwork Box. *Outer lid and sides delicately depicting the following figures: man, woman and dog strolling, trader on donkey-back, a leaping stag, a horseman and a galloping horseman. Inner lid with a scene depicting a horse, carriage and driver. Four inner compartments with bone-lined holes for silk threads. 3¾ x 8 x 6 in.*

and forty thousand francs by the time of their release.

From the early days of the confinement in Britain of continental prisoners of war, a lucrative trade had been carried on within the closed prisons, not only in producing straw plait, but in the manufacture of the finished articles for which the plait was intended – the straw hats and bonnets which were so popular in those times. Straw hats or bonnets of one sort or another were the normal headgear of the labouring classes, but fashionable and sometimes very expensive creations were also much sought after. This was by no means a recent fashion. In 1630, Ben Jonson addressed an epigram to Lady Mary Wroth, author of *'Urania'*, which ran: 'He, that but saw you wear the wheaten hat, would call

Strawwork Tea Caddy. *Hinged lid with countryfolk on the outside and a floral scene on the underside. Interior divided into two compartments with nicely fashioned and decorated lids. Note that some of the work is 'straw engraving' which is rarely found. 4½ x 7 x 5½ in.*

Strawwork Box. *Hinged lid with a harbour scene surrounded by floral motifs. Interior divided into five decorated compartments.* 3 x 8¾ x 6 in.

you more than Ceres', and in 1667 Samuel Pepys observed, after watching the ladies in his party trying on straw bonnets: 'which did become them mightily, but especially my wife'.[2]

The best of the prisoner of war straw workers were well qualified to satisfy this demand for 'fashion millinery'. Before the war, much of the finest plait used in the design of hats for the upper end of the market had been imported from France and Italy, 'Leghorn' plait being amongst the most popular. Therefore, the continental touch and technique of the prisoner–plaiters made their product desirable to both the millinery manufacturers in the nearby towns and the visitors to the prison markets. It was natural that a lady in proud possession of a newly acquired and fashionable Sunday bonnet, should look forward to showing it off on her next visit to church; but, in one place at least, she probably went to church rather than to the milliner to purchase her bonnet in the first instance. In 1797, the Agent for the prisoners of war at Portchester Castle complained to the Transport Board that many Portsmouth townsfolk, visiting under the pretence of attending Portchester Parish Church, which was within the Castle bounds, came really to buy straw hats and bonnets from the prisoners.

The captives did not enjoy this profitable occupation for very long – at least, not legally. From the latter years of the eighteenth century and afterwards, the prison trade in and manufacture of straw hats, caps and bonnets was strictly forbidden by country-wide Government Order; although, for a time, they were allowed to continue in the production of the *brasses* for sale to the local bonnet-makers who made up the finished article. This prohibition was not quite so unreasonable or small-minded as it may at first appear.

Strawwork Drop-Front Chest. *A rare dated box with the inside of the drop-front inlaid with masonic symbols and the masonic date 'Anno 5808' (1808). Hinged lid with a mythological character on the outside and an oval mirror, surrounded by scroll designs on the underside. Interior consists of six lidded compartments and three drawers.* 6 x 19 x 12 in. *(See also opposite.)*

The making of baskets, hats, bonnets and similar straw manufactures was a very important cottage industry in a number of counties, particularly in the Midlands. Daniel Defoe, who made a journey through the English counties early in the eighteenth century,[3] noticed that 'the Manufacture of Straw Work, especially Straw Hats, spreads itself from Hertfordshire into this County [Bedfordshire] and is wonderfully increased in a few Years past.' And even earlier, in 1689, it was estimated that some 14,000 people in the Luton/Dunstable area, were entirely dependent on the income from straw plait and hat making. Now, the heavy duties on imported plait from Italy and France, and the fact that the outbreak of the Revolutionary War had almost completely cut off supplies from abroad anyway, had been a boon for the poor countryfolk who carried on the craft, and inspired a rapid expansion of the trade to towns and villages in other parts of the country. The actual work of preparing the straw and making the plaits was carried out, in the main, by the women and children; the latter attending a 'plaiting school', the boys until they were about fourteen years of age, when they were old enough to be employed as farm labourers.

'School' was hardly an accurate description of these cottage sweat shops, where little children were sent to learn the craft of manipulating straw. They were sent there as soon as they had learned to walk and were placed under the care and supervision of a 'schoolmistress'. No lessons were given in the generally accepted sense, the 'teachers' were often illiterate and some could not even plait. Their real task was as overseers to make certain that each child produced its quota of saleable *brasses*. As many as fifty or sixty children were crowded into rooms often no larger than twelve feet square, the only heat supplied by charcoal 'dick pots'. By the time they were eight or nine years old they were earning about nine-pence a week (roughly 4p in today's money), of which two or

Strawwork Box. *Hinged lid with scenes of buildings on both sides. Interior divided into three compartments which are decorated in building and floral motifs. 3¼ x 10 x 7 in.*

Strawwork House Model. *A model of the front of a house with windows, chimneys, balconies, steps, etc. Overlaid with light and dark pieces of natural coloured straw. In original glazed case. 9½ x 7 x 6 in.*

three old pence went to the school as fees. The girls left when they were old enough to work without an overseer, usually when they were thirteen or fourteen, at which age they could be earning as much as three shillings a week (15p). As late as 1874, there were still seven plaiting schools at Tilsworth, Stanbridge and Eggington – but no day school. The plaits from the cottages or in the plaiting schools were made up in coils, or 'scores', of twenty-yard lengths. These were sold to the travelling dealers who made the rounds from village to village, or were taken to one of the Plait Markets which were a feature of nearly all of the straw towns.

War, which had at first produced the conditions which made the cottagers' work so much in demand, now produced a rival who was likely to bring about their ruin – the prisoner of war plaiter. The vast output of under-priced but quality handiwork which

Bone Calvary Model. *Superbly carved and coloured model of the Crucifixion with all the symbols of a cockerel, flowers, three dice, spears, supporting figures, etc. All contained within a straw marquetry case with a clear glass front and sides. 10½ x 6½ in.*

began to issue from the prisons caused serious loss of work and essential income to these poor people, and something had to be done about it. The Government Order banning the making of straw millinery – though not at first straw *brasses* – was promulgated through the Transport Office to all depots and prison ships throughout the country. Whilst incidentally providing some protection for the cottage hat-makers, if not for the plaiters, the Order contained more than a hint that a more important reason was a technical one: that as the articles made by the prisoners were of foreign manufacture they were

Bone Calvary Model. *Similar to the one opposite but slightly less elaborate. Also in a strawwork case with a glass front and sides.* 10 x 7½ in.

therefore taxable items. Part of the Order, which was issued in 1799, read:-

'Being informed that the Revenues and Manufactures of this country are considerably injured by the extensive sale of Straw Hats made by the Prisoners of War in this Country, we do hereby require and direct you to admit no Hat, Cap or Bonnet manufactured by any of the Prisoners of War in your custody, to be sold or sent out of the Prison in future, under any pretence whatever, and to seize and destroy all such articles as may be detected in violation of this Order.'

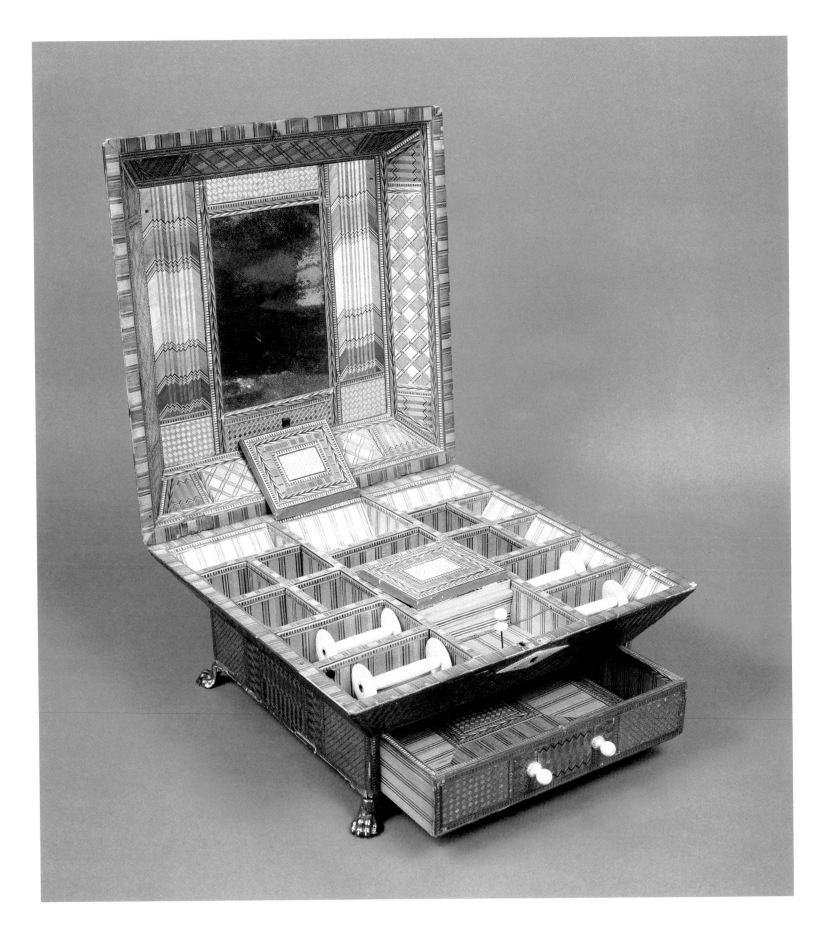

Strawwork Sewing Box. *Rare 'cushion-top' design with parquetry, herringbone and chevron designs throughout. Upper section divided into nineteen compartments and is outfitted with four bone thread bobbins. Lower drawer with bone 'secret pin' for locking purposes. Bone key escutcheon, drawer pulls and lid knob. (See also previous page 64.) 7 x 12½ x 13 in.*

Although the 1799 ban on all finished millinery manufactures was a blow to the industrious prisoners of war, they enjoyed another seven years of profitable straw plaiting; seven sad years for the plaiting schools and cottage industry. Then, as the war dragged on and the Government looked around for more sources of revenue, imported un-made-up straw plait was added to the long list of dutiable items. A tough duty of 7/- per pound was imposed on Hat and Bonnet Plait – and the finished headpiece was additionally taxed according to the width of its brim!

From July, 1806, when the new tax was introduced, a total ban on the production of all straw plait produced by prisoners of war was strictly imposed. It was reasoned that as the plait, like the hats, was a foreign production, it was subject to a tax which it would be almost impossible to collect from prisoners of war, and the only solution was to ban its production completely. However good the reasons for imposing this ban, it cannot be expected that the prisoners would appreciate its necessity. It was resented and crops up in prisoners' critical memoirs of the following decade. Their feelings can be summed up in the comments of just two of them, one French, the other American: Captain (later

Strawwork Box. *Hinged lid with floral designs on the outside and a harbour scene with Danish flags on the underside. Interior divided into three decorated compartments which sit over a single drawer.* 4½ x 11½ x 8 in.

Strawwork Box. *Two-level construction with the upper section divided into three decorated compartments and the lower portion being a drawer. Hinged lid with floral decorations on the outside and a harbour scene on the inside. 4¼ x 10⅜ x 7¼ in.*

Strawwork Chest. *Miniature size with hipped outer and inner lids both of which are friction fitted. Interior divided into four compartments and has a pincushion. Lower section has a small drawer with a bone pull. Drawer and inner lid have printed strips with French phrases. Floral designs both inside and out. 3½ x 5 x 3 in.*

English Prisoner of War Work. *Seven miniature carts and carriages made from a pack of 18th century playing cards. Contained in a wood box with other cards being used as dividers. With a provenance card reading: 'Toys made by my G.G.G. Grandfather Captain William Lewery R.A. while prisoner of the French at Verdun. T.R. Blackley 15 Feb. 72.'*

Baron) Charles Dupin, of the French Corps of Naval Engineers, wrote in disgust of the prohibition of hat making in the prisons:

> ' …by a Restriction which well describes the mercantile jealousies of a manufacturing people, the prisoners were prohibited from making for sale woollen gloves and straw hats. It would have injured in these petty branches the commerce of his Britannic Majesty's subjects.'

Later, the American prisoner of war, Charles Andrews, wrote sarcastically:

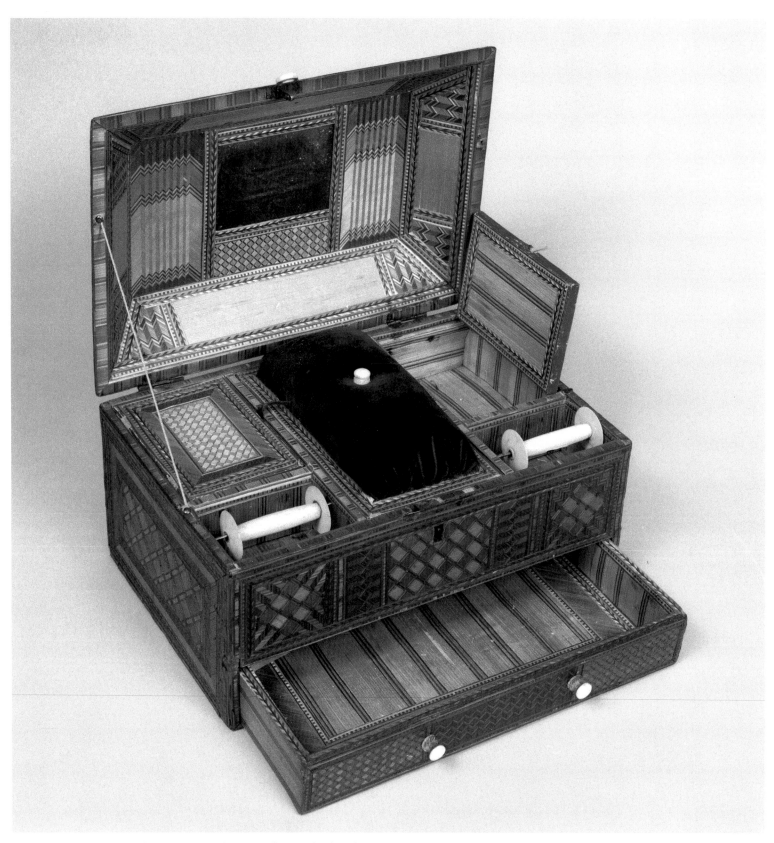

Strawwork Box. *Constructed on two levels with the upper section being divided into five compartments that are outfitted for sewing uses. Lower section is one drawer. Hip-shaped upper lid. All the strawwork done in herringbone and parquetry designs. 5¾ x 9½ x 6½ in.*

Strawwork Box. *Built on two levels with an upper section divided into three compartments and a lower section having two drawers. Hinged lid decorated on the outside with a farm scene and on the inside with a harbour scene. 5½ x 14¼ x 9 in.*

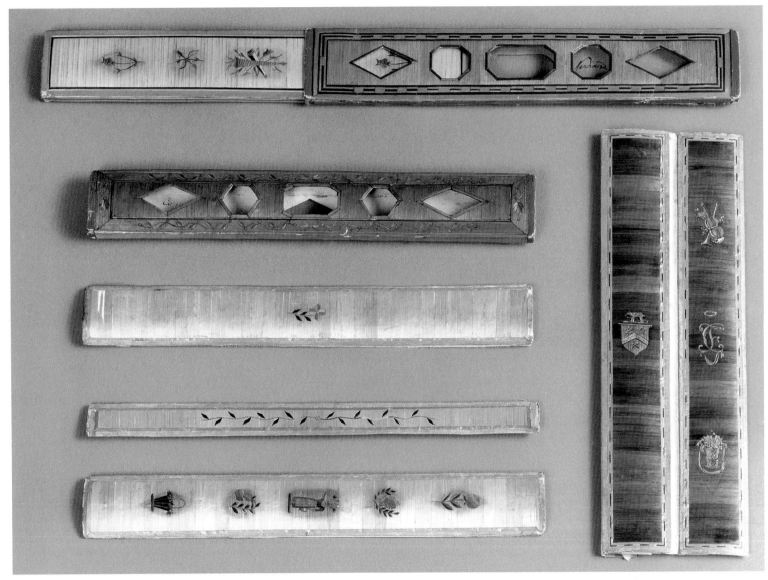

(Top) **Strawwork Silk Holder.** *Outer sleeve with decorated open frames that reveal delicate floral and archery motifs that have been applied to the inner sleeve. Signed on the pink lining within the inner sleeve. 9 x 1⅝ in. (Below left)* **Strawwork Silk Holder.** *Outer sleeve with decorated open frames that reveal delicate floral, etc. scenes that are applied to the inner sleeve. Signed on the inside of the outer sleeve. 9 x 1½ in. (Below right)* **Strawwork Silk Holder.** *Delicately done with strawwork designs of musical instruments, a monogram, a floral basket and an emblem. 9 x 1½ in.*

'The honorable Board had indulgently permitted the American prisoners to establish and carry on any branch of manufacture, except such as netting, woollen fabrics, making straw hats or bonnets &c. &c.; or rather they prohibited every branch of manufacture which they were capable of pursuing. At this time [by Charles Andrews' time the making of straw plait had been interdicted for many years] they could have carried on the making of straw into flats for bonnets with very considerable advantage, as almost every sailor was more or less capable of working at this art.'

It would seem that before making their derogatory comments, neither of these men considered the fact that a great many profitable activities were *not* prohibited, and that

Strawwork Cigar Case. *Two piece, friction-fit case completely covered in minutely detailed mosiac and marquetry designs. Closed: 4½ x 2½ in.* ***Strawwork Cigar Case.*** *Very similar in construction and design to the previous item. Closed: 4½ x 2½ in.* ***Strawwork Trinket Box.*** *Outer shell decorated with herringbone designs. Has two, circular shaped, swing-out trays. 1 x 3½ x 2 in.*

almost every depot in Britain had the advantage of a properly set up daily or weekly market to dispose of their wares. Both quotations are taken from their post-war reminiscences, so they would have known that the British prisoner of war in France or America, particularly the former, had nothing to compare with the privilege of the prison markets in this country. When Captain Dupin's memoirs were published, the *Quarterly Review*[4] replied to his 'prohibition' comments:

> 'It was so. These "petty branches" of manufactures were the employment of the wives and children of the neighbouring cottagers, and enabled them to pay their rent and taxes: and, on a representation by the magistrates that the vast quantities sent into the market by the French prisoners who had neither rent, nor taxes, nor lodging, firing, food or

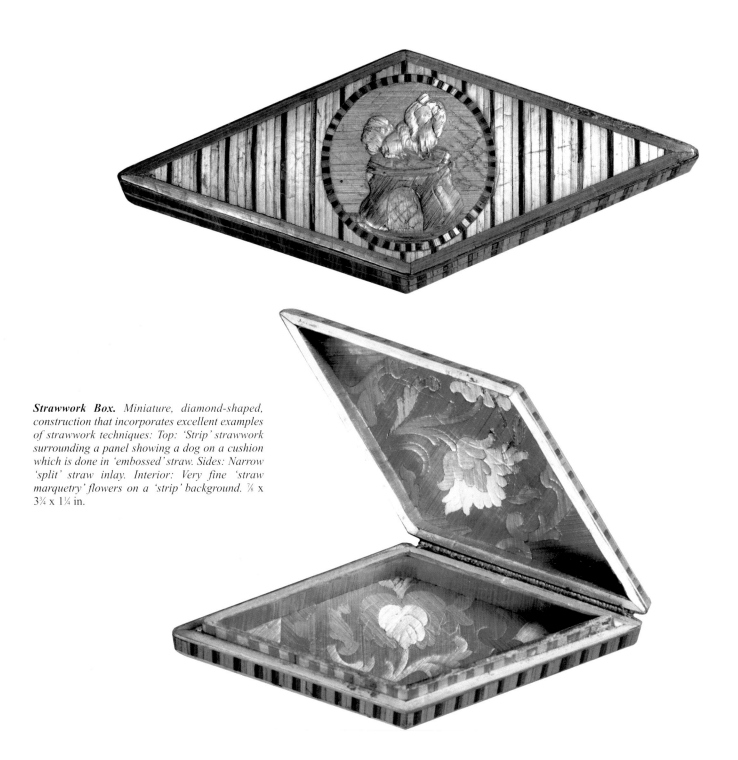

Strawwork Box. *Miniature, diamond-shaped, construction that incorporates excellent examples of strawwork techniques: Top: 'Strip' strawwork surrounding a panel showing a dog on a cushion which is done in 'embossed' straw. Sides: Narrow 'split' straw inlay. Interior: Very fine 'straw marquetry' flowers on a 'strip' background. ⅞ x 3¾ x 1¼ in.*

clothes to find, had thrown the industrious cottagers out of work, an order was sent to stop the manufacture by the prisoners.'

There is no shortage of evidence to show that the ban did *not* stop the trade. Prisoners had plenty of encouragement from financially interested British merchants outside the depots, and it was not difficult for them to produce the goods in secrecy. Neither was it difficult to find guards who, in return for cash, would risk the severe flogging which was inevitably meted out to the detected soldier-smuggler.

One very prominent – and indeed very long – name was linked with an evasion of the

'Book' Type Strawwork Boxes.

Order – Stephen John Batiste de Galois de la Tour, the Bishop of Moulins. This gentleman, who was a political exile deported from France because of his allegiance to the Bourbons, came to England as chaplain to the French prisoners of war at Norman Cross. He lived outside the depot, at the Bell Inn in Stilton and, through the influence of English friends in high places, was granted the privilege of the release of a young French Norman Cross prisoner to act as his servant. The Bishop let his British friends down badly, as the following shame-faced and apologetic letter from a very important one of them clearly shows. The embarrassed Sir Rupert George, the Transport Board Commissioner, wrote to the Secretary to the First Lord of the Admiralty:

'Dear Sir, TRANSPORT OFFICE. *19th March, 1808.*

[After explaining that he had been introduced to Bishop de la Tour by the Bishop of Montpellier, he went on to say…]
I prevailed upon my colleagues to release a Prisoner of War to attend upon him [the Bishop of Moulins]; this I am sorry to acknowledge, was irregular and unauthorised, but I was actuated by motives of humanity, as the Bishop complained that his finances were

'Book' Type Strawwork Box. *A silk thread box with four bone lined holes through which the threads pass. Constructed to resemble a book. Hinged lid with geometric and striped designs on both sides. Interior divided into five compartments covered by two decorated lids. 3 x 7½ x 5 in.*

so limited that he could not afford to keep any servant of a different description.

'This should have influenced the Bishop to keep his servant from carrying on any improper traffic with Prisoners; on the contrary he became the instrument of introducing straw, manufactured, to the Prisoners for the purpose of being made into hats, bonnets etc., by which the Revenue of our country is injured, and the poor who exist by that branch of the trade would be turned out of employ, as the Prisoners who are fed, clothed and lodged at the public expense would be able to undersell them.

'I must observe that this is the only article which the Prisoners are prevented from manufacturing. [Sir Rupert must have known that his statement was inaccurate.] When the Bishop's servant had established himself in their trade the Bishop wrote to me, that he [the servant] had found a means of getting his livelihood and desired that he might remain at large, and that another Prisoner might be released to serve him, neither of

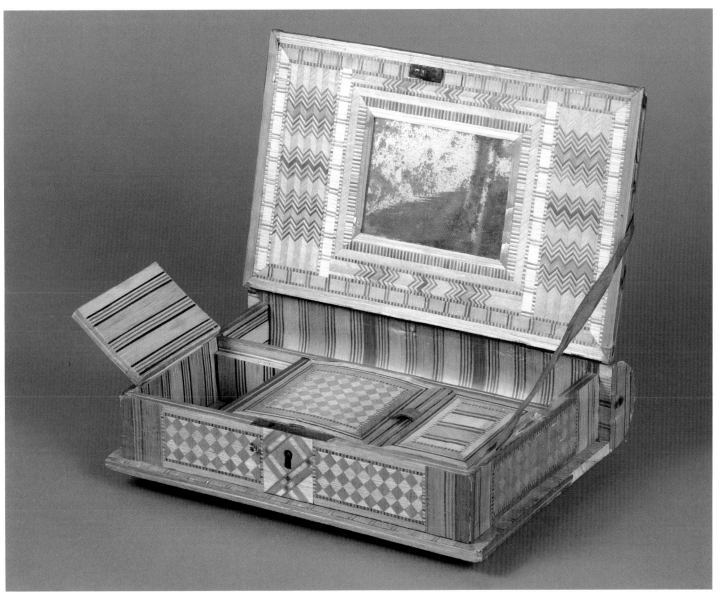

'Book' Type Strawwork Box. Decorated in and out with parquetry, herringbone and chevron designs. Hinged lid with a mirror on the underside. Interior divided into four compartments. 2 x 8½ x 6½ in.

which the Board thought it proper to comply with, for the foregoing reasons.[5]

I am Dear Sir,
Very faithfully yours
RUPERT GEORGE.'

The outcome was that the Bishop lost his privilege of having a servant, and the servant lost the privilege and comparative freedom of his parole. He was returned to Norman Cross Depot – probably to face a period of reflection and regret in the Black Hole, or *Cachot.*

All prohibitions give birth to illegal evasions and new under-worlds are born. The banning of prison-produced *brasses* was no exception; neither the captives nor their

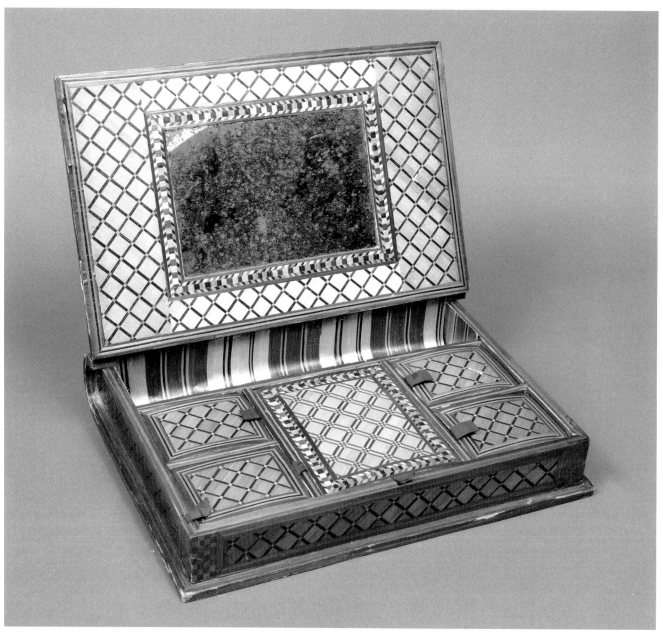

'Book' Type Strawwork Box. *Completely overlaid in various strawwork patterns and designs. Hinged lid with a mirror on the underside. Interior divided into six compartments with decorated lids.* 2 x 11 x 8 in.

British clients were willing to tamely submit to the interdict. A Huntingdonshire man, the Revd E. Bradley, incumbent of the village of Denton, near Norman Cross, left an unpublished manuscript which told of the cooperation of prisoner and soldier to beat the ban:

> 'The French prisoners at the prison made beautiful straw plaits, which were purchased by the people of Stilton and sold at a high rate. For a long time they were forbidden to sell these plaits, but they found means to do so through the soldiers. No doubt the soldiers made a great deal of money in this way, although the plaits were sold so cheaply many people in Stilton made very respectable fortunes in their sale.'

Whilst most of the prisoners' output – which, through quality and price-cutting, often won over that produced by the country's own cottage industry – was sold to be made up as near to the depot as possible, much was hawked around the neighbouring towns or sold to the wholesalers in London or elsewhere. The Revd Bradley said that the guards, who smuggled the contraband straw-work out of the prison yards, delivered it direct to the purchasers' houses or workplaces, sometimes with the plait wrapped round their bodies; in which case they would retire upstairs to undress, and then descend with the goods. The reverend gentlemen added that he had no direct knowledge of the means by which the captives obtained their raw material, 'but as they could no more make plaits without straw than the Israelites could make bricks', he came to the rather obvious conclusion that militiamen and guides were the handlers in both directions.

Every garrison had the problem of dealing with two-way smuggling on a grand scale; great quantities of the raw material had to be smuggled into the depots and equally unwieldy bundles of *brasses* smuggled out. Apart from the French workers and their organisers, a large number of British participants were involved in the illegal traffic. There were the merchants and wholesalers, who put immediate profit before the long-term injury to the trade in general and their cottage workers in particular; their crooked agents who took the actual risks of dealing; the militiaman or guard who would do the in-and-out smuggling, and others of the depot staff who found it worth their while to turn a blind eye. There are stories of steely-nerved visitors to the prison markets who bought finished plait from the prisoners, or took in cut straw as exchange, which they then delivered to unscrupulous hatters in the nearby town.

As the prisoner-made merchandise was sold at a bargain price, the quantities must have been truly great for so many people on either side of the wall to have risked the

'Book' Type Strawwork Box. Decorated on the outer lid and sides with strawwork framing and watercolour panels of floral and harbour scenes. Interior divided into three compartments covered by two decorated lids. 3½ x 8¼ x 5 in.

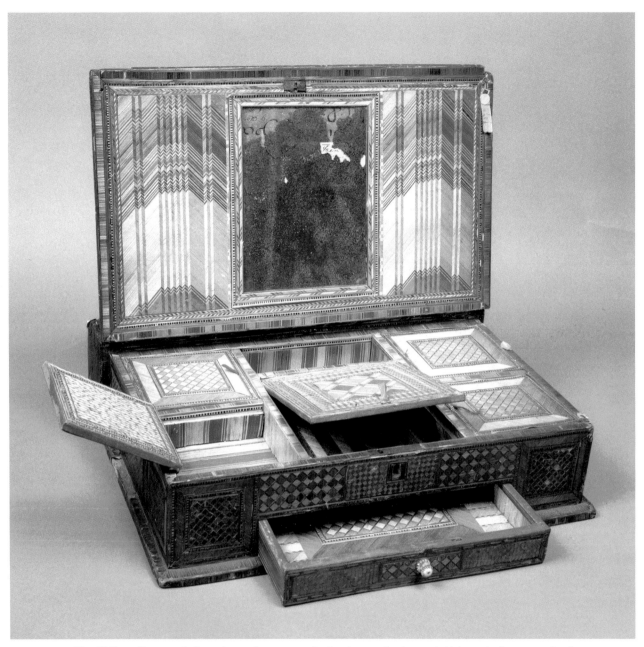

'Book' Type Strawwork Box. *A very large example that is completely overlaid in typical strawwork of varying patterns. Hinged lid with a mirror on the underside. Interior divided into six compartments with decorated lids. Lower front fitted with a drawer and bone pull. 3¾ x 14¼ x 11 in.*

fierce punishments laid down for the offence. A convicted soldier or militiaman could receive a flogging of anything up to five hundred lashes, whilst a civilian offender would be sentenced to six or twelve months, probably fettered, in an unpleasant local gaol. The civilians who were caught and charged were usually small-fry and go-betweens. The merchants themselves, however, were most often of sufficient wealth and importance to avoid arrest, sheltered as they were under the guardian angel of the bribe.

There were many courts-martial, and militiamen and soldiers were sentenced to vicious floggings; but the ring-leaders and dealers usually – but not always – got away with it. With so many interested parties at all levels of local society, it was difficult to get juries to convict, or judges to pass more than token sentences. Although it was common knowledge that the licensees of some of the Peterborough and Stilton inns were deeply involved in the straw plait racket, a local legal ruling was obtained which ensured that a publican could not lose or be refused a licence because of an offence connected with the straw trade! – whereas, it should be remembered, a common soldier could be given a sentence of lashes by the hundred.

Captain Pressland, the Agent for Norman Cross Depot, was seriously concerned at the number of local dealers who, with apparent impunity, ignored the Government Orders and engaged in the smuggling business; some even boasting openly of their certainty of never being brought to trial. In 1809, Pressland told the Transport Board that no matter how hard he and the Commander of the Garrison worked to suppress it, the illegal traffic would continue until the merchants and dealers were prosecuted. He had a further worry:

> ' …already eight or nine soldiers have deserted because of their dread of punishment, having been detected by those they knew would inform against them, and I shall leave the Board to judge how far the discipline of the regiment has been hurt, and the soldiers seduced from their duty by the bribes they are constantly receiving from Barnes, Lunn, and Browne [Huntingdonshire straw dealers].'

Strawwork Tea Caddy. *Hinged, dome-top, lid with parquetry designs on the exterior and chevron motifs on the underside. Interior divided into two foil lined, lidded, compartments. Bone keyhole escutcheon. 6¼ x 9 x 4¾ in.*

Pressland then made a strong point, far more important than lost revenues:

> ' …if these persons can with so much facility convey into the Prison, sacks of 5 to 6 feet in length, they might convey weapons of every description to annoy those whose charge they are under, to the detriment of HM's service, and the lives of his subjects most probably.'

Barnes, the dealer mentioned in Captain Pressland's accusatory letter, was the brother of a Baldock straw dealer and seems to have had the illegal side of the straw business nicely sewn up. He had gone so far as to purchase five wheat fields near the depot so that he could grow his own raw material – here was one man who did not mind how long the war lasted![6] This type of grow-your-own venture was not peculiar to Norman Cross. A Bedfordshire man bought wheat and barley fields near Penicuik, in Scotland, for the purpose of supplying straw to the plaiters in the great depot at Valleyfield.

The merchants had great influence and made it difficult for Pressland to get convictions. Whilst bribery bought the services of the corruptible among the soldiers, intimidation was just as effective to persuade their more honest fellows to keep their mouths shut. In February 1812, a local newspaper, reported that a Sergeant Ives of the West Sussex Militia, who had been active in the attempts to suppress the trade, was stopped by a gang who did not stop at beating and robbing him. More significantly and

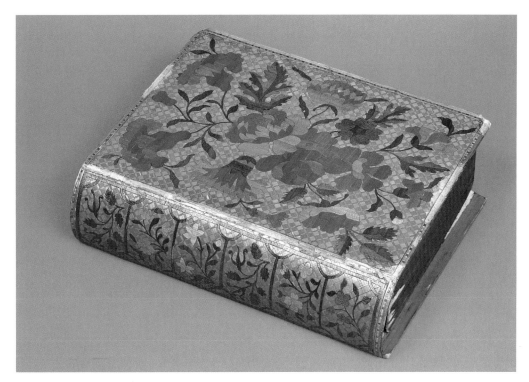

Strawwork Love Token. Constructed in the form of a book with floral strawwork throughout. Interior is divided into sixteen sections: two holding beautifully decorated oval boxes, five lidded compartments with watercolour hearts and French messages of love and dedication, a bottle holder and bottle and two ring slots. In the back of the spine is another message in French. 2 x 8 x 6½ in. (See also page 82.)

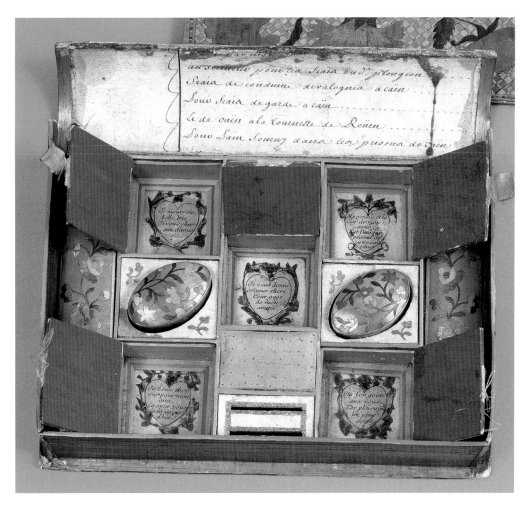

painfully, they forced open his jaws and cut off the tip of his tongue.[7]

Accusations of meanmindedness greeted every effort to stop the illicit industry, but it must be acknowledged that, apart from all other considerations, a very real security problem did exist. The criticisms came not only from the depots and the hulks (for the plait industry had spread to the prison ships), and those members of the prison staff with a vested interest, but also from well-meaning people on the outside, who thought they knew better how to run a prisoner of war establishment than did the Transport Office or the Commandant in charge.

George Borrow, the author, traveller and philologist, in the third chapter of his *Lavengro*, gives a vivid, though one-sided, account of a 'straw-plait-hunt'. His unpatriotic prejudice on this occasion may be explained by the fact that, in his ninth and tenth years he lived in the great Norman Cross Prisoner of War Depot. His father was a lieutenant in the West Norfolk Militia, stationed there from July 1811 until April 1813, and young George no doubt got to know, and like, many of the French prisoners. One can well imagine that, with their own families so far away, they would have been kind to the lad and enjoyed the pleasure of his company. One can imagine, too, that he would have been fascinated and flattered by the attention of his new and exotic warrior friends. If, when he wrote *Lavengro* forty years later, the following passage had been set down as the impressions of a ten year old, rather than the completely biased view of a fifty year old man, it would make better reading:

> 'Much had the poor inmates to endure, and much to complain of, to the disgrace of England be it said – of England, in general so kind and bountiful: rations of carrion meat and bread, from which I have seen the very hounds turn away, were unworthy entertainment even for the most ruffian enemy, when helpless and captive. And such, alas! was the fare of these *casernes*.
>
> 'And then, those visits, or rather ruthless inroads, called in the slang of the place "straw plait hunts", when, in pursuit of a contraband article, which the prisoners, in order to procure for themselves a few of the necessaries and comforts of existence, were in the habit of making, red coated battalions were marched into the prisons, who, with the bayonet's point, carried havoc and ruin into every poor convenience which ingenious wretchedness had been endeavouring to raise around it; and then the triumphant exit with the miserable booty; and worse of all, the accursed bonfire, on the barrack parade, of the straw plait contraband, beneath the view of those glaring eyeballs from those lofty roofs, amidst the hurrahs of the troops, frequently drowned in the curses poured down from above like a tempest shower, or the terrific war-whoop of *'Vive L'Empereur.'*

Undoubtedly there were 'straw plait hunts', and it is natural that the captive workers would have felt both despondency and rage; understandable, too, that their young friend, George, should have remembered their protestations and distress; but T.J. Walker, in his history of Norman Cross, points to a coincidence which allows us to judge the historic worth of Borrow's account. Captain Pressland had retired in 1811, and the new Agent, Captain John Draper, carried on in his place from August 1811 until February 1813, for almost exactly that same period when Lieutenant Borrow was serving at Norman Cross Depot – and his young son was storing away the memories which he was to set down four decades later. Captain Draper would have been deeply involved in all aspects of discipline and control at the Depot, including 'straw plait hunts'. A marble plaque in St Peter's Church, Yaxley, gives a more reliable indication of the Captain's character:

> Inscribed at the desire and the sole expense of
> the French Prisoners of War at Norman Cross

'Morengo' Snuff Box. *Superbly carved from a Coquilla nut into the form of a prison hulk. Hinged lid with a carved portrait of Napoleon. Figurehead of a seated Roman soldier. Bottom embellished with scroll and leaf carving of the highest quality. Nicely carved stern with 'Morengo' on the underside.* 2 x 5 x 2⅛ in.

to the memory of
CAPTAIN JOHN DRAPER
Who for the last eighteen months of his life was
Agent to the Depot,
in testimony of their esteem and gratitude for his
humane attention to their comfort during that too
short period.
He died Feb.23, 1813, aged 53 years.

It is true that prisoners of war would often have had good reason to complain of the quality of their food ration, and George Borrow may have sincerely believed what he wrote about 'carrion meat' from which the 'very hounds turn away'; but there may be a more believable explanation: I recently read somewhere that dogs would seldom go near

A Straw Splitter. *Undoubtedly the greatest innovation in the art of straw marquetry. Many Englishmen claim its invention but it is generally accepted as being the idea of a French prisoner. Has splitting holes to produce 4, 5, 6, 7, and 8 strips from each piece of straw.* Height: 4 in.

the scraps from meat cooked with herbs and spices – such as the Frenchmen's highly-seasoned *ragoûts*!

As I have quoted from George Borrow's gloomy account, it is right that I should balance it with the impression of another visitor to that same Depot; an account which probably leans as much in one direction as George's leans in the other:

> 'Having disposed of our horses at the inn, we walked back a mile or so to Norman Cross to see the barracks for the French prisoners, no less than 6,000 of whom are confined there. It is a fine, dry, healthy spot. Among them is little disease... their dexterity in little handicraft nick-nacks, particularly in the making of toys of bone, will put many pounds into the pockets of several of them. We were credibly assured that some of them will carry away with them £200 or £300. Their behaviour was not at all impudent as we passed the palisades within which they are cooped.'

The desirability of the prisoner-made product over its English counterpart lay not only in its cheapness, but as much in the superiority of its workmanship. The French craftsmen employed a great deal of ingenuity and a wide variety of techniques in the preparation of their *brasses.* Sometimes they used the outside of the straw, or alternated the white inside with the shiny yellow outer face; at others they produced what was known as 'rice' plait, which was achieved by showing the white inside alone. Many of their methods and techniques were improvements on our own native plaiting and the French prisoners are generally credited with the invention of the greatest innovation ever to be introduced into the straw trade – the 'Straw Splitter.'

The invention of this ingenious little tool completely changed the possibilities of artistic achievement in the craft – and made possible the finest of the masterpieces of straw marquetry illustrated in the next chapter. Its invention has, from time to time been

A Straw Plait Mill. *Plait mills were used to soften and make pliable dampened straw plait which was then used to produce various articles. Heavy wood construction with a crank handle and a tightening clamp.* 20 x 12 in.

attributed to at least half a dozen different Englishmen. However, popular belief has it that it originated among the French prisoners of war straw workers in this country, and it may be of significance that it first made its appearance at the beginning of the Napoleonic Wars. A Luton man, A.J. Tansley, wrote, 'It is generally supposed that the French prisoners at Yaxley Barracks, near Stilton, first made it in bone between the years 1803 and 1806. This instrument was soon imitated. A blacksmith at Dunstable, named Janes, made them in iron...'

Before the introduction of the 'splitter' whole straws were used in English plaiting, or were reduced in width only as far as was possible by the use of a knife. Now, with this new tool, it was possible to slice a single straw into a number of narrow slivers which, in the hands of a skilled straw worker, could be turned into incredibly fine plait. Like so many great inventions, the principle of the 'splitter' is so simple that anyone *could* have thought of it. It consisted of a central pin over which the hollow straw was placed. Radiating out from the centre pin were a number of small knives or blades – from three to ten of them. Using the centre point as a guide, a properly dampened straw was pushed onto the blades, which sliced it into the requisite number of strips.

The earliest type of 'splitter' was made from bone and set on to a wooden shaft. It says much for the skill and accuracy of the prisoner craftsman that he should have been able to produce, in bone, this tiny tool with its razor-sharp cutting edges, capable of splitting a single straw into as many as sixteen equal slivers. These tools would, of course, have been made for the straw workers by the bone carvers and model makers in the depots and, after seeing the delicacy of detail in ship models and automata produced by these artist-craftsmen no one could believe that the original idea of the 'splitter' would have been beyond their ingenuity.

A later version – which may or may not have been a prisoner of war innovation – took the form of a wooden stand about four inches high, with up to seven circular holes cut into it. Built into each of these apertures were brass or iron knives with spoke-like blades, varying in number according to the number of straw sections each was designed to produce. After splitting, the dampened straw was ready for the 'Splint-mill'. This tool was nothing more than a miniature mangle, the pressure on its boxwood rollers being variable by means of a thumb-screw. Its purpose was to flatten the straw ready for plaiting. On completion, the plaited lengths were passed through a similar press called the 'Plait-mill', which softened and made the *brasses* more pliable for the bonnet makers to manipulate into their creations.

The smuggling of plait and millinery-making was never completely stamped out, despite all the 'straw plait hunts', the floggings and the prison sentences. Sometimes the prison markets were closed down for short periods, but this was as punishing to the honest civilian traders as it was for the captives. Even the gruesome prospect of spending the rest of the war on a prison hulk was not an intimidating enough punishment to deter the most persistent offenders. The visitors to the depot markets so admired and desired the fine French plait that some took considerable risks in obtaining small quantities for their own use. In his *Historical Sketch of the Old Depot, Perth*, William Sievwright tells the story of one such visitor, who must have been either severely henpecked or particularly loving, to have taken such risks merely to satisfy his wife's demands for a new hat:

> 'As much straw plait as made a bonnet was sold for four shillings, and being exceedingly neat, was much inquired after. In this trade many a one got a bite, for the straw was all made up in parcels, and for fear of detection smuggled into the pockets of the purchasers.
> 'An unsuspecting man having been induced by his wife to purchase a quantity of straw plait for a bonnet, he attended the market and soon found a seller. He paid the money, but lest he should be observed, he turned his back to the prisoner, and got the things slipped into his hand, and thence into his pocket. Away he went with his parcel, well pleased that he had escaped detention – for outsiders found buying straw plait were severely dealt with by the law – and on his way home he thought he would examine his purchase, when, to his astonishment and no doubt his deep mortification, he found instead of straw plait, a bundle of shavings, very neatly tied up.

Norman Cross Model. *Unique model of the block house at the Norman Cross depot for prisoners of war in Huntingdonshire. Octagonal shaped wood construction with bone decorations and bone swivel guns in the upper windows. Originally made for Archdeacon Strong and was purchased at the Norman Cross prison market. From the collection of Colonel Strong, grandson of the Archdeacon, and lent by him to the Peterborough Museum (museum label still affixed to the base) for many years. Exact piece is illustrated on plate III in Dr T. J. Walker's book on the Norman Cross depot. Published 1913. A historic and well-documented piece.* Height: 13 in.

Straw Marquetry Box. *Very colourful, broad, split strawwork depicting flowers, flags and miscellaneous border designs. Two inner compartments and two lower drawers. 4 x 9 x 6 in.*

THE STRAW MARQUETRY ARTISTS

The same cheap material which was fed to cattle, used to thatch a cottage, make an archery target, reinforce a brick, stuff a palliasse, make a mat or a hat, could, with skill and ingenuity, be put to remarkable ends. It was employed in the beautification of furniture and everyday items such as snuff-boxes and screens; book-covers and boxes; silk-holders and fans; work-boxes and bureaux; pictures and frames; Noah's Arks and other toys – the list is endless.

The previous chapter has shown the importance of straw in the lives of two very different categories of people in this country during the late eighteenth and the early nineteenth centuries. The many native countryfolk whose very subsistence depended on the cottage industry of bonnet-making – and the foreign prisoner of war who was nimble-fingered enough to master that craft. That the latter often disobeyed the prohibitions of the Transport Office and abused the privilege of the prison market is perhaps not surprising; for of almost equal importance to the captive as financial gain – which made possible the purchase of additions to his rations and occasional luxuries such as tea or coffee – was the fact that the work itself provided a valuable relief from the boredom of his restricted and otherwise idle world. It is, of course, possible that he had no talent for any of the great number of other occupations which were legitimately open to the industrious captive; or he may have been under the influence of the powerful *armateurs* who ran the lucrative racket within the depot yards.

There was, however another class of straw worker whose handiwork did not come under the hat, plait and bonnet ban. This was the artist in straw, whose finest works were truly masterpieces of inlay and design. The authorities, with admirable fairness, considered that the remarkable creations of the marquetry artists were of such a high standard of craftsmanship as to be in a classification to itself and did not conflict with the interests of our local craftsmen. It is easy to understand that the British visitors to the depots should have found these prisoner of war artefacts irresistible, laid out in wide variety and in all their glistening attractiveness on the market yard stalls. The number of examples which have survived to this day in almost perfect condition, is evidence that they were never considered as 'fairings', or soon-forgotten souvenirs; but became treasured possessions of the families of their purchasers. It is not so easy to imagine how the rough fingers of soldier or sailor, working in the most uncongenial of surroundings, could have fashioned some of these little marvels of delicate perfection. However, as mentioned more than once elsewhere, it should be remembered that conscription had scooped into the armies and navies of Napoleon and his allies, men from just about every trade, profession and craft imaginable.

The Dutch and the French had for long been famed as cabinet makers and marquetry artists and, in the eighteenth century and early nineteenth, miniature furniture and other small inlaid pieces enjoyed a considerable vogue. It is fair to assume that, amongst the many thousands of prisoners of war flooding through our depots and prisons, there would have been conscripted marquetry workers and straw craftsman, who would have pooled their skills and knowledge and substituted straw for the costly and almost unobtainable wood veneers. There would also certainly have been some prisoners who had worked in the already well-established straw marquetry trade in their own country before the wars. It may come as a disappointment to some collectors and dealers to learn that not all beautiful pieces of eighteenth or nineteenth century straw inlay can be attributed to the work of prisoners of war, and that the art of straw marquetry was certainly not prison-born. Neither can the genuine article always be accurately described as 'French'. A visual verification of these facts can be seen in the illustrations to this chapter.

The Dutch, French and Italians were already producing high quality work in this

Straw Marquetry Picture. *A well-executed marine scene with a French vessel off a developed point of land with numerous buildings and a clock tower. In a lemon gold frame. 12½ x 16 in.*

medium long before the wars, and in England itself the art can be traced back at least as far as the early seventeenth century. The design motifs incorporated in much of the earliest continental examples show a strong eastern influence, and it may well be that the art itself originated in the Far East. That some prisoner of war straw marquetry also displays this same 'oriental' approach may be attributable to the perpetuation of a tradition – for marqetry workers were not necessarily original designers, but often worked to variations on a basic usage. And it should also be considered that there were many orientals, captured whilst serving on Dutch East Indian vessels, amongst the dozens of nations represented in our prisoner of war establishments.

An interesting article in the *Annual Register for 1805*, proves that the craft of straw inlay was well-established in England at quite an early date. It tells of the work of a most unusual practitioner, Samuel Best, an eccentric Londoner of local fame, better know by the strange sobriquet 'Poor Help', who also professed to be a prophet. When not prophesying, he occupied himself profitably as a skilled straw marquetry worker. For fifteen years he was an inmate of the Shoreditch Workhouse, where his ward was 'dedicated to the exhibition of a great number of works executed by himself in straw'; and his bed-head was decorated with straw chequer-work. Appropriately, 'the subjects he effected were taken from scriptural history. No trace, however, of this personage is left at the Workhouse [in 1805] he adorned with his presence and his skill, and his works are scattered wide and far'. It would be interesting to know if any of these works have survived; to compare them with the prisoner of war specimens produced at that time.

Apart from animal fodder, grasses and straw-like vegetation had always been an

Straw Marquetry Picture. *Companion to the other Straw Marquetry Picture. A sailing vessel off a different point. Turkish flags are flying. Lemon gold frame. 12½ x 16 in.*

important raw material since the earliest times and in many parts of the world. It had been put to use as bedding, floor-covering, thatching and other obvious and simple purposes. Later it was employed in more ambitious adaptations and during the fourteenth and fifteenth centuries, straw was extensively used in the manufacture of furniture. The kings and nobles of France had beautifully decorated 'foot-warmers' of straw, which encased their legs up to the thighs and kept out the chill as they dined in the draughty banqueting halls of their castles. Such luxury items in straw were well-known and popular enough to inspire an old French expression – *estre dans paille juste vertre* – literally, 'in the straw completely green' – descriptive of a family of substance – and other expressions which could be roughly, and rudely, translated as 'up to their arses in straw!'

During the eighteenth century the art of straw marquetry, parquetry and other variations was well advanced and generally popular. In 1759, a Sister Gervain of the Rue Tiquetonne, in Paris, was selling sweetmeat boxes lined with designs in straw, 'imitating the flowers and ornaments which the Chinese employ'. And, in 1782, the *Journal Generi de France* advertised that a nun from Lasson was about to open a shop for the sale of such straw-decorated articles as: *'table à l'Anglais', 'commode pour dame'*, fans, sacs, shuttles, boxes, tables and screens. Some very much larger articles were included in a sale at the Hôtel Bullion in 1785. The catalogue lists full-sized bureaux, corner cupboards and cabinets, covered with floral designs worked in coloured straw and furnished with bronze mountings and marble tops.

By the nineteenth century a few private collections of the best of straw marquetry were

Bone Ship Model in a Straw Marquetry Case.

already being formed in England and in France. Probably the finest in this country was that of John Eliot Hodgkin FSA who, between 1859 and the end of the century, got together some eighty fine examples of the art and recorded his collection in his book, *'Rariora'*. In a chapter entitled 'Marquetry in Coloured Straw of the Sixteenth, Seventeenth and Eighteenth Centuries', he described a number of the specimens in his collection, which featured boxes of all kinds, plaques, small cabinets, mirror frames, caskets, book-bindings, étuis, bonbonnières, encrusted bottles and delicate necklaces of straw and tinsel.

Hodgkin's collection began when, in the 1850s, he came across a cabinet 'in a broker's shop' which, when he opened its doors revealed on their reverse –

'...six beautiful miniatures, each representing a *grande dame de par le monde* and a cavalier, perhaps the Roy Soleil himself... All the detail of the pictures on the panels (except for the faces and hands of the figures, which were on vellum) is executed in filaments of wheaten or oaten straw, dyed for the most part with the most delicate tints... whilst the fronts of the numerous drawers are encrusted with tracery of the same material in its natural colour so exquisitely wrought as to resemble chiselled gold'.

With the discovery of this first and, for him, never surpassed, example of the art, Hodgkin was hooked, and went on to study the subject and build his collection. He

Bone Ship Model in a Straw Marquetry Case. *A fully outfitted, 74-gun, ship-of-the-line with nice carving details and a polychrome figurehead. A solid hull with brass cannon. Set in a fine strawwork case with a mirror back and hinged doors.* Model: 6½ x 8 in. Case: 9½ x 10½ x 4½ in.

visited collections in Paris, where, he said, there was more knowledge and greater appreciation of an art which 'time does not sully the tints or dull the polish made permanent by nature's own brilliant silicious enamel'. Reading his words more than one hundred years after they were written, and from the evidence of my own collection, I can confirm that, even today 'nature's own brilliant solicious enamel' retains its pristine freshness and shows no sign of age.

Anyone who has never possessed, or had the opportunity to handle and examine closely a straw marquetry masterpiece, will probably, and understandably, consider Hodgkin over-effusive and eulogistic when he wrote:

' …neither description nor illustration can give the reader unacquainted with the best specimens of this fascinating fabrique any conception of the charm of a fine example. There is in this humble material when artistically treated, a semi-transparency more chastened and far more satisfying than that of translucent enamel, a brilliancy without glitter, less fatiguing to the eye than that of glass or burnished metal and which soothes and yet perplexes; a new effect presents itself with every change of angle at which the surface is viewed, and a certain comfortable mellowness of tone endears the object thus adorned to every beholder'.

After re-reading my transcription of Hodgkin's words, I must admit that I found them rather overpoweringly enthusiastic and flamboyant, but I took a closer look at one of the finest pieces in my own collection, and can only agree that the more one sees of the best of these works of art and craftsmanship, the less believable seems the achievement – and that, after all, they deserve every word of his eloquence.

No matter where or when the art of straw marquetry originated, only the very finest of civilian-produced work from the Continent can compare with what would seem to have been the standard quality of prisoner of war work, particularly after the introduction of the 'straw-splitter' described in the previous chapter, which brought great refinement to the art and made possible the minute detail and extraordinary delicacy previously unachievable. It has generally been supposed that the very finest examples of straw marquetry, civilian or prisoner of war, could, with some degree of certainty, be dated no earlier than the beginning of the nineteenth century – after the invention of the straw splitter. I would have fully subscribed to that belief, until a recent visit to Luton Museum. There, the Principal Keeper, Marian Nichols, brought up from the cellar a small round box with an irrefutable provenance which dated it to the late seventeenth century. It was covered with a simple design in straw cut into finer slivers than I had ever seen. Someone, therefore, *did* have a means of splitting straw into minute strips much earlier than had been supposed. However, this example seems to be unique, even in that centre of the straw industry, Luton. Perhaps like the techniques of the Murano glassblowers, the secret of splitting straws into ultra-fine strips was preserved by a select group of craftsmen.

There are many popular misconceptions regarding the source of the raw materials and the methods employed by the marquetry-masters of the hulks and depots. One of the most prevalent, even today, is that all the wonderful little straw-work gems which were offered for sale in the depot markets, were made from the straw obtained from the prisoners' bedding! Had that been so, the vast quantities of articles displayed in the regular, and sometimes daily, prison markets, would have soon been responsible for the emptying of all prison palliasses and made for a general hard-lying of the prisoners. Whilst it cannot, of course, be stated that no hard-up prisoner of war ever did convert his bedding into knick-knacks in this way, we can be certain that, once sufficient funds were available, good quality straw of many kinds – some superior to that generally used in straw plaiting and hat making and many times better than his bed-stuffing – was used!

Even further from the truth than the 'mattress-into-masterpiece' stories, are some of the theories advanced as to the means by which the prisoners achieved the almost magical colourings – from vivid greens and brilliant reds to the most delicate of tints and shades of brown and gold. The most often repeated – and most ridiculous – is that they dyed the split straws by steeping them in colours obtained by soaking and boiling their socks, caps, shirts and other clothing. A close second is that the shades of gold were achieved with stains obtained from tea. Even had the prisoners possessed the secret of extracting dyes from tea, it would have been useless to any but the most extravagant of workers. Tea was never issued to prisoners of war, except medicinally to the hospitalised sick. Neither would it have been readily available in any great quantity in the depot markets; for tea at that time was too expensive for even the ordinary free Englishman to often enjoy – and those who could afford it kept it under lock and key. For the latter purpose the lockable tea-caddy and three-legged 'teapoy' had come into being. Prisoner of war examples of tea caddies are sometimes – though rarely – discovered, decorated with straw-marquetry, bone or rolled-paperwork. These two, and other theories of dye-extraction methods can be confidently dismissed and, if I am correct, few examples of prisoner of war marquetry were made from *dyed* straw. I say 'few' rather than 'none', as

Framed Diorama. *A model of a village near Shrewsbury. Consists of a canal, coal barge, an inn, houses, trees and several country folk. Well executed by someone with an understanding of vanishing points. Old provenance slips affixed to the back. 12½ x 14½ in.*

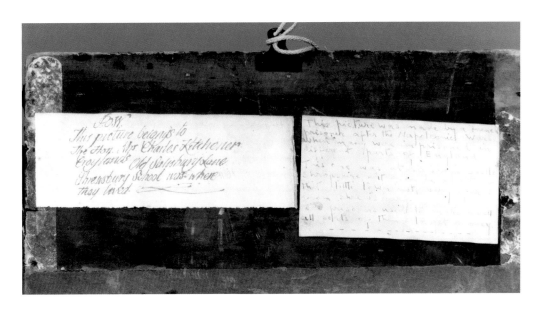

Straw Marquetry Box. *Superb example with the front and sides decorated with Napoleon's coat of arms and masonic compasses. Inner lid decor of a building, horses, coach, etc. Inside divided into four sections with decorated lids depicting navigating instruments, musical instruments, Nelson memorial and fruit in a basket. Lower side drawer lined with a Middle Eastern scene. 4 x 12 x 9 in.*

it is possible that some commissioned works were made from pre-coloured straw brought into the market by the subsequent purchaser, but not in the wide range of colours used in many of their works.

The *bleaching* of straw would have presented no great difficulty, as straws for plaiting had been treated by being dampened and placed in boxes with molten sulphur since the beginning of the eighteenth century; but *dyeing* was a very different matter. The dyeing of straw is a complicated process, as the hard siliceous surface has to be specially treated before the colour can penetrate, and even then basic or acid dyes have to be employed. Until a quarter of a century after the period of our study; only a small amount of simple dyeing was carried on by a few hat-makers; then, between 1845 and 1857, three professional dye-works were founded in the Luton area; but the range was still limited to a few colours obtained from wood- or vegetable-dyes. All this is mentioned as a matter of possibly general interest, but the prisoners had no need to tackle such an almost insurmountable problem, or even experiment with the outlandish methods attributed to them. Their answer lay in the tinted or tintable varnishes which would supply the desirable transparency which gave such sparkle to their colourings, and were easily and legitimately obtainable through visiting market contacts.

In addition to the varnishes, the artists took full advantage of the wide colour range of natural straws. Rye provided the pale tones of whites and creams. Red Wheat, the light browns and the rich deep browns. Oats, the many natural shades of golds and bronzes – and some of the greens were obtained from immature straw or grasses. However, the most magical effects were achieved by the angle at which the straw was laid down. All other necessary materials could be purchased from traders and visitors to the depot markets – in the case of the hulks, from the bum-boatmen who traded alongside. Louis Garneray, obtained his paints and brushes through prison ship officers and the bum-boats to set himself up as an artist on the hulk *Prothée*, at Portsmouth. That there were practitioners of the marquetry art aboard Garneray's prison ship is known from the fact that, once he had drawing materials, he financed an escape attempt by designing ship motifs for them at three sous apiece. Until that time they had concentrated on flowers, birds and geometric patterns in their compositions.

What could be arranged on a prison hulk could be accomplished with so much greater ease in a depot ashore, and it is known that prisoner of war work of all types was often bespoke. Visitors brought all manner of articles into the markets to be repaired or decorated by the prisoner craftsmen. In the museum at Peterborough there is a telescope which once belonged to the last Brigade-Major of Yaxley Barracks, Major Kelly, who took it into the market to be covered with straw marquetry. The materials used in many commissioned works were supplied by the buyer, and although most of the components of pieces bought in the markets would have been manufactured within the walls, the authenticity of a piece need not be in question because a lock, a hinge, or some other detail of its make-up is of obvious English manufacture.

The diary of Dr Strong, Archdeacon of Northamptonshire, reveals that he was a visitor to and patron of the Norman Cross market over more than a decade. He mentions the purchase of a number of pieces which were made to his order, and have survived to this day. More than one hundred and fifty years after he carried them home, I was able to add two of his purchases to my own collection: an eleven-figure one 'Spinning Jenny', and the model of the Block House, which is illustrated in J.T.Walker's history of the Depot, 1913. Of the Block House, the Archdeacon noted:

'23rd October 1801 – Drove Margaret to ye Barracks.
Bought the model of the Block House and supplied the Mahogany, £1.11s.6d,. sergt.1s.,
man.1s., soldier 1s 3d.'

Those two pieces were bequeathed to the reverent gentleman's grandson, Colonel Strong, and were on loan to Peterborough Museum for many years; but they eventually turned up in a London auction room, which I attended. There are, however, a couple of other versions of the wooden artefact, one of which can be seen in the hand of the prisoner-dealer in A.C. Cook's painting of the Depot Market.

The Archdeacon also bought straw marquetry, and recorded that, in October 1811, ten years after buying the Block House model, he paid two guineas for a fine straw-work depiction of the West Front of Peterborough Cathedral. It would seem that straw pictures of the Minster were best-sellers; which leads us to a known straw marquetry artist who executed more than one of them. He was one of the few whose name has been preserved in the form of now rare examples of the compulsory labels which had to be attached to work offered for sale in the markets. The artist who created the Archdeacon's panel (19in. x 16in.) was Jean De la Porte, a French corporal who was captured in 1805.

Even in such a great collection as that at Peterborough with its more than one hundred and fifty straw marquetry artefacts; no more than half a dozen names can be attributed to individual items with any certainty: Godfroy, Corn, Grieg, Ribout and Jacques Gourny. However, of la Porte we are more sure, as the museum has a number of his works, either signed or attributable and the Victoria and Albert Museum has a marquetry portrait panel entitled 'Monbars Leader of Buckaneers'. An inscription on the reverse reads:

> 'Monsieur De la Porte
> Prisonnier de Guerre
> Norman Cross
> Le Quarterzième d'Août
> Mille huit cens dix.'

Corporal Jean De la Porte was serving on the French 74-gun *L'Intrépide* at the Battle of Trafalgar, the 21st October, 1805, when she surrendered to HMS *Britannia.* and was put to the torch. With other prisoners taken in the battle, la Porte was landed at Portsmouth. From there he was transferred to Norman Cross Depot, where he arrived on the 8th January, 1806, to spend the next nine years of his life within its walls. The fact that, as a non-commissioned officer, he would have been quartered in the somewhat superior conditions of the Petty Officers' Block in the Depot, and enjoyed the remuneration from his undoubtedly superior craftsmanship, probably means that he lived as comfortably as any man could be who had been deprived of his freedom for so many years. It is also possible that many examples of his art are still possessed, perhaps unwittingly, by families in Huntingdonshire (now Cambridgeshire).

Except for the most simple or primitive pieces of straw-decorated articles – which could be the product of a one-man enterprise and which often have a naïve charm of their own – the obviously 'professional' prisoner of war products in straw inlay were the result of well-organised team-work; each member important in his contribution to a finished quality product. In the case of a casket, miniature bureau, multi-drawered box or any other wood-based article, the woodworker came into his own at the outset. The carcase was constructed by the carpenter or cabinet-maker, usually from pine recovered from depot-delivered packing-cases, or from rarer woods supplied by visitors or British retailers.

I have examined a number of badly damaged boxes and panels, too far gone for restoration. Incidentally, the lids of many damaged boxes, are often in an excellent state of preservation on the underside, and these are often framed up and offered by dealers as 'Prisoner of War Straw Pictures' which, of course they are in a sense, and are well worth including in a collection in their own right. In almost every case where prisoner of war work of this type was found in poor condition, the damage had come about through wear-and-tear, accident, or neglect, and seldom through warping or inferior workmanship. It is rare to find a piece where the marquetry is in good condition but the bodywork has warped or split – even after a couple of hundred years!

The donkey-work, the soaking, bleaching, splitting, milling and general preparation of the straw would have been carried out by semi-skilled members of the team who would keep the marquetry workers supplied. We know that many designs or part designs were repeated over and over again, but one-off pieces would have required the artist or designer who, like Louis Garneray, designed the pictorial panels and their intricate surrounds. From my study of broken-down pieces I have reached certain conclusions as to the methods used in their original manufacture, and have come to believe that the making of a straw-inlay covered casket and the like would have proceeded more or less as follows:

Straw Marquetry Box. *Outer lid decorated with an oval harbour scene showing a ship, buildings and English flags. Sides overlaid with floral and scroll motifs. Fancy bone key escutcheon. Inner lid superbly done with brightly coloured strawwork scenes of an officer, a lady and a bowl of flowers. Inside divided into four compartments with decorated lids. Two lower drawers with floral and border designs on the inside. 5½ x 14 x 9 in.*

1. After building the bodywork from wood or thick card-board, it would be sanded to a fine finish and possibly sized with thin glue.

2. Although some workers appear to have applied straw directly onto this smooth surface of the wood or card, the following procedure would most often have been followed.

3. All the surfaces, interior and exterior, would then be covered with thick absorbent paper (usually pink or pale blue).

4. The methods of adhesion were varied. A waxy, paste-like substance was often employed and stronger adhesives could have been bought in, but this would hardly have been necessary. Prisoner-made glues could be made up from the bones, horn and hooves, obtained by arrangement with the prison cooks and butchers.

5. Extremely accurate measurements would then be taken of all the surfaces to be covered. That these measurements were critical can be seen from the hair-line accuracy with which the finished veneered panels joined and matched up.

6. Armed with these measurements, a master design layout was made for each of the surfaces to be decorated, and these were then transferred by 'pouncing' or tracing on to the thick absorbent paper covering of the casket.

7. Copies of the designs would then be prepared on thin sheets of paper which were to take the straw. All would now be ready for the marquetry artists to go to work. I use 'marquetry' here as a generic term to cover all decorative straw-inlay work, but, as we shall see, the prisoners had a number of techniques at their disposal.

8. Most work would be carried out in much the same way as wood veneers would be used in marquetry proper. Straws opened out to their full widths, or in a great number of slivers side by side, were then glued onto the thin papers. Sheet was laid over appropriate sheet so that the craftsman could cut through both sheets in one operation, thus ensuring that inlay and apperture were a perfect match. The thin sheets of paper-backed straw would often be coloured or tinted before cutting, but superb effects could be achieved by the careful placing of the natural straws with their grain at right-angles to one another, or by 'herring-boning'.

9. With great precision and dexterity, each cut-out piece would then be fitted in its place, and eventually it would emerge as yet another prisoner of war collector's piece.

The techniques employed as variations on straightforward MARQUETRY were at least six in number:

PARQUETRY – where geometric patterns were used to cover all the surfaces with straight-line designs.

LOW RELIEF – where elaborate designs were made by the building up of great numbers of tiny pieces of straw to create very low-relief contoured surfaces.

EMBOSSING – High or low relief embossing was achieved by pasting the flattened straw to the thin sheets of paper in the normal manner and then pressing or stamping the requisite design from the underside. Sometimes embossed artefacts were further embellished with the next technique:

ENGRAVING – This technique is encountered more often than some of the others, as it was an 'extra' which took the form of incising or indenting with fine lines, cross-hatching or additional design features on to otherwise finished marquetry pieces.

MOSAIC – Some of the finest straw mosaic work is, at first glance, hardly distinguishable from 'Tonbridgeware', and must have been far harder to produce than the latter. Tiny pieces of plain or coloured straw were placed with incredible accuracy next to each other, and these brilliant craftsmen even managed to use the direction of the grain to great effect when positioning these minute pieces, sometimes no larger than a sixteenth of an inch square.

CLOISONNE – I have only seen two examples of this technique; where, in an imitation of the oriental art, brass has been replaced by straw to build the 'cloisons', or walls, which surrounded the areas later to be filled with enamel.

In so many words can be described the basic principles and techniques of a now neglected craft; but mere words and even the finest illustrations cannot do justice to the finished article. Only by seeing for oneself – in one of the museums listed at the end of this book, in auctions, or by lucky chance discovery in antique emporium or junk-shop – can the works of our wartime prisoners be truly appreciated.[8]

'Book' Type Straw Marquetry Box. *Outside overlaid with various parquetry and mosaic designs. Inner lid has a straw framed watercolour of "A View of Beaufort Castle." Interior with multiple compartments and nicely decorated lids. Two small drawers at the lower front.* 3¼ x 13 x 9½ in.

1. Captain Boteler's *'Recollections'*: Navy Records Society. 2.

2. *'Luton and the Hat Industry.'*

3. DANIEL DEFOE: *A Tour Through England.* 1725.

4. *Quarterly Review.* Vol.XXVI. December, 1821.

5. T. J. Walker, M.D. *Appendices.*

6. Barnes did not escape all punishment. He and his two colleagues were tried at Huntingdon, the 20th May, 1811. Barnes was sentenced to twelve months gaol and his friends to six months each.

7. *The Stamford Mercury.* 12th February, 1812.

8. Straw decorated artefacts comprise a far wider range of prisoner of war work than any other. An earlier chapter told of the 'General' who ruled over the violent *'Romans'* in Dartmoor Depot, whose regalia appeared from even a short distance to be a uniform of glittering golden lace, but was really a coat, hat, waistcoat and trousers, covered with ingeniously executed strawwork.

Bone Model of a Fortress. *Intricately designed and carved model of a fortified castle with twenty-two guns.*
Three-level construction mounted on a pierced base and with a balustraded enclosure. 8 x 7 x 6 in.

Chapter Five

Part One

The Prisoner Bone-Workers

[Germain Lamy, prisoner of war in Forton Depot had prospered as a straw plaiter until the production of plait was interdicted] 'But Germain was not thereby discouraged, but quickly learned another trade, forming a partnership with a comrade already skilled in the business. This new industry consisted in manufacturing bones into work-boxes, combs, different types of toys, more especially boats and ships. Material never failed: a market was held twice a week, to which the different messes contributed all the bones they could collect; competition was strong, and the old bones increased in value.'

Doisy de Villargennes visiting his
foster-brother Lamas, at Forton

BY FAR THE MOST EASILY OBTAINABLE of all the raw materials available to prisoner of war craftsmen and workers, was bone. It was even easier to come by than some types of straw, as the less common varieties of that material, which were employed in the creation of marquetry, had to be brought in from outside the prison walls.

It has been estimated that to satisfy the culinary needs of Norman Cross alone, meat equivalent to the weight of five or six bullocks must have been delivered to the Depot each day[1] [assuming that they always got their full ration!]. Over the eighteen years of its existence, therefore, a veritable mountain of bones would have passed through the kitchens of just that one depot, to re-emerge as masterpieces or knick-knacks in the prison market.

As was the case with strawwork, misleading statements regarding articles made from bone are not infrequent. With the same inaccuracy that masterly examples of straw inlay have often been described as 'made by prisoners with straw from their mattresses', one fine ship model was labelled, 'made from bones left over from his meagre ration'. In one sense that may be true; but it does rather invite us to picture a poor devil picking out pieces of bone from the mess served up to him, whereas it is more probable that he seldom, if ever, found worthwhile bones in his ragout. The meat ration for each six-man mess was cooked with that of the others, in huge copper boilers, the bones becoming the common property of each individual mess. The larger and better bones, like the 'boiler-skimmings', would have been valuable 'cooks' perks'.

The manufacturing of artifacts from the skeletal remains of prison food – mainly beef and mutton – provided work for every class of bone-worker among *les laborieux*. The unskilled would have collected the bones from the kitchens in order to make them ready for further treatment. Their primary task would have involved any or all of a number of preparatory steps. Re-boiling would have been essential, to remove the oily fat present in the bone – and incidentally to collect as a useful adhesive residue thus produced;

Bone Watch Stand. *Domed top with tapered support columns and decorative finials. Surrounding the watch holder is a pierced filigree screen of delicate design. Lower section is fitted with a drawer. Watercolour of a lady set in the back of the watch holder. Back decorated with paintings of a soldier and a river and village scene. Original wood and glass case. 11 x 9 x 5in.*

(Above right) **Miniature Bone Furniture.** *Three edged shelves with twist-carved support columns. Lace carved bone backing fitted with two circular mirrors. Shelves contain cups, saucers, bowls and pitchers. 4 x 2¼ x 1¼ in. (Above left)* **Miniature Bone Furniture.** *Three curved shelves with turned support columns and mirror back. Lace carved bone backing for the top shelf. Shelves contain bowls, bottles and candlesticks. 4 x 4 x 1 in. (Centre bottom)* **Miniature Bone Furniture.** *Three edged shelves with pierced aprons and superbly turned support columns. Top shelf fitted with an open carved backing. Shelves contain wine sets, glasses, bowls, pitchers, urns, and vases with flowers. 4¼ x 2¾ x 1⅜ in. (Centre top)* **Miniature Bone Furniture.** *Three curved shelves with turned support coloumns and a mirror back. Lace carved bone backing for the top shelf. Shelves contain bowls, bottles and candlesticks. 4 x 4 x 1 in. (Centre right)* **Bone Case.** *Turned, cask-shaped, case with incised horizontal lines and a threaded lid. Contains tiny dominoes. Height: 1¾ in. (Bottom left)* **Bone Case.** *A cask-shaped case with vertical line piercings and a screw-off top. Contains doll house cups, saucers, bowls, etc. Height: 2¼ in.*

Bone Watch Stand. *An arched roof resting on nicely turned support columns and bases. Surrounding the watch container is a fine screen of delicate, pierce-carved, scroll work.* 8 x 6¼ x 3 in.

Bone Watch Stand. *An arched roof sitting on turned columns and full-figured carvings of Roman soldiers. Surrounding the watch holder is a fine screen of delicate, pierce-carved scroll work.* 11½ x 8½ x 5 in.

Double Watch Tower and Ship Model. *Elaborate architectural-style cabinet overlaid with intricately carved and pierced bone of various designs and motifs. Upper portion with two arched roofs supported by turned columns and three full carved bone figures. Two watch holders surrounded by screens of pierce-carved and fretted bone. Middle section houses a fine wood model of an 82-gun ship. Lower section contains three drawers with strawwork inner linings. 21 x 13 x 10 in.*

although a stronger glue was easily obtained by boiling down hides and hooves into a thick gelatinous liquid, which was left to set into brittle brown slabs until needed. Next came the scraping, cleaning, drying, smoothing and later the bleaching. The bones would then be ready for the semi-skilled workers, who cut, sliced and pared them into width, length and thickness as required. Some pieces were pared to suitable thicknesses for the makers of games-boxes, watch-stands, guillotines, ship models, toys and all manner of decorative and marketable articles. Other, and less valuable, pieces were left for the skilful but less ambitious button-makers and makers of spillikins and miniature

Wood and Bone Watch Stand. *Constructed in the form of a grandfather clock. Decorated with inset bone designs and a bone-framed watercolour of a British man-o-war. Lower section fitted with a drawer.* 12¼ x 5½ in.

Bone Ordnance Model of a Mortar. *Well-shaped bone carriage with a turned barrel and several accessories that are set on a balustraded, square, checkerboard base. 4½ x 4½ in.*

playing cards. That some of the parers must have been craftsmen in their particular field is evidenced by the unbelievably paper-thinness of shaved bone sails to be seen on miniature models no more than a few inches long. These semi-skilled workers may also have worked their material into rough shapes before passing them on for the artists and craftsmen to work their wonders.

It is probable that the bleaching came about after the master-craftsman had completed and polished the component parts of his creations. Unprepared bone has a natural yellow tinge about it and soon takes on a drab appearance even after boiling, yet most bone artifacts, unless neglected and exposed to dust and dirt, have retained a look of 'ivory' whiteness, even after two hundred years or more. So some sort of bleaching *must* have been employed. We know that the straw-plaiters used bleaching-boxes of molten-sulphur and the long-drawn-out process of exposure to sunlight may sometimes have been resorted to; however, the unpredictability of our English summers must have necessitated the introduction of more reliable methods. The late Ewart Freeston, whose knowledge of ship models and model-making was probably unsurpassed, had a number of theories as to how that 'whiteness' was achieved. Freeston conjectured that soaking

French 'Dieppe' Type Wall Mirror. *Intricately bordered with carved and applied bone leaves, armorial devices, Eagles, Lions and a scroll with the legend 'Montroyt St Denis'. Mounted on a heavy wooden frame. Bevelled glass mirror. 36 x 24 in.*

in a strong alkaline solution of potash could have done the trick; or lime in the form of a wet paste or solution may have been used to coat the artifact. Hydrogen peroxide was also used by straw workers, so would have been easily obtainable for use with bone; but sulphur dioxide sounds the most probable, as sulphur was used as a disinfectant in all the depots and prison ships, and 'when burned in the vicinity of water, dilute sulphuric acid is formed which acts as a bleaching agent'.

French 'Dieppe' Type Wall Mirror. Bordered with applied bone leaves, marine creatures and other decorative motifs. A bone scroll bears the inscription "Scotorum." Mounted on thick wood covered with old velvet. Bevelled glass mirror. 34 x 20 in.

There is good reason to believe that many of these prisoner of war productions were the result of teamwork, rather than individual effort. In many instances, the carpenters and cabinet-makers would have come into it at an early stage, as bone-work decoration was often applied to wooden carcasses of one sort or another, and marquetry or parquetry inlays of wood or straw are often to be seen on the baseboards of bone ship models. The contribution of the artist in the team can be seen in the many little

French 'Dieppe' Type Wall Mirror. *Covered with applied bone carvings of a crown and shield, winged gryphons, a carved head and a banner inscribed "Lausdeo." Mounted on a thick oval board with a pale gold, velvet covering. Bevelled glass mirror.* 36 x 22 in.

watercolour panels, protected under glass or mica, which occur so often on games-boxes and other bone artifacts. Careful examination will sometimes reveal the efforts and skills of a half a dozen variously talented men in the creation of a single market curio.

Most of these industrious groups would have been managed by one of the entrepreneurs among their fellow captives: men who ran everything, from the gaming tables and brokering, to retailing in the inner and outer markets of the depots. These

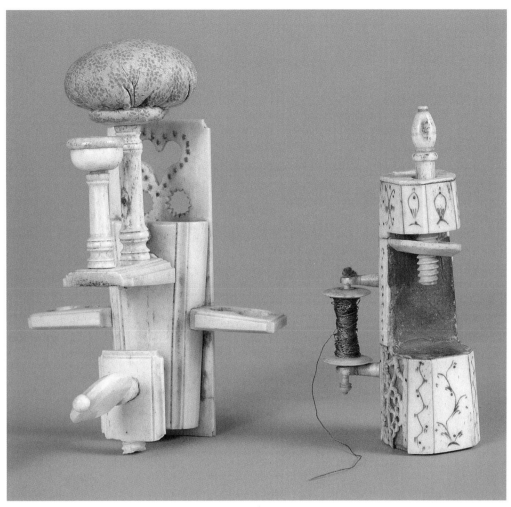

Bone Sewing Aid. *Outfitted with a pin-cushion and a turned needle-holder. Screw-type clamp for table attachment. Bone backing with a pierced heart and an inset mirror. 5½ x 3½ in. (Right)* ***Bone Sewing Aid.*** *Outfitted with two thread reels and a pin-cushion on the top. Screw type clamp for table attachment. Applied bone overlay with open carved and etched designs. Red and green colouring. 5 x 2¼ in.*

were the *capitalistes* or *armateurs,* who were certain to be present wherever the chance of making an honest (and sometimes dishonest) *sou, franc* or *louis*, presented itself. In the present case, the *armateur* would have had to be in cahoots with the cooks in order to obtain the bony raw material in bulk, to distribute among his workers; but, of course, not all workers in that medium were part of a team.

Some simple and less rewarding types of prisoner of war work in bone seem obviously the work of individuals, a case in point being the ubiquitous 'knuckle-bone apple-corers'. I have found examples of this artifact, sometimes carved or engraved but most often plain and undecorated, in the vicinity of most of the old depot sites which I have visited. Another widespread, cheap and even more popular scrap-bone offering, was the 'lady's leg pipe-tamper'. In the eighteenth and early nineteenth century, when the nether limbs of ladies were less in evidence than today, it was something of a 'macho must' for Jack-the-lad to tamp his pipe with a leg-shaped tamper, carved by a prisoner of war taken from Napoleon.

After the source of the raw material, comes the question of the tools with which to work it. Just as the once-held popular idea of the 'artist' was that of an impoverished,

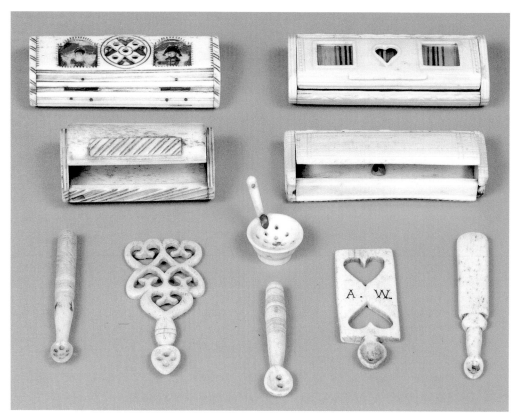

(Top left) **Bone Snuff Box.** *Fitted with a hinged lid with open carved hearts and frames with paintings of a boy and girl. 1⅝ x 3⅜ in. (Top right)* **Bone Snuff Box.** *Fitted with a hinged lid with an open carved heart and two frames that reveal a panel of strawwork. 1½ x 3½ in. (Centre left)* **Bone Snuff Box.** *Fitted with a curved lid with simple, diagonal line, carvings. 1⅜ x 2½ in. (Centre)* **Bone 'Colander Ladle' Snuff Spoon.** *Perforated bowl with a bone handle and a copper rivet. Diameter: 1 in. (Bottom far left)* **Bone Snuff Spoon.** *Turned handle with a bowl perforated with seven holes. Length: 3 in. (Bottom centre left)* **Bone Snuff Spoon.** *Open carved, heart motif, handle with a perforated bowl. 1¼ x 3¼ in. (Bottom centre)* **Bone Snuff Spoon.** *Turned handle with a two-hole perforated bowl. Length: 2½ in. (Bottom centre right)* **Bone Snuff Spoon.** *Pierced handle with open hearts and the initials 'A.W.' Bowl with a single perforation. 1 x 3 in. (Bottom right)* **Bone Snuff Spoon.** *In the form of a cricket bat with a four-holed bowl. Length: 3½ in.*

undernourished romantic, living in an unheated garret in Montmartre or some other bohemian location, doomed to die before his genius was recognized – so was the romantic view of the prisoner of war artisan who, despite *his* genius, would have had to live and work in miserable poverty, bravely facing up to the odds against him. Thomas W. Bagshaw,[2] writing in *Apollo* magazine in 1935, said that many collectors and dealers hold the false impression that the 'delicate work was made with the roughest of tools under the worst of conditions, and picture a half-starved prisoner slaving with a home-made tool in the dingy light of a dungeon to produce a model which will delight some child or a casket to hold my lady's jewels'.

Even if it deprives the collector of an addition to the already romantic story behind his treasured possession – and the honest dealer of a strong addition to his sales puff – this is a point which should be set straight. Unlike *les indifférents,* who existed on admittedly meagre rations, no captive who was able and willing to work even in a menial capacity, need ever have gone even half-starved. The more the financial position of a skilled craftsman improved, the better was his opportunity to buy space in which to work. Almost anything could be bought at a price – including almost any type of tool which could be obtained through the market traders or visitors. Furthermore, it is to be doubted whether there would have been much objection from the guards or depot officers, as legitimate prisoner of war work was encouraged rather than frowned upon, and counted as a quietening influence. However, one has only to remember that in any of the large depots, the skills of just about every trade and profession were there to be called upon: jewellers, watchmakers, instrument-makers, metal-workers, blacksmiths and other specialist occupations, so it was probably seldom necessary to send beyond the walls for any special working implement.

Most small tools could be made from nails, wire, bolts, needles and other metallic odds and ends – and most model-makers would agree that, whilst a well-equipped tool-chest would be a desirable luxury, their basic requirements are simple and few indeed. With no more than a knife, a saw, a file and some means of drilling, almost any craftsman could get by. The principle of the Archimedean drill is as old as the hills and easy to make, and gimlets and bradawls are even simpler hole makers. A serrated cutting edge to make a saw would have presented no great difficulty. Many escapes from the prison hulks were achieved, or attempted, with the aid of home-made 'tools'. Tom Souvuille and his fellow absconders made gimlets from an old fencing foil, and saws from barrel-hoops while Bertaud and Garneray, after making a wooden mallet, turned odd pieces of metal into chisels, and made miniature saws from their knife blades.

It will be seen among the examples of bone-worker masterpieces illustrated in the

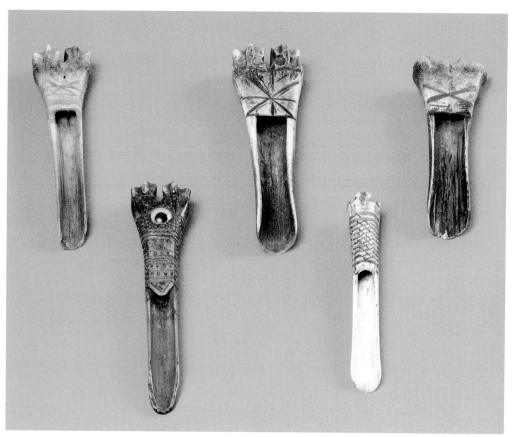

'Knuckle-bone apple-corers'.

Bone Covered Box. *Norman Cross type. Wood construction with pierced and etched bone overlay. Green and brown colouring. Hinged, hip-shaped lid. 6 x 11 x 7½ in.*

Bone Covered Box. *Norman Cross type. Similar to the previous item but smaller in size. Hinged, hip-shaped lid, for access to three inner compartments. 5 x 8½ x 6 in.*

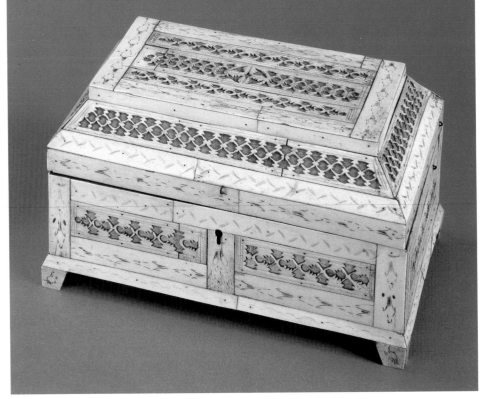

Bone Covered Box. *Norman Cross type. Wood construction with pierced and etched bone overlay on the outer surfaces. Green colouring (see Dr T.J.Walker's* Depots for the Prisoners of War at Norman Cross, *page 131). 3¼ x 6¼ x 5 in.*

'Norman Cross' Bone Covered Box. Wooden box with elaborate bone carving applied over all the outer surfaces. Copper lining between the wood and bone. Hinged lid with carved figures of a man and woman hunting on horseback, two dogs and a deer. It is generally believed that this type of work came from the Norman Cross prison. 2⅜ x 8¼ x 6¼ in.

following pages, that some parts seem to have been turned on a lathe. Closer inspection has often revealed that the tiny components of balustrades and balconies were in some cases the result of painstaking labour with knife and file; but in others, such as guns, barrels, pillars and bowls, some type of turning equipment had certainly been employed. Over the years, article-writers for newspapers and magazines have commented on this latter fact, and usually concluded that the prisoners sent prepared bone out through the markets for the local professional British turners. to provide the finishing touch. I am surprised that Freeston, in his excellent book, should have given even some slight credence to this possibility as a widespread practice – although one cannot say it *never* happened.

Having watched native craftsmen in India – working in conditions not much better than the depot prisoners would have endured a couple of hundred years ago – turning ivory or wood on simple lathe-like equipment, powered by nothing more than a bow, the string of which was looped round the spindle, I rather doubt that many French prisoner of war artifacts contain British civilian parts!

After studying a number of tiny prisoner-made automaton 'toys' – with their complicated mechanisms, driven by a thread round a main wheel operated by cranked handle or treadle, which set geared cog-wheels into motion and turned the spinning sails of windmills or pirouetted dancing figures – it is hard to believe that, with all the talent and cheap labour on offer around them, the craftsman captives would have found the construction of a full-scale automaton – a lathe – beyond their ingenuity.

Bone Covered Sewing Box. *Norman Cross type. Wood construction with pierced and etched bone veneer over the outer surfaces. Hinged, hip-shaped lid with a large cushion on the top. Recently restored feet and some bone repairs (see Dr T.J.Walker's* Depots for the Prisoners of War at Norman Cross, *page 131).* 6 x 8½ x 6 in.

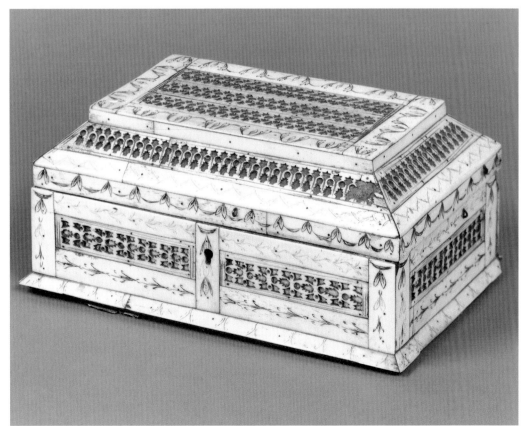

Bone Covered Box. *Norman Cross type. Wood construction with pierced and etched bone overlay. Red and green colouring. Hinged, hip-shaped lid for access to a large, single compartment (see Dr T.J.Walker's* Depots for the Prisoners of War at Norman Cross, *page 131).* 4 x 8¾ x 6 in.

Bone Calvary Model. *A fine model of The Crucifixion with all the symbols of a cockerel, supporting figures, three dice (13), spear, flowers, etc. Light polychrome colouring and worn paintings on the sides. Strawwork panel in the base. 9 x 5¼ x 3⅛ in.*

Bone Calvary in a Bottle. *Crucifixion model inside an early bottle with a painted, wood-topped, cork. Crudely carved and coloured with all the symbolic forms. 8 x 2½ in.*

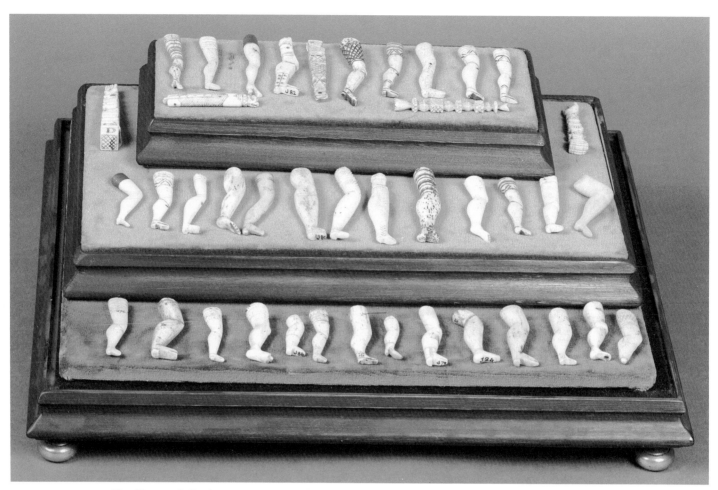

Pipe Tamper Collection. *A grouping of forty tampers that are mostly carved from bone and the majority in the form of ladies' legs. Some carved with fist motifs. Something every 'macho man' of the period had to have to tamp his smoke.*

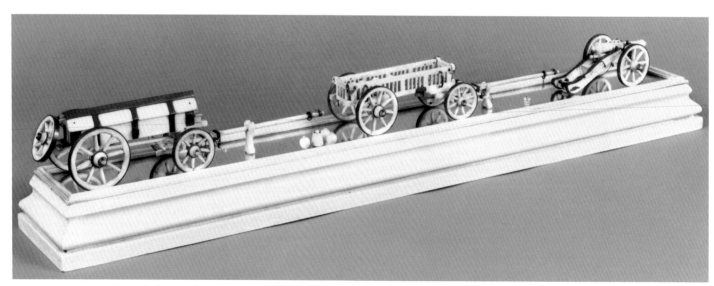

Bone Ordnance Group. *Includes a field gun and carriage, a four-wheeled ammunition cart filled with balls and another cart with a hinged roof. All bone construction with copper reinforcements. Overall length: 24 in.*

Bone Teetotums. *An interesting collection of twenty-five teetotums of various shapes, sizes, designs and colours.*

Bone Ammunition Wagon. *Bone body with a hinged, copper-covered roof that allows access to four cannon and a rope and bone ladder. Bone spoked wheels that have been copper shod. Length: 9 in.*

Prisoner of War Bone Ship Model. *Superbly carved and detailed model of a 74-gun vessel. Planked and pinned hull with horn gunwales and an open section of planking to expose the bone hull ribbing. Retractable bone cannon. Carved female figurehead and a very elaborate stern. Mounted on a bone and horn base with decorative floral carvings. 22½ x 28 in.*

Chapter Five

Part Two

The Prisoner Ship Model Makers

ODE TO A PRISONER OF WAR BONE SHIP MODEL

The Fighting *Téméraire*

No tusk from trackless jungle brought,
   No bone of slaughtered whale
Her wreathed and Tritoned sterrnposts wrought
   And bulwarks eggshell frail.

No warm dog-watch her building whiled
   Away in tropic seas,
For no shore-anchored salt beguiled
   His unaccustomed ease.

Mellow as ancient ivory
   And fine as carven jade,
From beef-bones of captivity
   The shapely hull was made,

Whose making helped upon their way
   Such limping hours and slow
As measured out the leaden day
   That none but prisoners know.

Old wars, old woes, old wasted years,
   Old causes lost and won,
Old bitterness of captives' tears
   As dreams – as dreams are done.

As dreams the stubborn hulls, the pride
   Of masts that raked the sky,

Sea-shattering bows and oaken side
   Of fighting fleets gone by.

Yet still, though thrones and systems shake
   And pass and are no more,
The spars a casual touch might break
   Unharmed by Time endure.

Still, though the world in change bewhelmed,
   From the small mimic bows
The antique warrior, mailed and helmed,
   Looks out with frowning brows,

Like those beneath whose sightless stare
   The sullen smoke-drift rolled
Round her, well-named the *Téméraire*,
   In famous fights of old.

What of her builder? Did he sail
   Home to his France at last,
To tell in happier times the tale
   Of wars and prisons past?

Or is, upon some gravestone hoar,
   The legend plain to see:
'He was a Prisoner of War,
   But Death has set him free'?[1]

THE SHIP MODEL, IN ITS EARLIEST FORM, IS AS OLD as the hills. I have yet to meet a man who had never, as an excited youngster, followed a paper boat as it bobbed and tossed along a storm-gully till it reached a drain. I have seen my grandson, deeply engrossed and obviously enjoying an electronic game, but that pleasure does not compare with the sheer joy with which he launches a pencil-masted chunk of wood onto the stream which runs through my garden, then dashes from bridge to bridge, to watch as it passes under.

   Ship and boat models, as toys, votive or funeral offerings, have featured among archaeological finds relating to most ancient civilizations; many found in Egyptian tombs

Prisoner of War Bone Ship Model. *Fine quality model of a 52-gun ship. Planked and pinned hull with extra carving detail on the planking below the bone cannon. Carved Roman figurehead and a nicely detailed stern. Mounted on a planked bone base with surrounding balustrade. 18 x 24 in.*

dating back four thousand years or more. In the modern world, ship models have been produced for a variety of purposes: as scale models for use in shipbuilding yards; as mementoes of great naval occasions, sometimes employing material from the original vessel in their construction; as museum pieces of historic interest and works of artistic fantasy, such as trophies and silver *nefs,* elaborate early German containers for salt and tableware.

The National Maritime Museum at Greenwich, houses one of the world's finest collections of ship models, dating from the mid-seventeenth century. An excellent and well-illustrated book *Ship Models* by Lavery and Stephens,[2] has been published, which

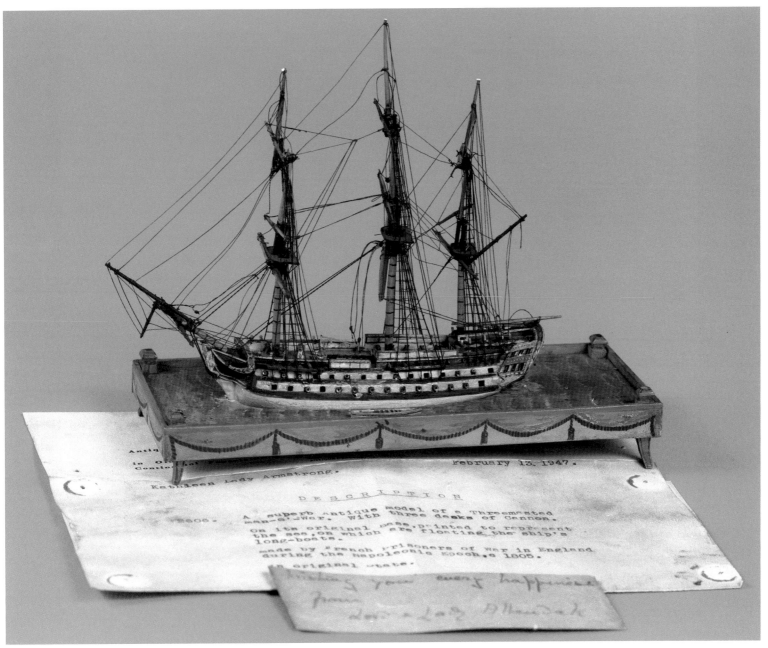

Prisoner of War Ship Model. *A very fine miniature model of an 88-gun ship-of-the-line. Carved stern and figurehead and fitted-out with brass cannon. Set in a nicely painted baseboard. Recently re-rigged and placed in a fine contemporary glass case with bone fittings. Has a provenance label and a presentation label from "Lord and Lady Allendak." 5½ x 6½ in.*

details that vast collection, but concentrates on scale models and makes only passing reference to prisoner of war work. This is understandable, as prison-made models were seldom made to scale or pretended to be accurate portrayals of the vessel they had graced with its name.

In general, the prisoner of war ship model should be regarded as a wonderful memento of one or other of the wars of the period and, at their best as amazing works of art. We do have one book devoted to our subject. Twenty-five years ago, the late Ewart C. Freeston published his *Prisoner-of-War Ship Models. 1775–1823*.[3] The author was a

Bone Model of a Whaleboat. *Very well-carved model from a solid piece of whalebone. Nicely detailed with oars, harpoons, buckets, ropes, etc. Mast is up and vessel is fully rigged. Mounted on a whalebone base with turned feet. 6½ x 9 in.*

model maker and restorer of ship models, as deeply interested in that aspect of prisoner of war work, as I am in the subject of the prisoner of war generally. He wrote a prologue to his book which, I reproduce here:

'It is a curious fact that many of the greatest works of art have been created in places and under conditions which, one would think would have mitigated against any success in the construction of a masterpiece. This applies to all forms of art whether it be literature, painting, music or, in the case of the subject under review, the making of model ships and boats.'

Prisoner of War Bone Ship Model. *Quality constructed bone and wood model of a 12-gun cutter. Planked and pinned clinker built hull. Brass cannon. Restored rigging.* 16 x 16 in.

Although the accomplished craftsman can work with tools and equipment which would spell failure to the unskilled amateur, yet even so it would seem to be necessary for the skilled workman to possess the best tools and work under the best conditions in order to create something of beauty. For though the expert is master of his tools and trade, and can produce with inferior equipment a result which the novice would find impossible with the very best, there would seem to be a minimum necessary for even ordinary productions. Therefore, granting this premise the results we see in the subject now being discussed can fill us only with wonder and amazement at the skill, patience, ingenuity and fortitude displayed by these unknown, but now I hope not unsung, seamen

Prisoner of War Bone Ship Model. *Unusual model of a mid-17th century English, 94-gun, ship-of-the-line. Planked and pinned hull. Primitively carved stern and a figurehead of a man on horseback. 13 x 14 in.*

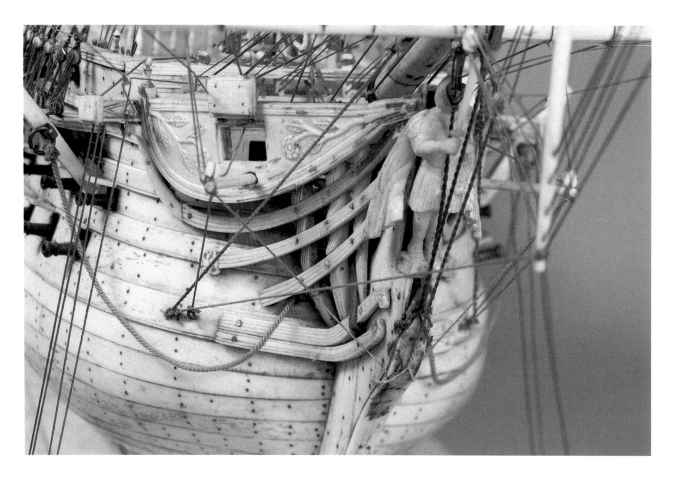

Prisoner of War Bone Ship Model. *A fine large model of a 116-gun vessel with a planked and pinned hull. Very well carved and detailed with an elaborate stern and a figurehead of a Roman soldier. Mounted on a bone planked baseboard. 28 x 36 in.*

of an era long since past, who did their work under the most distasteful, sordid and terrible conditions of body and mind, with tools and equipment of a most primitive sort. Many of the most elaborate would never have been started had the prisoners believed they would soon be released.

Among the bone ship models in the Victoria and Albert Museum is the smallest I have seen. Although the models are not on display, I was privileged to visit the store where, after ploughing through lists and catalogues, I was intrigued by one entry which noted 'ship model in walnut'. Three times we went through every cupboard and case; then

Prisoner of War Bone Ship Model. *Good quality, small size, model of a 70-gun vessel. Nicely carved figurehead and stern. Bone cannon and two life-boats. Well detailed throughout the deck. Planked and pinned hull with carved rope designs along the topside. Mounted on an oval base with bone planking and an ebony edge band. 9 x 11 in.*

suddenly spotted a large pip, or tiny nut (not walnut), no more than an inch in length. It bore the correct number, and after a few minutes' scrutiny the attendant noticed a tiny line near one end. Carefully twisting at that point, the nut came apart to reveal a rigged and sailed bone ship, no more than three-quarters of an inch in height!

1. These words are taken from an epitaph inscribed on a headstone in an Odihan, Hants, churchyard. It was raised in memory of a French paroled prisoner of war: Pierre Julian Jonneau, who died in that town, aged 29 years, on the 4th September 1809.

2. Brian Lavery & Simon Stephens: *'Ship Models, Their Progress and development etc,* Zwemmer. 1995.

3. Ewart C. Freeston: *Prisoner-of-War Ship Models 1775–1823.* Nautilus. 1975.

Prisoner of War Bone Ship Model. *Extremely large model of an 86-gun ship with a planked and pinned hull and baleen wales. Superbly carved throughout with an elaborate stern and a large figurehead of a Roman soldier. Retractable bone cannon. Mounted on a bone and baleen checkered base. 38 x 48 in.*

Prisoner of War Bone Ship Model. *A very fine model of a 104-gun ship-of-the-line. Planked and pinned hull with baleen gunwales. Brass cannon. Good bow carving and a figurehead of a Roman. Very ornately detailed stern. Mounted on an eight-sided bone and baleen base with surrounding balustrade. 24 x 29 in.*

Prisoner of War Bone Ship Model. *A very colourful model of the 110-gun vessel 'Ville De Paris' which was built at Chatham, Kent in 1796. It was Lord St. Vincent's flagship in 1799 and from 1803-1805 carried the flag of Admiral Cornwallis. Planked and pinned hull. Retractable brass cannon. Carved stern, deck fittings and figurehead all with polychrome colouring. The model has an unbroken provenance from its first owner after manufacture to this present day.*

Admiral P. Fraser: The first purchaser left it to his wife ... The Hon. Elizabeth Lucy: Sister of Viscount Torrington. Upon her death in 1840 the model went to her second husband ... The Revd George Goodenough Lynn: He gave it to his brother-in-law ... The Revd Augustus Gedge (1827-1909): Then to his son ... The Revd Arthur A.L. Gedge: Then in 1946 to his daughter ... Miss I. Gedge: Then in 1972 to her niece ... Mrs. M. Keeling: Then in 1984 to her daughter ... Dr C. Keeling: Then to ... The Comtesse De Kerdrel: Then to ... Arthur Davidson: Then to ... Clive L. Lloyd: Then to ... John F. Rinaldi.

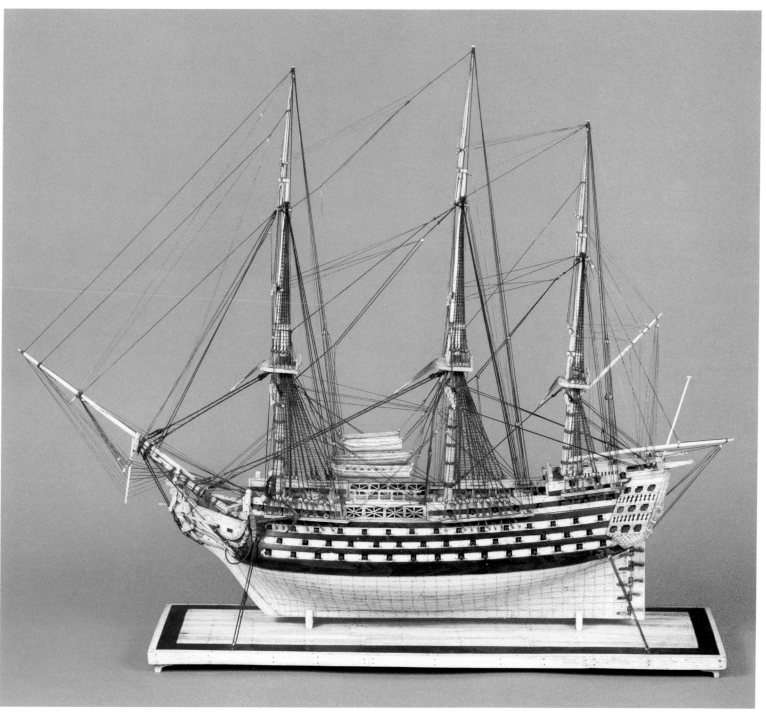

Prisoner of War Bone Ship Model. *Superbly detailed model of the 118-gun vessel 'Achille'. Finely planked and pinned hull with horn and baleen gunwales. Brass cannon. Elaborate carving throughout with a figurehead of a Roman soldier and the stern bearing the vessel's name. Mounted on a planked bone and horn baseboard. 25 x 30 in.*

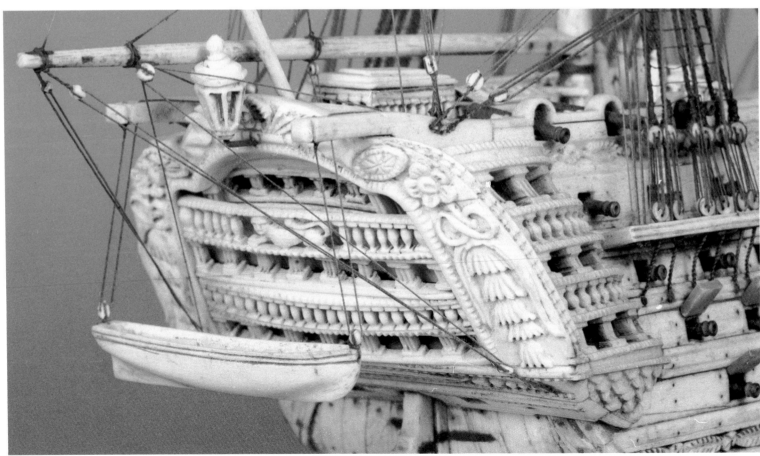

Prisoner of War Bone Ship Model. *Beautifully detailed model of a 116-gun vessel. Planked and pinned hull with an elaborate pierce-carved plank below the brass cannon. Polychrome figurehead of a Roman warrior. Very ornate stern carvings. Mounted on a planked bone and horn baseboard. 21 x 27 in.*

Prisoner of War Bone Ship Model. *A beautifully detailed model of an 86-gun ship. Almost miniature size with a planked and pinned hull with baleen gunwales. Carved figurehead of a Roman and a meticulously executed stern. Brass cannon. Mounted on a planked bone baseboard with surrounding balustrade. 13½ x 16 in.*

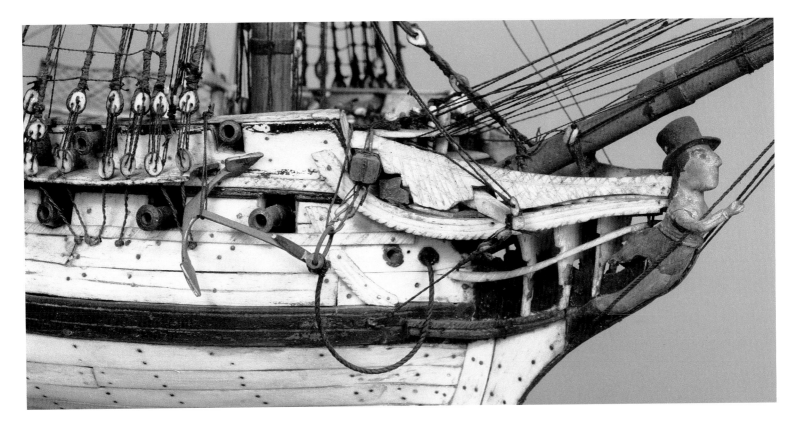

Prisoner of War Bone and Wood Ship Model. *A very interesting and attractive model of a 44-gun frigate. Retractable brass cannon and a painted figurehead of a top-hatted gentleman. Wood masts and other miscellaneous wood fittings. The model was first purchased in 1810 for 12s/6d by a resident of Poole, Dorset. It was later loaned to the Poole Museum but in 1970 a family descendant who inherited the model found it not on display but in the basement with a broken case. It was then withdrawn and sold to Clive Lloyd. 27½ x 36 in.*

Prisoner of War Bone Ship Model. *A very fine model of a 100-gun ship-of-the-line with a planked and pinned hull. High quality carving with a female figurehead and an elaborate and ornate stern. Mounted on an excellent bone and horn baseboard with turned posts. 22 x 28 in.*

Prisoner of War Bone Ship Model and Base. *A superb example of prisoner of war ingenuity and craftsmanship. An 86-gun vessel of whalebone construction. Solid carved hull with a well-detailed stern and a carved figurehead of a Roman warrior. Bone cannon and four lifeboats. Mounted on a marvellous, two-tier, whalebone base with surrounding balustrade and nicely fashioned posts with turned finials. Set on four large, turned bone feet. Overall: 13 x 13 in.*

Bone Model of a Merchant Vessel. *A large plain model with a planked and pinned hull. Simple carving designs throughout. It is doubtful that this model is Napoleonic prisoner of war period work. It shows nice age and may date in the Victorian era.* 23 x 36 in.

Miniature Bone and Ivory Ship Model. *Very well-detailed model of a 72-gun vessel with full rigging and ivory sails. Carved stern and figurehead. On an ebony base with bone inlay and ball feet. Original storage box with bone fittings. 5¼ x 5½ in.*

Bone Prisoner of War Ship Model. *A small model of an 86-gun vessel. Planked and pinned bone hull with baleen gunwales. Simply carved stern and a polychrome figurehead of a Roman warrior. Brass retractable cannon.* 10 x 11½ in.

Prisoner of War Bone Ship Model. *Planked and pinned hull with baleen gunwales. Retractable brass cannon. Simply carved figurehead, stern and deck fittings. Mounted on a bone trimmed baseboard with applied marbled paper.* 12½ x 18 in.

Prisoner of War Bone Ship Model. *A small model outfitted with thirty retractable brass cannon. Planked and pinned hull with nice carving throughout. Mounted on a planked bone baseboard with rope-carved edging and four turned finials. 9½ x 12½ in.*

Rolled-Paper Tea Caddy. *Octagonal wood construction with raised edges to hold the inlays of rolled paper. Numerous different scroll and filigree patterns. Hinged cover for access to a lidded compartment. 4¾ x 5½ x 3⅛ in.*

Chapter Six

Part One

Rolled Paper Work and Paper Sculpture

LIKE THE USE OF BONE AS A SUBSTITUTE FOR IVORY, and straw as an alternative to fine wood veneers, rolled paper work was an imitative art. In this it was ideally suited to the prisoner of war craftsman's ingenuity in creating saleable trinkets from inexpensive materials. Sadly, however, examples in this category of their work are rarer than most, because of the more perishable nature of the fragile raw material. Some specimens are preserved in museums and collections.[1] Peterborough has a number of examples, some of which may have been made by a prisoner of war who was known to practise the art in Falmouth, before being transferred to Norman Cross.

In the hands of an expert artist-craftsman, rolled paper could, according to the technique employed, give a convincing appearance of delicate metal filigree, mosaic, ivory carving, or even simulate bas-relief by the use of 'cones'. The basic preparation of the segments was simple enough, though exacting. Sheets of paper, vellum or other animal parchment, were cut into strips not much more than one eighth of an inch in width, using a very sharp knife. These strips were then tightly rolled round a pin or nail into concentric coils, scrolls, cones, spirals, or bent in layers round leaf or petal-shaped templates. Conical pieces were achieved by raising the centres of coils with a tweezer-like tool. The American name for the craft is 'quilling' or 'quill-work', which might suggest that at an early date the paper may have been rolled round a quill stripped of its feathers.

The paper or parchment itself was usually left white or natural, but different effects were achieved according to the treatment of the edges of the strips. The most usually employed technique was to gild or gold-leaf the top edges, but in some cases they too were left plain or tinted red.

All manner of articles were decorated with rolled paper work; but perhaps the most popular was the tea caddy. If one is lucky enough to find a caddy the body of which is made of pine, there is a good chance that it was made in one or other of the prisoner of war depots. Most civilian-produced tea caddies were made from mahogany or other less common woods but, as we know, the basic structure of most prisoner of war work was made from deal recycled from the provision crates and boxes delivered to the depot stores. However, that is only rule of thumb and does not exclude *all* caddies made from superior materials. *The Gentleman's Magazine* for 1791 mentioned that large numbers of tea-caddies were being decorated with filigree-paper panels in English homes. If they were commercially in demand over the following years, there is good reason to suppose that some may have been farmed out to take advantage of the cheap but high quality work of the prisoners – a labour force which the English milliners had exploited in the case of straw plait.

Once the paper or parchment components had been produced and ready, the next stage, that of arranging them into some sort of design, was as simple as the first. If we take, for example, a typical tea caddy – almost invariably of Sheraton hexagonal design – each of the thirteen panels which made up the body and lid of the caddy would be surrounded by a raised frame, usually of a hardwood, of a depth slightly greater than the widths of the paper scrolls and larger motifs.

First, each shallow sunken panel would be lined with silver, gold or copper foil, or perhaps paper or cloth, The pieces which made up the bold general design layout of flowers, swags, scrolls, drapes, etc., within each panel would then be glued into place; after which the interstices would be packed tight with the small paper coils. One (non-prisoner of war) cabinet in the Port Sunlight Collection, is decorated with tiny parchment rolls – 135 to the square inch! A simple enough technique – but, as with every other art or craft, the difference between the masterpiece and the mediocre depended on the taste, vision and dexterity of the practitioner rather than the cost or simplicity of his medium.

G.C.Rothery[2] says that in cases where the edges had been heavily gilded and well burnished, the finished work 'so nearly approaches the aspect of gold filigree, that specimens have actually been described by experts as "metalwork"'. Another paper *trompe-l'œil* came about when thick cream paper or vellum had been left completely untouched, and the finished work had taken on the appearance of delicately carved and fretted ivory.

Although described as an 'imitative art' whereby paper could take on the aspect of gold, ivory or jewel, it should not be assumed that rolled paper work was an economically inspired prisoner of war invention, far from it. Mary Delany 1700–1788, friend and correspondent of Dean Swift, is noted in many biographical dictionaries as the 'inventor' of paper filigree; but whilst she was famed for her excellent 'paper mosaics' in her day, we know that this minor art predated her – perhaps by a couple of centuries. Jane Austen, in *Sense and Sensibility* (1811), makes it seem not at all unusual that Elinor Dashwood should take on the task of 'rolling the papers' for Lucy Steele, who was making a 'filigree basket' for the daughter of Lady Middleton. Rolled paper filigree – or more often parchment – dates back to mediaeval times when it was something of an ecclesiastic art. In the fifteenth century it was used in some church decoration as economical accessories to religious pictures and ornaments and, from even earlier times, European nuns made convincing substitutes for the expensively ornate reliquaries, normally covered with gold and silver scroll-works and curlicues [fancy twist work and curls]. During the seventeenth century the religious influence was less in evidence: pictures, portraits, cabinets and even rolled-paper-bedecked furniture made their appearance.

By the late eighteenth century the art had become an amateur, ladylike pursuit in Britain, though profitable to the London cabinet-makers. They soon began to advertise all manner of objects, including of course 'tea caddies of all sizes and shapes', with recessed panels to be decorated at home, and women's magazines advertised patterns 'of ingenuity and delicacy suitable for tea caddies, toilets, chimney-pieces, screens, cabinets, frames, picture ornaments etc.'[3]

This type of paper decoration was not a ladies-only craft. A number of men are known to have practised it professionally; but I shall end this brief history by mentioning yet another example of the ubiquitous tea caddy. This one is on display, anachronistically it might at first seem, in the Science Museum, London, amongst pick-proof locks made by the great inventor and locksmith, Joseph Bramah (1749–1814) – who in his spare time was a maker of rolled paper filigree!

---

1. Lady Lever Art Gallery, Port Sunlight, Liverpool.

2. *'Antiques' Magazine'*, July 1929. G.C.Rothery: *'Rolled Paper Work'*.

3. *'New Ladies Magazine'*. 1785.

Chapter Six

Part Two

Automata and Mechanical Toys

During a television programme featuring a class of school children, a small boy was asked: 'Why do you think God put people like us on the earth?'
After thinking for a moment his expression brightened, and he replied: 'I suppose he got bored, so he made little miniatures of himself – just to amuse himself.'
The same answer might be given as the reason for man having made automata.

Hillier. *Automata & Mechanical Toys.*

ALTHOUGH THE FINEST OF THE BONE SHIP MODELS may be classed as the classics of prisoner of war craftsmanship, the ingenious creations of the captive makers of automata or mechanical toys are the most intriguing – and must have been among the best-selling.

From early times almost everyone, young or old, has been captivated by apparently inanimate objects which spring into life at the turning of a wheel, lever, or the touch of a button. Although we may daily pass by a static sculptural group, which we appreciate as a work of art but no longer stop to admire, it is always tempting to pause, perhaps for the hundredth time, if on that same journey we pass by an automated Town Hall clock with figures which emerge and disappear on the hour – however crude their carving.

Five thousand years ago, small figurines of servants, with articulated limbs, accompanied the Egyptian pharoah on his journey to the nether world. The ancient Greeks took the art to the point of chicanery and deceit, with automated and talking statues – and the Dutch steam organs of today still attract as much for their dancing figures as for their music.

By the eighteenth century the manufacture of automata was enjoying a great vogue on the Continent, whether as small toys for children or life-sized 'collectors-piece' wonders for the adult market; a popularity which grew throughout the following century. However, there were few British makers, or even dealers, at that time. Those few were suppliers to either wealthy clients, or to businesses as eye-catching attractions for their window displays – and even so, much of their stock was imported from Europe. From this we may gather that the automaton – even as a toy – was a rare possession in the ordinary English family. The main centres of manufacture of this form of mechanical art were Germany, Italy, Switzerland and, of course, France. It is little wonder, therefore, that the French prisoner of war craftsmen should have imported their knowledge into their prisons and created their version of the craft, thereby cashing in on a virtually unexploited market.

One particularly gifted craftsman was a French prisoner of war by the name of Cruchet (his forename may have been Marie). It could be that his was a natural talent for carving and model-making, or he may have had some working experience in the Dieppe ivory or jet carving trade before the war. All that we do know is that he spent some time on

Bone Model of a French Guillotine. *Unusual small size with three tiers, a single figure and a victim. Copper blade with a pierced heart.* 11 x 5½ x 1½ in.

Bone Model of a French Guillotine. *Fine, two-tier, model with five soldiers.* 23 x 14½ x 5 in.

fishing vessels before being conscripted into the French Navy. His naval service came to an abrupt end when his ship, *l'Intrépide*, was honorably captured in the Battle of Trafalgar, in 1805. The crew were all taken to Norman Cross, among them the straw marquetry artist, Corporal Jean De la Porte, whom we have met in a previous chapter.

Cruchet made a name for himself by his skill as a maker of bone automata; complicated multi-figured 'Spinning Jennys' and, a specialty of his, working models of the Guillotine, which appealed to the Englishman's morbid fascination with the French Revolution and the 'Reign of Terror'. It would seem that Cruchet was also no mean maker of model ships, and that during his long captivity he made at least one which was acclaimed a masterpiece. A remarkable story is told regarding this man-of-war model – no doubt incorporating retractable guns – which was purchased by the Prince Regent. It

Bone Model of a French Guillotine. *Multi-tiered model with pierced and fretted galleries and gates surrounding each platform. A victim plus twenty-eight soldiers with moveable arms. Eighteen cannon. Polychrome colouring in red, black and green. Mounted on working wheels. 20 x 12¼ x 5 in.*

Bone Model of a French Guillotine. *Multi-tiered model with delicate fretted galleries and gates surrounding all the platforms. A victim plus forty figures with moveable arms. Eight cannon on the lower level. Full polychrome colouring plus several paintings and designs throughout. Originally purchased at the Dartmoor market by Coryndon Luxmore of Bridestowe. 23 x 14½ x 5 in.*

Bone Model of a French Guillotine. *Nicely made, two-tier, model with four top-hatted gentlemen, a soldier and a female victim. Some red colouring. 10¾ x 6⅝ x 3¼ in.*

is said that, besides the asking price, Cruchet was offered his freedom, but refused it, saying that he did not wish to leave without his shipmates; so perhaps he was released with la Porte, in 1814.

By the 1820s, he had found fame in France as the designer of mechanical spectaculars for the Paris Opera House; but he still made automaton figures – knife-grinders, drunks, spinners, snuff-takers, ladies at the harpsichord. These, however, would have been made on a larger scale than his wartime manufactures; using wood or papier mâché to make figures dressed in the costume of the day, and worked by levers or clockwork. A far cry

Bone Model of a French Guillotine. *Delicately made, two-tier, model with twenty-two soldiers and a victim. Finely fretted galleries and gates surround each tier. Four cannon on the lower level. Blade decorated with a somewhat worn painting of birds and scrolls. Some red colouring. 19 x 10 x 4 in.*

Prisoner of War Toy. *Unusual item with a domed wire cage over a bone floor and topped with a bone finial. Contains two painted birds and a windmill. Lower section is a soft leather bellows which mechanizes the item when squeezed. 4½ x 3 in.*

from, but no more wonderful than, the tiny working models he had made from bones at Norman Cross. In 1855, Marie Cruchet, a Parisian toy-maker who may have been a descendant or even the ex-prisoner of war himself, patented a 'talking device' for use with mechanical toys.

The prisoner of war 'toys' were, in the main, small; but there were a few built on a larger scale. Probably the largest is the model of a château in Peterborough Museum. It was made from bone over a wooden structure and is roughly two feet in height, twenty-eight inches wide, about eighteen inches from front to back, and houses a complicated mechanical system, operated in part by a waterwheel which is fed by a tank from inside. Between the towers a troop of soldiers move on an endless march, and a number of figures are engaged in various activities; from courting to sawing wood.

Such over-sized and bulky pieces are rare, although some of the delicate pierced-work guillotines, with their lace-like galleries (and gory heads in buckets!), rise to a height of two feet or more. Models of forts and others edifices seldom exceed a height of more than twelve inches. Spinning Jenny models vary in size from three to eight inches, but even these comparatively tiny examples of the mechanical toy-makers art may incorporate from one to a dozen moving figures.

Although these marvellous little manufactures were usually referred to in contemporary letters and literature as 'toys', it is to be doubted that many were purchased as children's playthings. Few country families who survived on pittances earned from cottage industries, could have afforded to buy market toys, however cheap, for their children, many of whom were put out to work as young as three or four years of age. So many of these delicate artefacts have survived in good condition, some complete with their original pine boxes, that whatever excuse the buyer who could afford them may have made at the time of purchase, they became an adult 'toy' and treasured curio.

The prisoner-mechanics were probably called in, at least in an advisory capacity, when a ship model with retractable guns was being constructed. I have seen a number of these, including a few in which the gun-ports also closed – and one rare example where a 'clapper' construction made a gunfire sound as the guns re-emerged.

And there were others in this specialist field of bone-work who, whilst no less ingenious, were perhaps less scrupulous in the choice of their artwork. These were members of the underworlds which existed in most depots, who made their money from erotica, not always crude in workmanship but in subject matter – the pornographers who could hardly keep up with the demand for their toys of copulating couples and the like. These operators, together with the 'purveyors of dirty books and drawings', were a thorn in the side of the Transport Office throughout the wars.

Pornographic Toy. *Wood carved figure of a Dartmoor countrywoman wearing a long skirt, a cloak and a hood. Skirt front is hinged and when lifted reveals the lady's charms. A rarity because troops were sent into the prisons to break up the workbench of anyone producing these items.*
3½ x 1½ in.

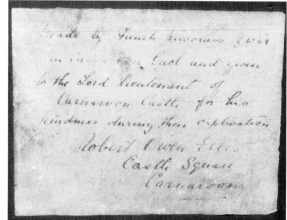

Presentation Bone Spinning Jenny. *Large mechanized model with seven figures, an infant, two birds and two dogs. Extremely high quality carving with full polychrome colouring. Upper and lower platforms made of wood with strawwork applications. Original case with affixed provenance slip on the back: 'Made by French prisoners of war in Carnarvon Gaol and given to the Lord Lieutenant of Carnarvon Castle for his kindness during their captivity... Robert Owen Ellis, Castle Square, Carnavon.'* 8 x 5 x 2¾ in.

Large Bone Spinning Jenny. *Mechanized model with eleven figures, an infant and two dogs. Superb quality carving and full polychrome colouring. Wood upper and lower platforms with applied strawwork decorations. Made at the Norman Cross depot and is from the collection of Colonel Strong. 7¼ x 5 x 2¼ in.*

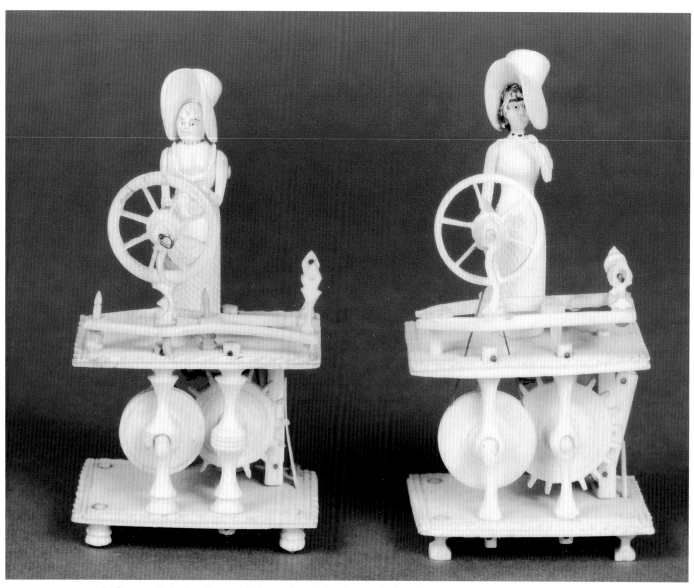

(Left) **Bone Spinning Jenny.** *Mechanized model with a single female figure working at a spinning wheel. The crank handle and distaff have recently been restored. 3¾ x 2 in. (Right)* **Bone Spinning Jenny.** *Mechanized model with a single female figure working at a spinning wheel. The crank handle and distaff have recently been restored. 4 x 2 in.*

Bone Spinning Jenny. *Mechanized model with a single female figure working at a spinning wheel. One cog wheel has recently been restored. 5½ x 2½ in.*

Bone Spinning Jenny. *Mechanized model with a single female figure, a spinning wheel and a windmill. 6 x 2½ in.*

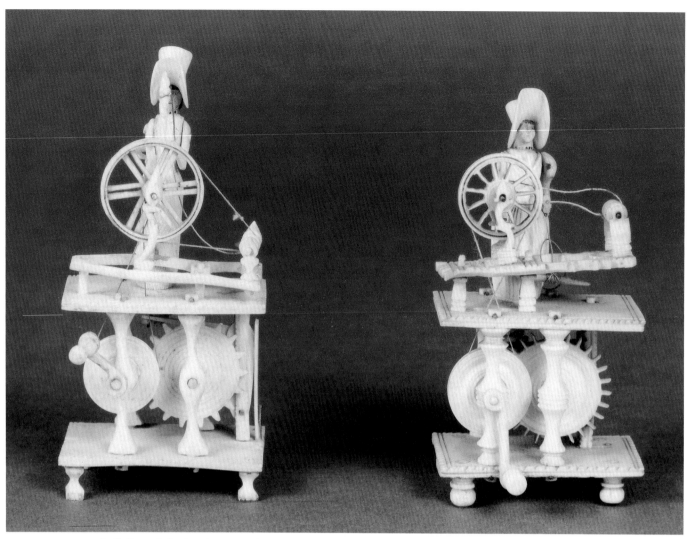

(Left) **Bone Spinning Jenny.** *Mechanized model with a single female figure working at a spinning wheel. Some red colouring. 4 x 2 in. (Right)* **Bone Spinning Jenny.** *High quality, small, mechanized model with a single female figure working at a spinning wheel. The distaff has recently been restored. 3¼ x 2 in.*

Bone Spinning Jenny. *Mechanized model with a single figure of a woman working at a spinning wheel. 4 x 2 in.*

Bone Spinning Jenny. *Mechanized model with a single female figure working at a spinning wheel. Mellow polychrome colouring throughout. 3½ x 2 in.*

Bone Spinning Jenny. *Mechanized model with three female figures working at a spinning wheel. Nicely fashioned wheels and fancy turned column supports. Two breton hats recently replaced. 5½ x 3 in.*

Bone Spinning Jenny. *Superb mechanized model with two female figures, a spinning wheel and a bird cage holding several small birds. Very high quality carving throughout. Some light polychrome colouring.* 5½ x 3 in.

(Left) **Bone Spinning Jenny.** *Mechanized model with a single female figure at a spinning wheel. Some red and black colouring. 4¼ x 2 in. (Right)* **Bone Spinning Jenny.** *Mechanized model with a single female figure working at a spinning wheel. 4 x 2 in.*

Bone Spinning Jenny. *Mechanized model with a single figure of a woman working at a spinning wheel. Wheels fabricated with circular type spokes. 5¼ x 2½ in.*

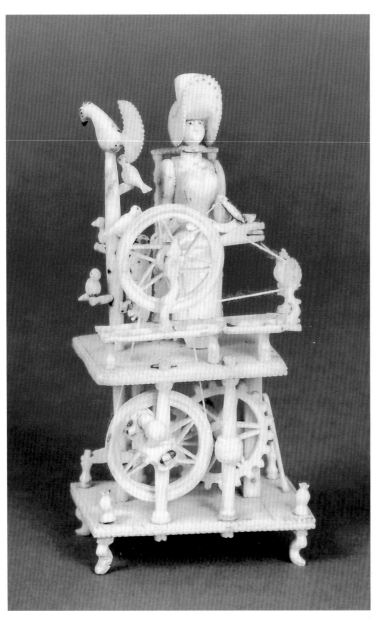

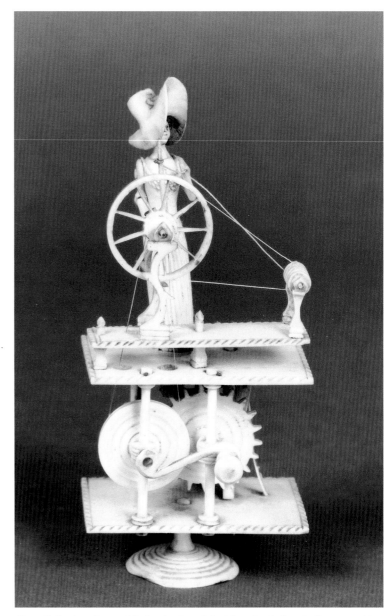

Bone Spinning Jenny. *Mechanized model with a seated woman, a spinning wheel and a tree with a cat, four roosting birds and a cockerel at the top. 4½ x 2¼ in.*

Bone Spinning Jenny. *Mechanized model with a single female figure working at a spinning wheel. 4½ x 2 in.*

Bone Spinning Jenny. *Mechanized model with a single female figure, a spinning wheel and a tower with a flagstaff on the upper platform. 4¾ x 2 in.*

Bone Spinning Jenny. *Mechanized model with a single, polychromed figure of a female working at a spinning wheel. The crank handle, spinning wheel arms and distaff have all been recently restored. 4 x 2 in.*

Bone Spinning Jenny. *Large mechanized model with two female figures, a spinning wheel and a windmill on the upper platform. 5¾ x 3 in.*

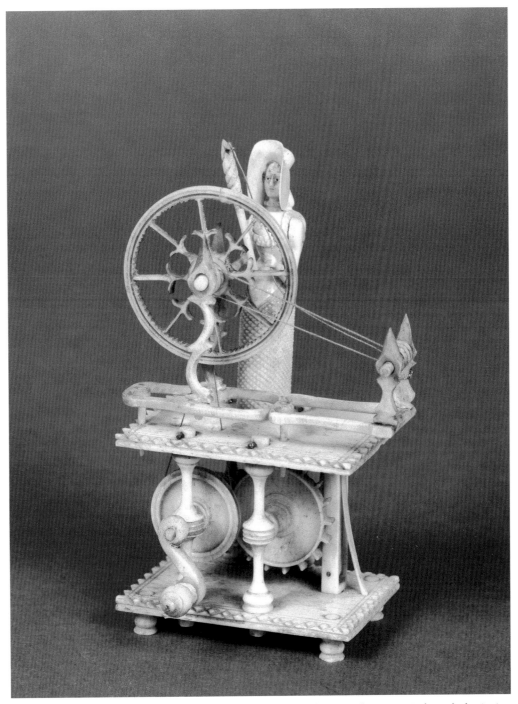

Bone Spinning Jenny. *Mechanized model with a single female figure working at a nicely spoked spinning wheel.* 3¾ x 2⅜ in.

Bone Spinning Jenny. *Fine mechanized model with a single female figure seated at a spinning wheel. Also on the platform is a windmill. Nicely fashioned wheel spokes and good polychrome colouring on the figure and windmill. 6 x 2½ in.*

Bone Spinning Jenny. *Mechanized model with three females, two children, an infant, a spinning wheel and a table. High quality carving with fancy wheel spokes. 5½ x 3½ in.*

Bone Spinning Jenny. *Mechanized model with a single, polychromed, female figure working at a spinning wheel. A turned, bone, pedestal base has recently been added. 5⅜ x 2 in.*

Bone Spinning Jenny. *Superb mechanized model with three female figures, an infant, a dog, a windmill and a spinning wheel on the upper platform. Nicely fashioned wheel spokes and good turned platform pillars. The crank handle has recently been restored and a turned bone pedestal base has been added. 5½ x 3 in.*

Bone Games Box. *Sliding dome-top with pierced and open-work carving and drilled holes for scorekeeping. Sliding inner lid with a painting of Britannia and other subjects. Contains dominoes. 4 x 6 x 2¼ in.*

Chapter Six

Part Three

Games, Games-Boxes and Pastime Trivia

AS THE FOLLOWING SECTION WILL REVEAl, great numbers of French prisoners of war displayed a passionate addiction to gaming and gambling, unmatched by punters from the many other countries represented in our depots and prison ships. The caterers to that addiction, the owners of the gaming booths and billiards tables, made large fortunes, whilst the luckless players often lost *their* small fortunes or pittances – and sometimes their lives – through the fickle fancy of Lady Luck.

Almost everyone, except perhaps those forbidden by their faith – or those completely without faith in their luck! – might enjoy the occasional flutter. Games of chance or skill have always had a universal appeal, and the canny and industrious prisoners of war who realised this and kept the depot markets stocked with appropriate artefacts were sure of regular and rewarding employment. Dominoes, playing cards, chess sets, teetotums, spillikins, all were to be found on the market stalls, in qualities which ranged from the crude to works of art and craft. The prisoners were most prolific in the production of games-boxes, made in a wide range of designs and presentations. The smallest – just a couple of dice in a simply decorated box – are often no more than an inch and a half long, whilst the true games-boxes may reach any length up to about a foot.

It is often difficult dating prisoner of war work to a certain period. We know that straw-work, ship models and other bone-work artefacts were being made during the whole period covered by this book, but most of the games-boxes can be dated to within twenty years of their manufacture! Some of the 'commemorative' boxes, such as those depicting the *'Death of Nelson'* and *'Nelson's Toomb'* [sic] can take us even closer, as they could not have been put on sale before November 1805, at the very earliest. However, an all-embracing clue to period is provided by the fact that the majority of these boxes contained sets of dominoes, so they could not have been made in a pre-Napoleonic era. Although a type of domino was made in China from the twelfth century onwards, dominoes, as we know the game, was not known on the Continent until the mid seventeen-hundreds, and was introduced, by French prisoners of war, into England only at the end of the eighteenth century.[1]

The larger games-boxes were usually compendia containing more than one game: dominoes, dice and sometimes sets of miniature bone playing cards, miniature skittles, score pegs, or small teetotums. Designwise, these boxes are usually found as a variation on one of four or five basic types. The most common – but often of no less artistic merit and achievement – is the hinged **'Dome-top'**. The origin of its name is obvious, as the arched lid was made from the shin bone, or tibia, of the ox – and perhaps sometimes the horse. The largest and rarest of this type are sometimes fitted with double or even treble 'dome-top' lids. Most of the lids of this group are pierced and fretted, some with a lace-

Games-Box with Watercolour Panels. *Fourteen, bone-framed, panels containing watercolours of flowers, people, villages and hearts. Peak-shaped sliding lid for access to hand-painted bone playing cards and dominoes. 4 x 9 x 3½ in.*

like delicacy, and the finest of them are superbly carved with figures or designs in low relief on a pierced ground.

Although no two dome-tops are exactly the same, the close repetition of one particular basic decoration might indicate that they all came from one place of origin and the work of one craftsman. However, we know that some prisoners had spent time in as many as three or four different depots or hulks over the many years of their captivity, and may

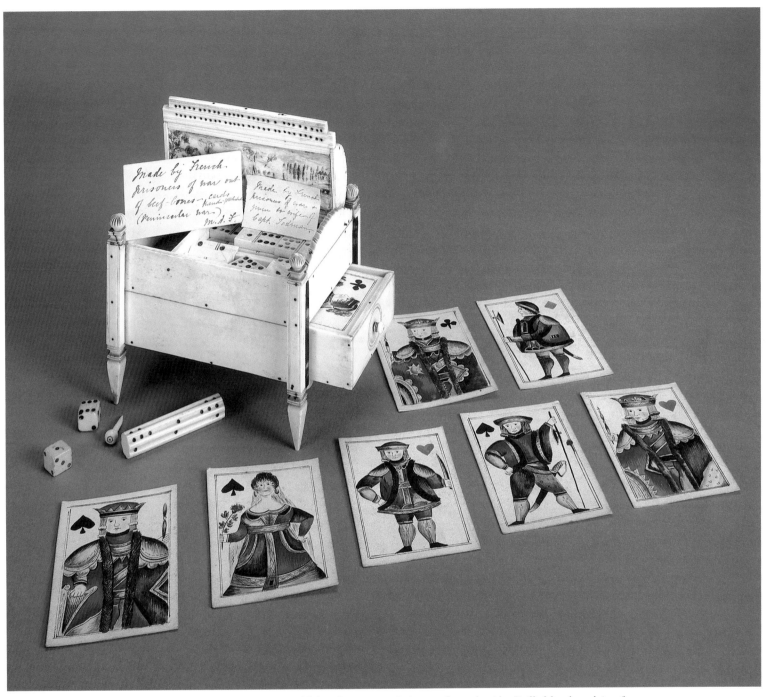

Unique Bone Games-Box. *Domed lid with a worn painting on the underside. Drilled border edging for scorekeeping. Inner compartments contain dominoes, dice and a roller type teetotum. Lower drawer contains a full set of normal sized playing cards that are completely hand-drawn and painted. Has a provenance slip stating that this item was presented to the wife of Captain Todman. 4¾ x 5 x 3½ in.*

have taken their craft along with them. Despite the similarity, a sufficient number of examples of that design have passed through my hands alone, to suggest teamwork and production-line, rather than the work of one man. Whatever its size, in every case where the lid is an open-work 'dome-top', there would originally have been a second, and flat, sliding lid to protect the dominoes and other contents, and this was often painted with flags, Britannia and commemorative details. Another prominent and almost invariable

Bone Games-Box. *Double dome-top lids with pierced designs of 'clubs and hearts.' Overhanging scoreboard and a sliding lid with a worn painting with 'Nelson's Toomb' motifs. Contains dominoes. Red and green colouring throughout. Includes a provenance slip with names and it states the date of manufacture to be 1814. 2¼ x 9¾ x 5 in.*

detail of this type of box, is the scoreboard which overhangs three sides of the base.

There is a sub-group which should be mentioned at this point, the **'Shallow dome-top'**. In this variation there is a single sliding lid of curved wood, covered with a veneer of finely fretted bone. Between the bone and the wood is an interlining of copper or 'gold' foil, which glows through the frets. The four sides of the box itself are almost always treated in a like manner.

Like the dome-top, there is another distinctive type which can easily be categorised by its lid, and can most aptly be called the **'Roof-top'**. These attractive manufactures are of

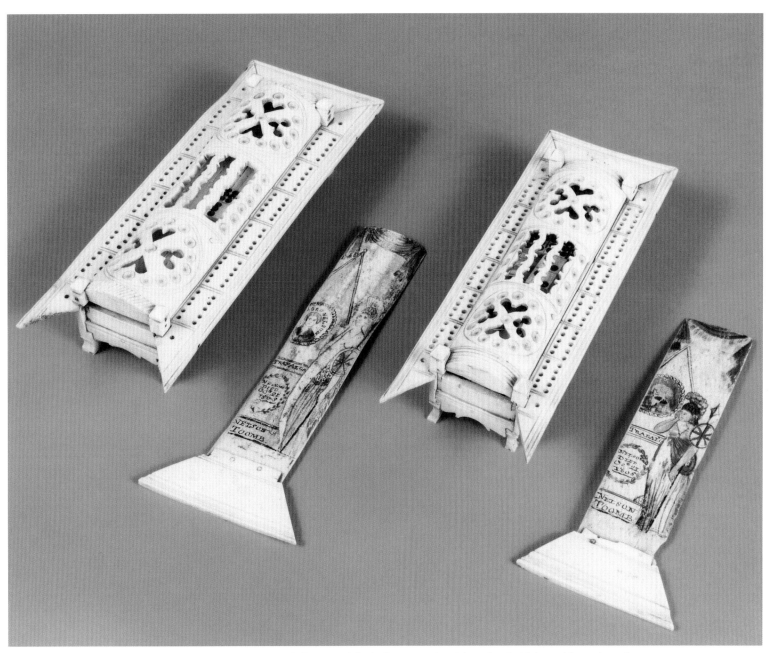

(Left) **Bone Games-Box.** *Hinged, dome-top lid which is incised and fretted with 'clubs and hearts' motifs. Sliding lid painted with 'Nelson's Toomb' subject matter. Contains dominoes. 2½ x 9½ x 3½ in. (Right)* **Bone Games-Box.** *Hinged, dome-top lid which is incised and fretted with 'clubs and hearts' motifs. Sliding lid painted with 'Nelson's Toomb' subject matter. Contains dominoes and dice. Probably by the same hand as the previous item. 2½ x 10½ x 3¾ in.*

particular interest as they are clear examples of teamwork; the skills of woodworker, bone-worker and artist, brought together in one comparatively small games box. The design concept was of bone-framed panels on all surfaces of the box – except of course the underside – the frames surrounding watercolours on paper or velum, protected by glass or mica. The sliding lids exhibited from four to six of these small framed pictures and the complete boxes from ten to fourteen. The subject matter of these fascinating and informative little works usually included full-length portrayals of civilian men and women; uniformed officers and their ladies; buildings and flowers.

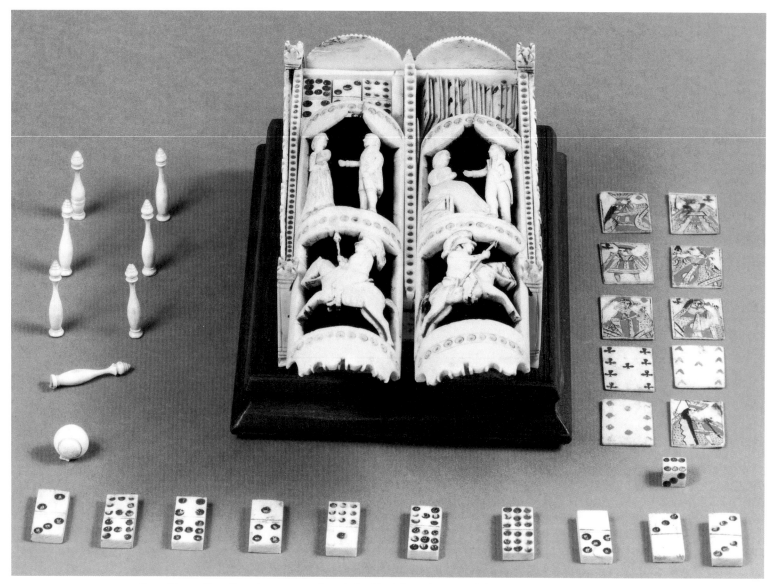

Bone Games-Box. *Superb rare example with double sliding, dome-top, lids which have been open-carved with ladies, gentlemen and equestrian riders. Slides are treated with circle and snowflake designs and a lower skirt with tassel motifs. Red, blue and green colouring throughout. Contains bone playing cards, dominoes, dice and skittles with a ball. 2½ x 7¾ x 5 in.*

The watercolour artists were also employed, though with greatly reduced scope for their output, in the production of another, but flat-lidded, bone **'picture-frame'** box. This was a far less elaborate production, the sides of the box itself decorated with minimal and sometimes crude engraving; but the sliding lid, which seldom had more than two panels, still retained something of the charm of the 'roof-top'.

Even in its simplest form, where the small domino box is no more than a rectangular container with sliding lid, there is usually an added decoration of some kind. In many cases the lids are drilled to act as scoreboards, the sides left plain or decorated using one or more of a number of techniques: engraving, straw-marquetry, fretwork, or naïve paintings of landscapes or battle scenes painted directly on to the bone, then varnished. Comparatively simple as they are in construction, many of these are delightful examples of the less expensive of depot marketware.

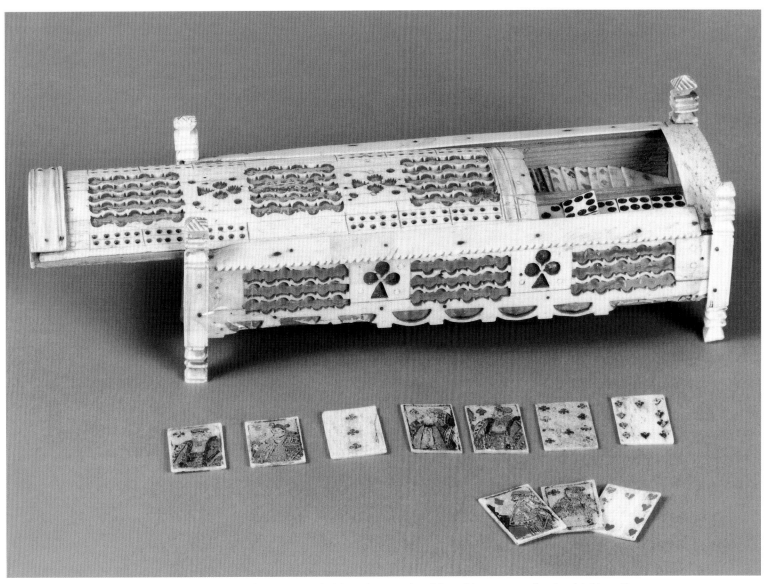

Bone Games-Box. *Wood structure with delicately pierced and fretted bone veneer forming 'club' motifs. Slightly domed sliding lid with scoreboard holes. Contains bone playing cards, dominoes and dice. Sections of the lower skirt have recently been restored. 2¾ x 8¾ x 3½ in.*

In general, 'bone' games-boxes will be found to have at least some wood in their composition and some, such as the 'Sissinghurst Shoe' type of box, are almost entirely of wood, except for their domino contents and a small amount of bone decoration. Whilst 'Sissinghurst' may describe wooden shoe-shaped relics of that Kent castle's time as a prisoner of war depot, it is a misnomer in the case of domino boxes, for reasons explained above. Sissinghurst Castle was demolished after the end of the Seven Years' War, in 1763.

It would be tedious to try to fit all the different kinds of games-boxes into thematic groups. Even the meanest of these artefacts is a record of some determined soul who may have spent the major part of his youth confined in prison camp or hulk – and the 'masterpieces' speak for themselves.

1. *Encyclopaedia Britannica*, Volume IV.

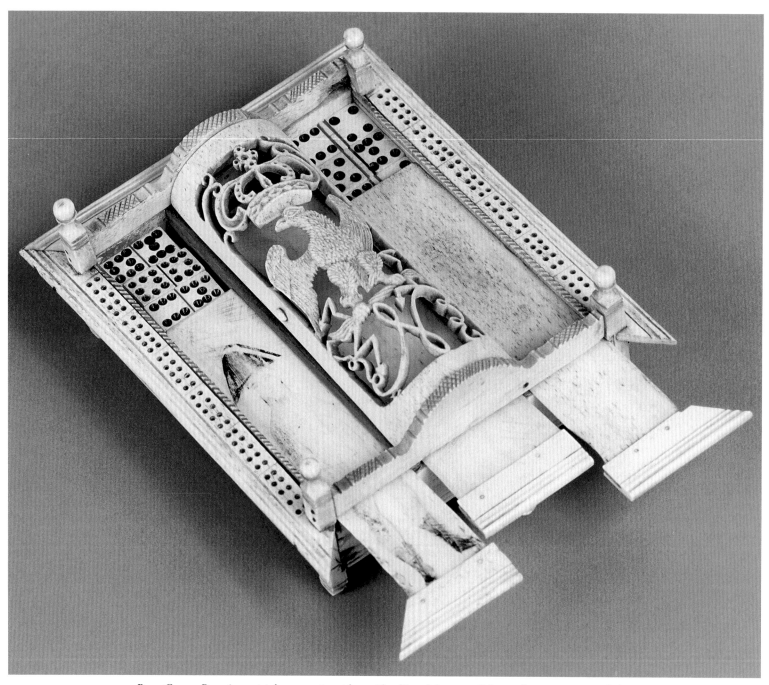

Bone Games-Box. *A rare triple compartment box with a hinged dome-top lid over the centre section. Lid is superbly open-carved with Napoleon's arms: crown, full eagle and 'N' in script. Overhanging scoreboards and sliding lids with worn paintings. Contains dominoes. 2½ x 6½ x 5¼ in.*

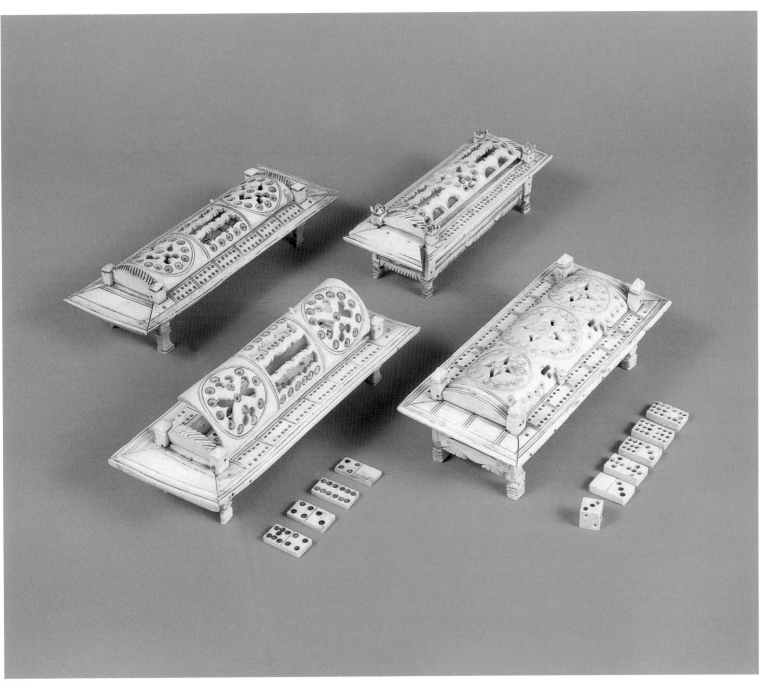

(Top right) **Bone Games-Box.** *Hinged, dome-top fretted and pierced with 'hearts and clubs' motifs. Overhanging scoreboard and a plain sliding cover. Interior is empty. Green, red and black colouring throughout. 2¾ x 8 x 3 in. (Top left)* **Bone Games-Box.** *Hinged, dome-top lid fretted and pierced with 'hearts and clubs' motifs. Overhanging scoreboard and a sliding lid with a painting of a lady that may not be period. Red and Green colouring throughout. Contains dominoes. 2½ x 9¼ x 3⅜ in. (Bottom right)* **Bone Games-Box.** *Hinged, dome-top lid with pierced 'hearts and clubs' motifs. Overhanging scoreboard and a nicely carved lower apron. Contains dominoes, dice and scoring pegs. 3 x 8½ x 3¾ in. (Bottom left)* **Bone Games-Box.** *Hinged, dome-top lid fretted and pierced with 'clubs and hearts' motifs. Overhanging scoreboard. red and green colouring throughout. Contains dominoes. 2½ x 9 x 3½ in.*

(Back left) **Bone Games-Box.** *Flat, sliding lid with circular tortoiseshell inlays. Sides decorated with incised circles and lines with red and blue colouring. Contains bone dominoes. 1⅝ x 6¼ x 1¼ in. (Back centre)* **Bone Games-Box.** *A simple, yet well-made, example with dovetailed ends and etched and coloured designs over five sides. Sliding lid for access to compartments that contain dominoes and dice. 1 x 5½ x 1 in. (Back right)* **Bone Games-Box.** *Flat, sliding lid with circular tortoiseshell inlays and drilled holes for scorekeeping. Sides and ends decorated with incised circles. Contains dominoes. ¾ x 5½ x 1½ in. (Front left)* **Bone Games- Box.** *Decorated with 'dice dot' designs over five sides. Sliding lid for access to three dice. 1 x 2¼ x ¾ in. (Front right)* **Bone Games-Box.** *Unusual shape with decorations of circles, dots and lines all of which are coloured in red and green. Sliding lid for access to dominoes and dice. 1¼ x 1¼ x 1 in.*

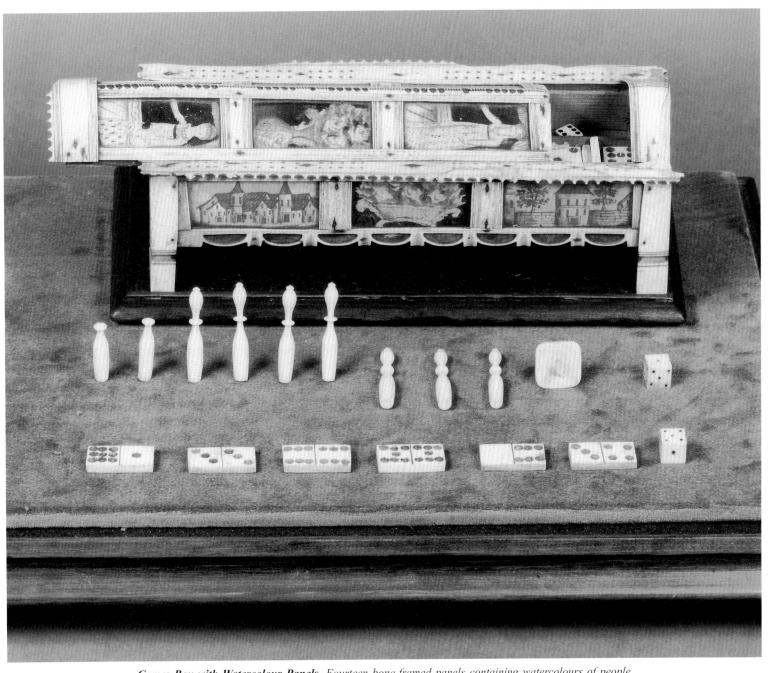

Games-Box with Watercolour Panels. *Fourteen bone-framed panels containing watercolours of people, buildings and flowers. Sliding, peak-topped, lid covering contents of dominoes, dice and other game implements. 3½ x 10½ x 4 in.*

Presentation Chess Set. *Complete set of well-carved bone chessmen coloured in green and white. Each piece fitted into a velvet-lined, strawwork box with a silver ring handle on top of the lid. This set was given to Lord Doneraile by the French prisoners at Dartmouth.* Chessmen: King and Queen 3¾ in. Box: 4½ x 13½ x 7 in.

Bone Carved Chessmen. *Complete set of thirty-two pieces. Plain workmanship and probably a set used by the prisoners rather than ones offered for sale in the depot markets. Reputedly from Porchester Castle. Kings and Knights: 2⅛ in.*

Bone Games-Box. *Superbly carved over five sides. Sliding, dome-top, lid with two carved scenes depicting: a classic maiden with a sheaf of wheat; a lady, seated beneath a tree, receiving offerings from Cupid. Sides and ends carved in bird and floral motifs. Contains dominoes. 2¼ x 6 x 2⅝ in.*

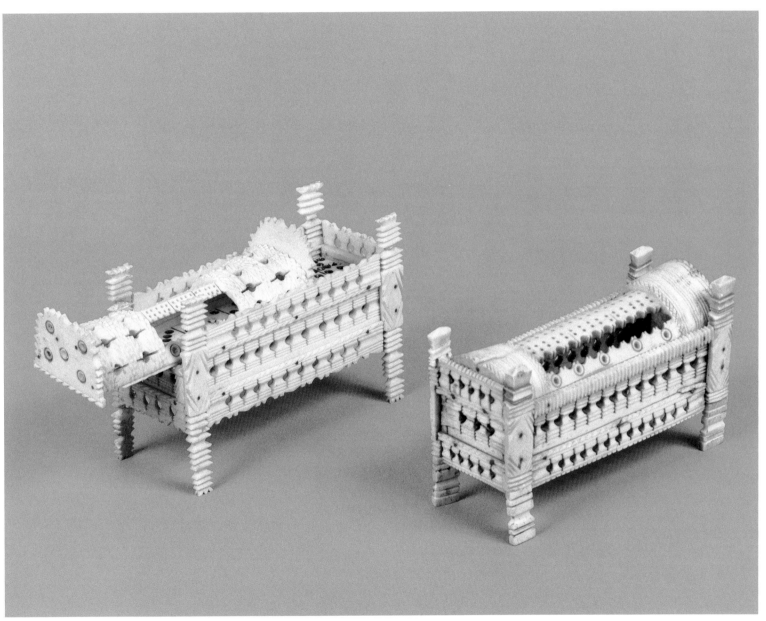

(Left) **Bone Games-Box.** *Sliding dome-top with pierced and open-work carving and drilled holes for scorekeeping. Sliding inner lid with a painting of Britannia and other subjects. Contains dominoes. 4 x 6 x 2¼ in. (Right)* **Box Games-Box.** *Sliding dome-top lid with open-work carving and drilled scoreboard holes. Pierced and slotted sides and ends. Underside with hand-written notes. Box is empty. 3½ x 5¼ x 2¼ in.*

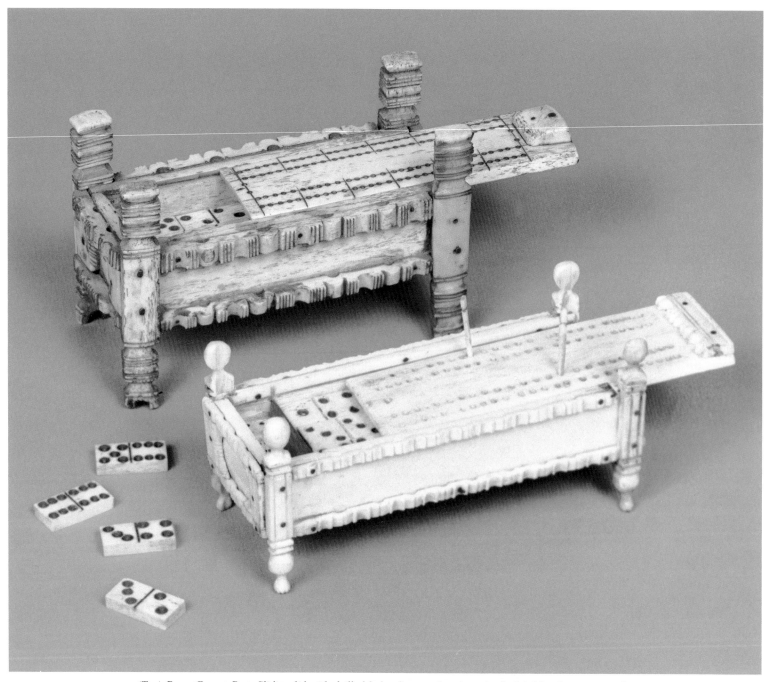

(Top) **Bone Games-Box.** *Sliding lid with drilled holes for scorekeeping. Applied 'ribbon' carving on the sides and ends. Nicely carved legs with half-ball tops. Contains dominoes, dice and score pegs. 2¾ x 5½ x 2⅜ in. (Bottom)* **Bone Games-Box.** *Sliding lid with drilled holes for scorekeeping. Tall pillar legs and 'ribbon' carving applied to the sides and ends. Contains dominoes. 3½ x 5½ x 2⅛ in.*

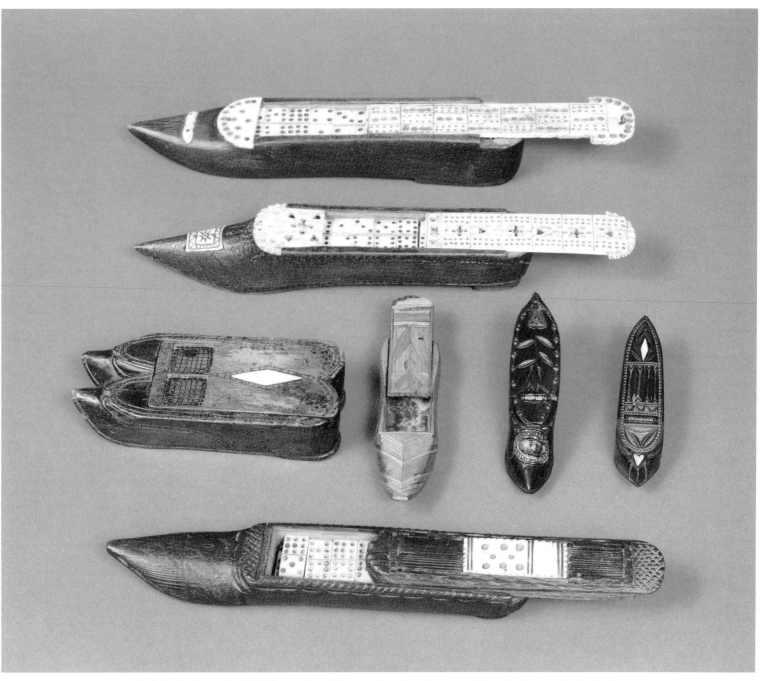

(Top) **Sissinghurst Castle 'Wooden Shoe' Games-Box.** *Bone top and sliding lid decorated with domino motifs and drilled for scorekeeping. Contains dominoes. 1½ x 9½ x 1½ in. (Centre top)* **Sissinghurst Castle 'Wooden Shoe' Games-Box.** *Bone top and sliding lid meticulously pierced and incised with various designs and scorekeeping holes. Toe of shoe inset with an incised bone panel. Contains dominoes. 1½ x 9 x 1½ in. (Centre left)* **Sissinghurst Castle 'Wooden Shoe' Games-Box.** *Unusual double shoe carved from a single piece of wood. Sliding lid with a diamond-shaped bone inset. Contains dominoes. 1¼ x 5¾ x 2¼ in. (Centre)* **Strawwork 'Shoe' Games-Box.** *A shoe carved from wood and overlaid with broad split starw of various colours and designs. Box is empty. ¾ x 4½ x 1¼ in. (Centre right)* **Sissinghurst Castle 'Wooden Shoe' Games-Box.** *Nicely fashioned from a single piece of wood. Decorated with floral and border design carvings. Hinged top. Strawwork insole. 1½ x 4½ x 1 in. (Centre far right)* **Sissinghurst Castle 'Wooden Shoe' Games-Box.** *Constructed like the previous item but with diamond and heart-shaped inlays on the lid and toe. Strawwork insole. 1 x 4 x 1 in. (Bottom)* **Sissinghurst Castle 'Wooden Shoe' Games-Box.** *Sliding wood lid with a bone 'domino' design application. Contains dominoes. 1¼ x 8¼ x 1½ in.*

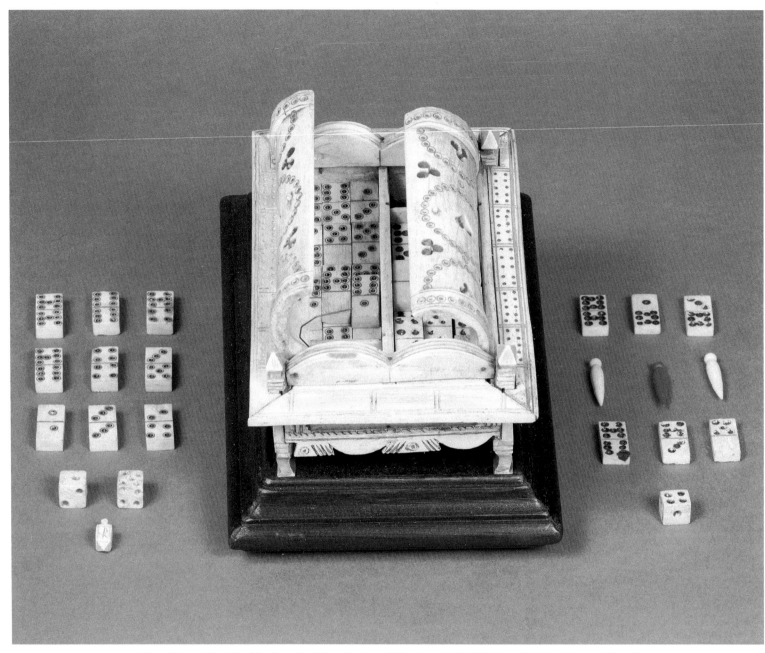

Bone Games-Box. *Double-dome-top lids with pierced 'hearts and club' designs. Overhanging scoreboard and lower apron with red, black and green colouring. Contains dominoes, dice, teetotum and scoring pegs. 2¾ x 7 x 4¼ in.*

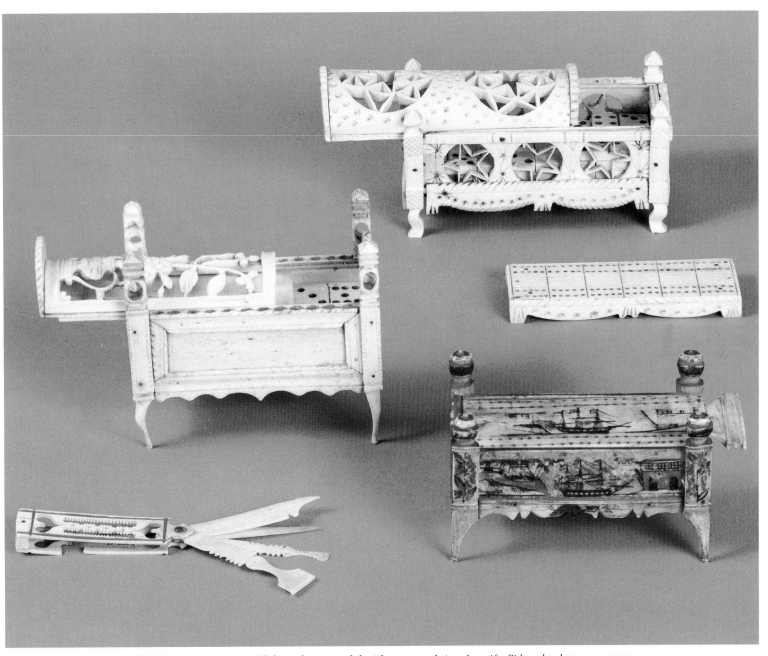

(Top) **Bone Games-Box.** *Sliding, dome-top, lid with open-work 'star' motifs. Sides also have open type 'star' motifs and a carved lower apron with tassel designs. Contains a separate scoreboard and dominoes. 3 x 5 x 2½ in. (Centre-left)* **Bone Games-Box.** *Sliding, dome-top, lid with fine open-work carving of a vase and flowers. Plain sliding lid covering a set of dominoes. One leg appears to be a replacement. 4 x 4¼ x 1⅞ in. (Bottom-left)* **Bone Necessaire.** *Resembling a typical clasp knife and having an openwork cover with heart motifs. Red incised lines. Contains four folding blades. Closed 3 x ¾ in. (Bottom-right)* **Bone Games-Box.** *Sliding lid with drilled holes for scorekeeping. All sides are completely covered with paintings of shipping and floral scenes. Interior compartment is empty. 2⅝ x 4¼ x 2 in.*

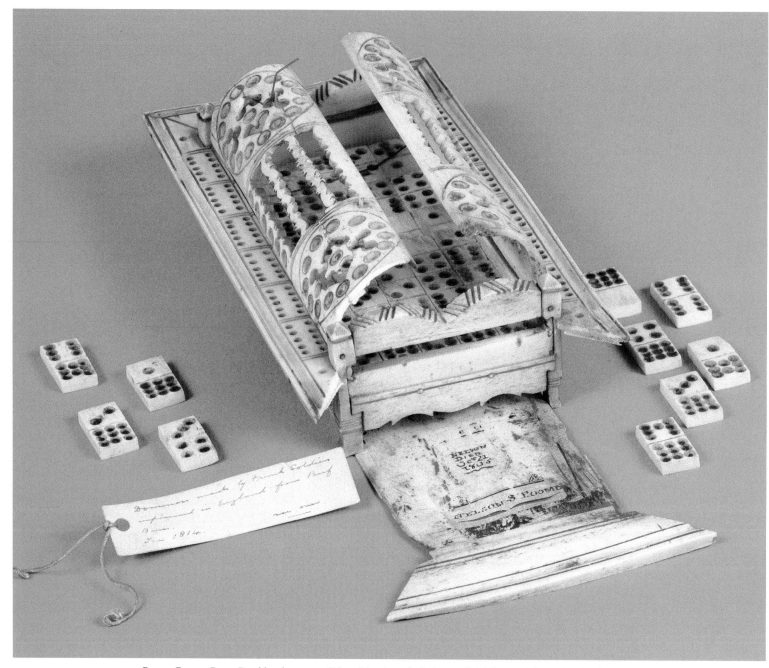

Bone Games-Box. *Double dome-top lids with pierced designs of 'clubs and hearts'. Overhanging scoreboard and a sliding lid with a worn painting with 'Nelson's Toomb' motifs. Contains dominoes. Red and green colouring throughout. Includes a provenance slip with names and it states the date of manufacture to be 1814. 2¼ x 9¾ x 5 in.*

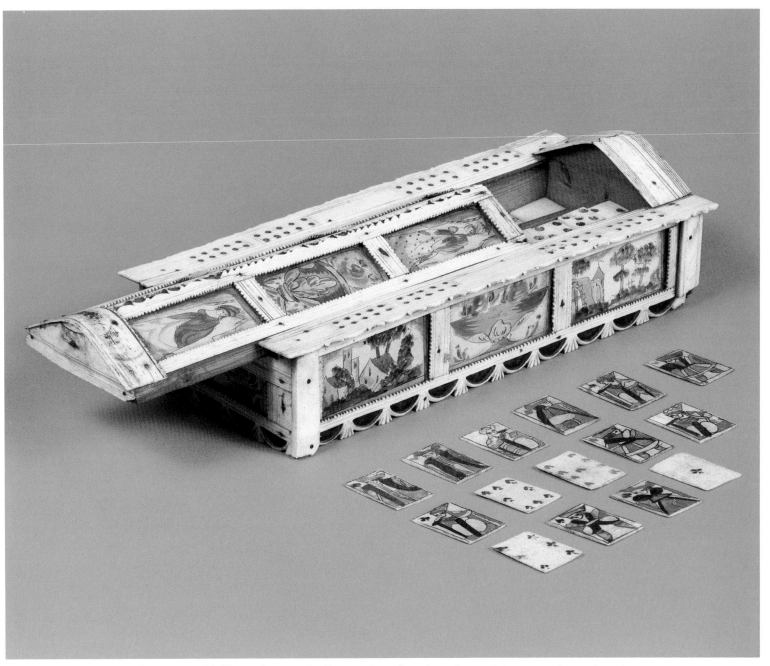

Games-Box with Watercolour panels. *Fourteen bone-framed panels containing watercolours of people, buildings and flowers. Sliding, peak-topped, lid covering contents of dominoes, dice and other game implements.* 3½ x 10½ x 4 in.

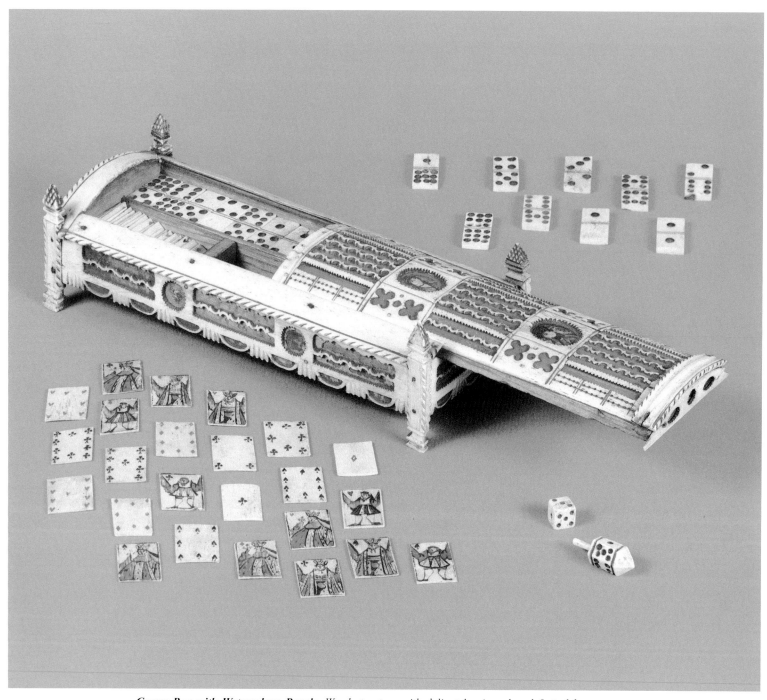

Games-Box with Watercolour Panels. *Wood structure with delicately pierced and fretted bone veneer forming small oval frames for watercolour portraits. Slightly domed sliding lid with scoreboard holes. Contains bone playing cards, dominoes, dice and teetotum. 2⅝ x 8¾ x 3½ in.*

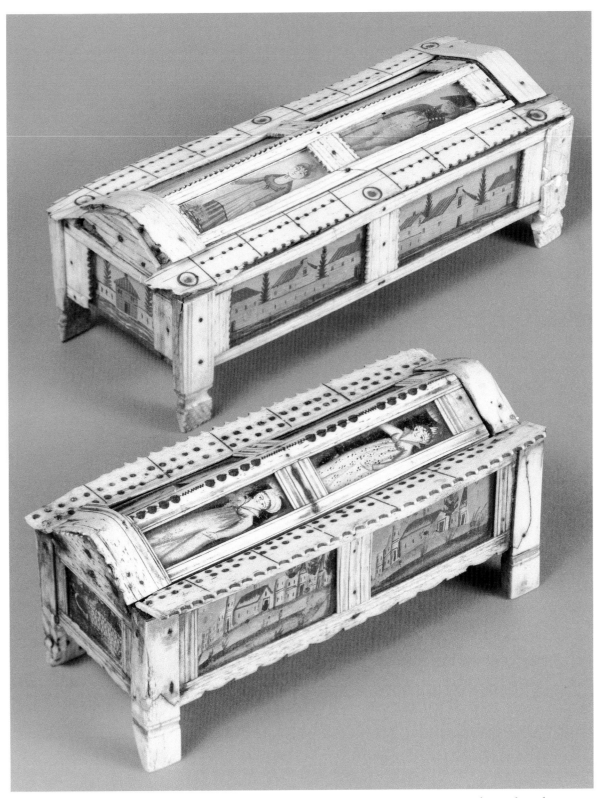

(Top) **Games-Box with Watercolour Panels.** *Ten bone-framed panels containing watercolours of people, soldiers and houses. Sliding peak-topped lid. Box is empty. 3 x 8 x 3⅛ in. (Bottom)* **Games-Box with Watercolour Panels.** *Ten bone-framed panels containing watercolours of people, buildings and flowers. Sliding, peak-topped, lid covering contents of dominoes and dice. 3 x 6½ x 3 in.*

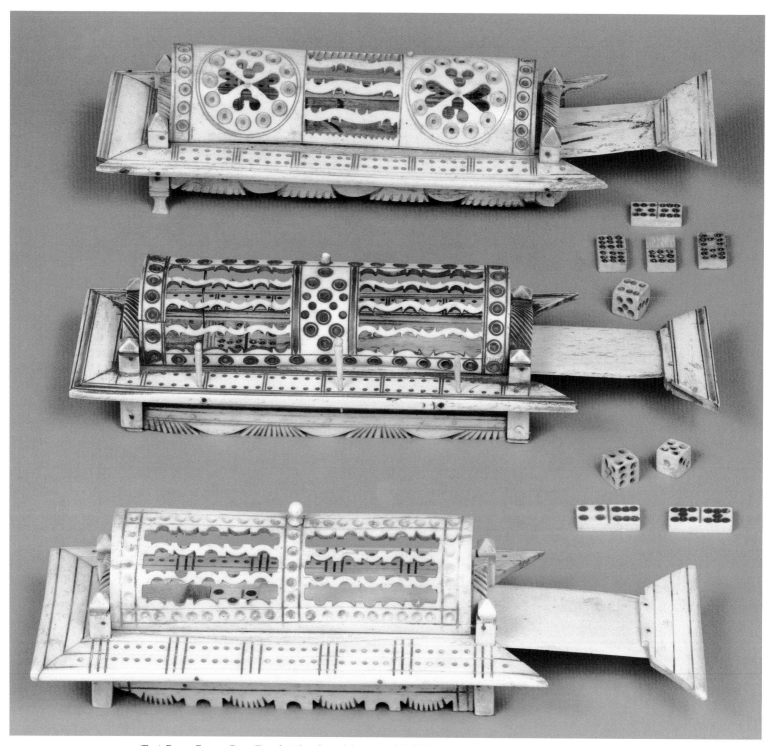

(Top) **Bone Games-Box.** *Fitted with a fretted dome-top lid. Sliding cover with a painting of a female figure and the inscription "L'ESPERANCE." Contains bone dominoes. 2¼ x 9½ x 3¼ in. (Centre)* **Bone Games-Box.** *Hinged dome-top lid with fretted openwork designs. Numerous incised lines with red and black colouring. Plain sliding lid covering a full set of dominoes, dice and cribbage pegs. 2¼ x 9 x 3¼ in. (Bottom)* **Bone Games-Box.** *Fretted dome-top lid and a bone slide for access to dominoes and dice. Incised lines with blue and red colouring. 2½ x 8 x 3¼ in.*

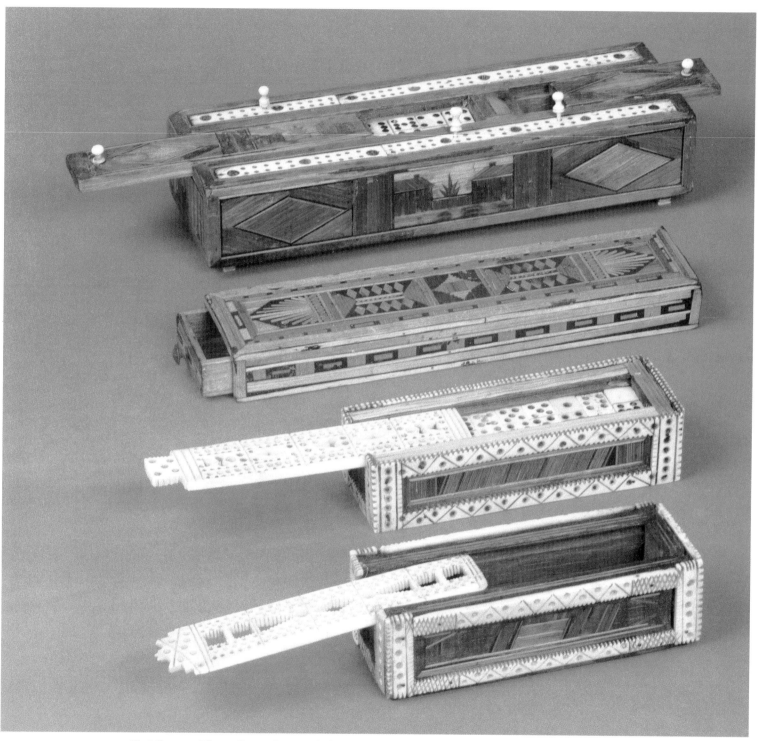

(Top) **Bone and Straw Games-Box.** *Made from a single block of wood with two recesses for dominoes and scoring pegs. Sliding lids and body of box with straw overlay of various scenes and designs. Bone scoring strip set into the top. 2 x 9½ x 3⅛ in. (Centre-top)* **Strawwork Games-Box.** *Wood construction with straw overlay forming various designs and patterns. Pullout drawer containing some dominoes. 1 x 9 x 2¼ in. (Centre-bottom)* **Bone and Straw Games-Box.** *Sliding lid with open-work carving of 'clubs, hearts and diamonds' all of which are surrounded by coloured dots and scorekeeping holes. Sides and ends decorated with bone framing and strawwork designs. Contains dominoes. 1¼ x 6 x 2 in. (Bottom)* **Bone and Straw Games-Box.** *Sliding bone top with cut-out designs and drilled holes for scorekeeping. Sides decorated with bone framing and strawwork of various designs. Box is empty. 1½ x 6 x 2 in.*

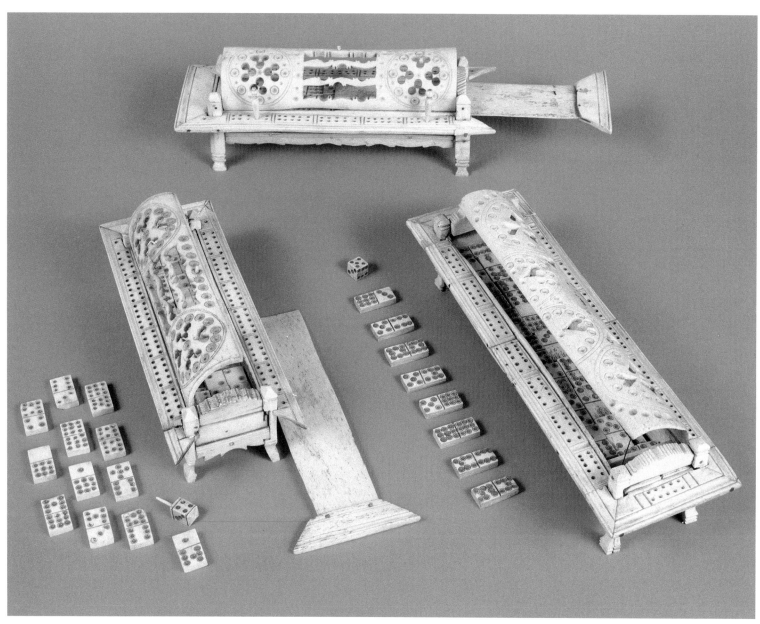

(Top) **Bone Games-Box.** *Hinged, dome-top lid with pierced 'club' motifs. Overhanging scoreboard and a sliding lid with traces of a painting. Contains dominoes, dice and scoring pegs. 2¾ x 9⅝ x 3½ in. (Bottom left)* **Bone Games-Box.** *Hinged, dome-top lid with pierced 'hearts and clubs' designs. Overhanging scoreboard and a plain sliding lid covering dominoes and dice. 2½ x 8¾ x 3¼ in. (Bottom right)* **Bone Games-Box.** *Hinged, dome-top lid with cut out 'heart' designs. Overhanging scoreboard. Contains dominoes and dice. 2¾ x 11¼ x 3½ in.*

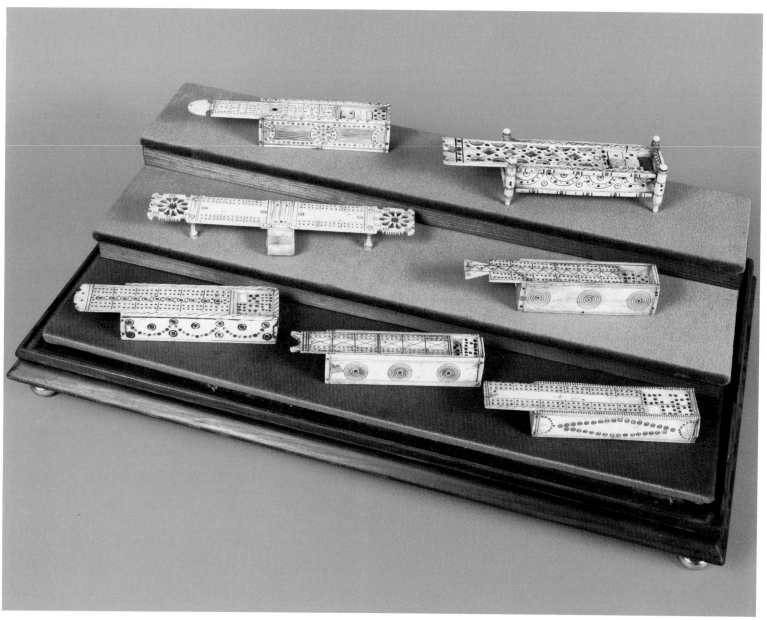

(Top left) **Bone Games-Box.** *Fine quality with a sliding lid decorated with circles, lines and holes for scorekeeping. Sides embellished with circles, dots, pin-wheels and incised lines. Everything coloured in red and blue. Contains dominoes.* 1⅜ x 5½ x 1¼ in. *(Top right)* **Bone Games-Box.** *Flat, sliding lid with openwork designs surrounded by dots and circles. Sides and ends decorated with incised circles, half-circles and lines. Red, green and black colouring. Painting of a lady and gentleman on the underside. Contains dominoes and dice.* 1⅞ x 6 x 1⅜ in. *(Centre left)* **Bone Scoreboard.** *Unusual item with pierced floral designs on each end and drilled holes for scorekeeping. Pivoting storage box on underside.* 1 x 9 x 1⅛ in. *(Centre right)* **Bone Games-Box.** *Flat, sliding lid with drilled holes for scorekeeping. Sides and ends decorated with incised circles. Contains dominoes.* 1¼ x 5⅜ x 1¼ in. *(Bottom left)* **Bone Games-Box.** *Flat, sliding lid with drilled holes for scorekeeping. Sides and ends decorated with incised circles coloured in red and black. Contains dominoes.* 1¼ x 5¼ x 1¼ in. *(Bottom centre)* **Bone Games-Box.** *Flat, sliding lid with drilled holes for scorekeeping. Sides and ends decorated with coloured dot and circle designs. Contains dominoes.* 1 x 5½ x 1⅜ in. *(Bottom right)* **Bone Games-Box.** *Flat, sliding lid with drilled holes for scorekeeping. Circle and dot designs on sides. Red and black colouring. Contains dominoes.* 1 x 5 x 1⅛ in.

Duke of Wellington's Calling Card Case. *The calling card case has been coated in black wax which has been stamped with the signets and seals of the Duke's friends and officers. Also included are forty-three of his hand-coloured playing cards. Also there is a written provenance slip dated June 4, 1897.*

Wellington Medallion. *Duke of Wellington bronze case medallion which opens and contains thirteen coloured prints of the battles of the British army in Portugal, Spain and France from 1808-1814. These battles were under the command of the Duke of Wellington.* Diameter 3 in.

Chapter Seven

Artists

Dominic Serres

We are able to open this section on the 'captive as artist', by introducing a French prisoner of war who came onto the scene at the very beginning of our period of study – and perhaps even a few years earlier. To say that this remarkable Gascon made a success of what most prisoners might have justifiably described as dire misfortune, is an understatement. Today he is remembered as an important eighteenth century marine artist, a Royal Academician, and listed in Benezit and most other art dictionaries as 'of the English School' of painters.

Dominic (Dominique) Serres, was born at Aux, the capital of Gascony in 1722. He came from a wealthy and distinguished family with a country seat at Beauperre, where Dominic spent his childhood. It was planned that he should make a career in the Church, the family no doubt hoping that he might follow in the footsteps of one of his uncles – the Archbishop of Rheims. Dominic was given an excellent education, at the English Benedictine School at Douai, where, fortuitously as it turned out, he was also given both

---

(Above) ***Dominic Serres.*** *'The passage of the Hudson River', oil on canvas, signed and dated 1777, 25 x 39 in. (63 x 99 cm.). Captain Hyde Parker wrote proposing to commemorate 'the good conduct and gallantry' of his younger son, Hyde, in North America, with 'four pieces to be done in the best manner', and continued: 'Serres is the best painter I know for this purpose'. This painting shows Hyde Parker's small squadron, in July 1776, approaching one of the forts at the mouth of the Hudson, or North, river, probably the Battery on the southern tip of Manhattan island.*

a good grounding in art and in the English language.

Despite years of training and parental wishes, the young Serres had dreams of a very different future than that of the priesthood. Whilst still in his teens he ran away, literally it would seem, as he 'made his way on foot into Spain.'[1] There, he signed on as a common sailor on board a vessel bound for the Americas. Edward Edwards, in his *Anecdotes of Painters*, published in 1808, says that Serres 'left his friends rather abruptly, and went to the West Indies, which voyage was occasioned, as he said himself, by a disappointment in a tender connexion.'

His education made certain that his acceleration up through the ranks of seamanship would be a rapid one and, whilst still in his twenties, he became master of a merchant vessel trading with Havana. At some time whilst he was plying these seas, his ship was captured by a British frigate and he was brought to England as a prisoner of war. It is at this point that dates become confusing. Redgrave says that his capture took place 'during the war of 1752', but as there was no 'war of 1752' as such, a little guess work becomes necessary. There were warlike actions taking place on the American side of the Atlantic at about that time, like the French and Indian War, but the general assumption is that Serres was taken early in the Seven Years' War (1756–1763). However, E.H.H.Archibald mentions the existence of a Serres painting dated 1754, which was undoubtedly painted in England, and considers the possibility that he was captured even earlier, possibly during the War of Jenkins' Ear (1739-43).[2] But whichever date is correct, captured he certainly was.

On arrival in England he was at first confined in the Marshalsea Prison in London, but, as an officer, was soon released on parole. After a short time in Northamptonshire, he returned to London and decided to try his luck as a professional painter, setting himself, and his English wife, up in a little shop on London Bridge, not far from the place of imprisonment which had welcomed him to this country. There he began to display his marine paintings, later moving to a shop in Piccadilly, opposite the Black Bear Inn, where he exhibited for sale both seascapes and a few landscapes. As his reputation grew, he was able to move up-market to Warwick Street, Golden Square.

Dominic Serres' pleasant personality and social graces soon gained him many friends and, of immediate importance, patrons. He was described as 'a very honest and inoffensive man, though in his manners *un peu du Gasco,*' and besides his native French, he was a 'tolerable Latin scholar, spoke the Italian language perfectly, understood the Spanish, and professed something of the Portuguese; add to this, that few foreigners were better masters of the English language'.[3] Among his new friends he was fortunate to count one of our finest British marine painters, Charles Brooking, who encouraged him and was a great influence on his success as a professional artist.

It is puzzling nationalistically, but says a lot for his personal attributes, that an enemy captive should have so quickly made his mark on the marine art of this country. Also that he should have himself become so Anglicized as to become the most important painter of naval actions as seen from the point of view of his country's traditional enemy. Over the years he was much patronised by a number of our great naval commanders, such as Lord Hawke, and carried out such exacting commissions as the British view of Lord Howe's engagement with the combined fleets of France and Spain off Gibraltar, in 1782. There is one passage in Edwards' *Anecdotes* which might betray one pang of conscience on the part of the Gascon:

> 'In the year 1785, Mr Serres painted a large picture of an engagement between a French and English frigate by moonlight, in which the former claimed some sort of merit in not being captured, as the English was obliged to retreat, in consequence of another French interfering.

This picture the artist carried to Paris, where it was left, but upon what speculation the author never could learn. This was the only time in which the painter ever saw Paris, although a native of France.'

He painted for Britain throughout the Seven Years' War (1756-63) and the War of American Independence (1775-83) and has left a record in paint 'possibly more accurate than the written accounts.'[4]

When, in 1768, the Royal Academy of Arts was established, with Sir Joshua Reynolds as its first President, Dominic Serres was a founder member. From the first opening exhibition until the last year of his life, Dominic's work was represented in every annual exhibition. Altogether, he exhibited 105 paintings at the Royal Academy as well as thirty or more in other London exhibitions. His final accolade, towards the end of his life, was to be appointed Marine Painter to George III.

Dominic Serres died at his home at St George's Row, Hyde Park, on the 6th November, 1793, the year that a new war had broken out between his native and adopted nations, which was to last for more than twenty years. He left two sons and two daughters – all artists of the 'English School'. Dominic Serres was buried in Marylebone Cemetery.

Lieutenant George Maurer

Lieutenant-Adjutant George Maurer of the Hess-Darmstadt Infantry Regiment, captured in Spain, was one of a dozen German officers who were paroled to the quiet Border town of Lauder, in Berwickshire in 1812. To describe the only example we have of George's artistic ability as a work of art, would perhaps be over-complimentary – but it is, nevertheless of great interest. In the bottom left-hand corner of this little watercolour is a self-portrait of the artist, dressed in a most peculiar get-up. There he sits, on a fine August day, in 1813, sketching Thirlestane Castle, the ancient seat of the Earls of Lauderdale; attired in a swallow-tailed uniform coat, knee-breeches and high boots, topped off with what looks like a Scottish bonnet. Maurer's 'self-portrait from behind' can be made more recognisable by adding his description according to Admiralty Records: a young man of twenty, with hazel eyes, fresh complexion, five feet nine and three-quarter inches in height, well built, but with a small sword scar on his left cheek. The story of the rediscovery of this little painting is told in Chapter 23 dealing with 'Parole in the Scottish Border Towns'.

Ensign Jean Marie Bazin

Ensign Jean Marie Bazin, who came from a wealthy St-Malo family, had a natural gift for drawing, painting and caricature which stood him in good stead when he arrived in England as a paroled French prisoner of war. Before his capture he had seen some action whilst serving on the corvette *La Torche* in the West Indies.

On the 19th July, 1805, the 18-gun *La Torche* was cruising in a small squadron comprising the *Topaz* (40), the *Faune* (16), and the *Département des Landes* (22), when they met up with the British frigate *Blanche*, north of Peurto Rico. The *Blanche* was on her way from Jamaica to Barbados with despatches for Lord Nelson. The French ships were sailing under false colours and, believing the English ensigns, Captain Zachary Mudge was taken by surprise. Before the British decks could be cleared for action, the enemy had opened fire The *Torche* and the *Département* began the action and after a two-and-a-quarter-hours battle the 36-gun frigate was forced to surrender, being 'in a thoroughly disabled condition, with several of her guns dismounted, her sails and rigging shot to pieces, her masts badly wounded, and her holds full of water'. The British prisoners were taken aboard the French vessels, and a few hours later the *Blanche* sank.

Dominic Serres. '*H.M.S.* Phoenix, *Captain Parker, the* Roebuck, *Captain Hammond, and the* Tartar, *Captain Ommaney, forcing their way through the* chevaux de frize, *the Forts Washington and Lee and several batteries up the North River, New York, October 9th. 1776', oil on canvas, signed and dated 1779, 27 x 45 in. (69 x 114 cm.). On a second expedition to cut Washington's lines of communication across the river, Hyde Parker found that an obstruction had been built to prevent him going further. He succeeded in breaching it by forcing its junction with the shore.*

MELFORD HALL. NATIONAL TRUST PHOTOGRAPHIC LIBRARY/JOHN HAMMOND

Four weeks later, the eighteen-gun *Torche* struck her colours – understandably without putting up a fight – to the 74-gun battleship, HBMS *Goliath*, and Ensign Bazin began his eight year stint as a prisoner of war.

As an officer, Bazin was granted the privilege of parole, first to the pleasant town of Wincanton, in Somerset, until 1812, when that parole town was cleared of prisoners. He was then sent to the equally pleasant Scottish Border town of Jedburgh. where he soon gained many Scottish friends and was often welcomed into their homes. In a short while, Bazin became one of a small group of parolee artists who sold their works and accepted commissions and he was almost certainly the painter mentioned in '*Memoirs of a Highland Lady*'. Mrs Grant wrote:

> 'Lord Buchanan, whom we met there [Jedburgh], took us to see a painting in progress by one of them; some battlefield, all the figures portraits from memory. The Picture was already sold and part paid for, and another ordered which we were very glad to hear of, the handsome young painter having interested us much.'

Louis Garneray. *French Prison Hulks in Portsmouth Harbour.*

Ambroise Louis Garneray

Louis Garneray as he was better known, was born in Paris on the 19th February, 1783, into a family of artists. His father, Jean François (1755–1837), was a painter of portraits and genre, and had been a student of the great French artist Jacques Louis David. Therefore, it was natural that Ambroise Louis should be expected to follow in the family footsteps. Reared in the midst of so many painters he inevitably absorbed a grounding in art from his earliest years. However, by the time he was thirteen, with his country at war, a secret longing for adventure came to the fore and he determined to go to sea. After overcoming parental opposition, they wisely decided to apprentice him to a vessel commanded by a close relative.

His first voyage took him to India, and between 1796 and 1806 he lived a life more jam-packed with high-seas adventure than he could ever have imagined – including surviving a number of shipwrecks and sea-fights. He served on at least a dozen vessels over those years, sometimes in the French Imperial Navy at others in privateers, but his most treasured memories were of his time as lieutenant on the *La Confiance*, under the command of the famous privateer – or, as some would have it, corsair or pirate – Captain Robert Surcouf. A year before his capture, Garneray had returned to Naval service, as quartermaster's-mate on the 44-gun frigate *Atalante* – just in time to experience yet another ship-wreck, this time off the Cape of Good Hope. Louis was drafted to her sister frigate, the *Belle-Poule*, which was to be his last posting in the service of France.

In March 1806 the *Belle-Poule* was off the African coast near the Azores, in company with the 78-gun ship-of-the-line *Marengo*, when they fell foul of a powerful British force under Admiral Sir J. B. Warren, which captured both French ships. Garneray and his shipmates were put onto the *Ramillies* and delivered to the prison ships at Portsmouth. Had Garneray been captured whilst serving as an officer on a privateer, he may well have been granted parole, and spent his captivity in the comparative freedom

of an English or Scottish parole town. As a quarter-master's-mate in a naval vessel, he was doomed to long years on prison ships.

Louis Garneray's story is one of victory over adversity, and the paintings which he produced during his long captivity are historic documents, invaluable additions to our knowledge of the prison ships. He did not confine his depictions to paint alone – the word-pictures which he penned in his 'Mes Pontons' are perhaps more vivid than those of the brush.

Whilst he was a prisoner he had always imagined that the sea would be his post-war career, had studied navigation and mathematics in the interests of promotion; but when, after eight years, he was released and returned to Paris in 1814, it was to belatedly realise his father's wishes; to set himself up as a professional artist. Characteristically, after making up his mind, he soon got down to work, making his debut at the *Académie des Beaux Arts* in 1816, with a painting of the Port of London. The following year he was appointed Painter to the Duc d'Angoulême, and was soon enjoying the patronage of Louis XVIII and his family. Among the many marine paintings shown at the Paris Salon during his forty-four years as a professional artist, was one which he exhibited in 1824, which took him back in memory to his days as a prisoner of war. It was entitled in the catalogue as *'The English Hulks'* with the additional interesting note: *'In the winter of 1810, a storm broke the mooring chains of one of the hulks in Portchester River and drove it onto the hulk next in line, thus endangering the lives of the French prisoners on board'*.

Garneray's paintings are to be found in a number of French and English galleries, but even more of his art can be seen in his published works. He wrote and illustrated a number of books, the most important being his 'Mes Pontons', already mentioned, and his two-volume 'Voyages, Aventures et Combats', but he also published 'Scènes Maritimes', and a number of volumes of aquatints, which included sixty-four views of

the principal ports of France. Apart from his oil painting, Louis was a fine engraver, aquatintist and watercolourist – and it is said that for six years he supplied the Sèvres factories with originals for their porcelain artists to copy. In 1833 he was appointed Curator to the Rouen Museum of Art, and twenty years later, in 1852, he was made a Chevalier of the Legion d'Honneur. Ambroise Louis Garneray died in Paris on the 11th September, 1857.

Footnote

A few writers have cast doubts on the authenticity of a series of Garneray paintings of the Portsmouth hulks, I think without good reason. Samuel Scott and other well-known names have at times been cited as possible copyists from a Garneray original – and more than one has said that 'at least one of the copies is by Daniel Turner'. As far as I can discover, three of these paintings are in the National Maritime Museum, two in Portsmouth City Art Gallery and one in the National Library of Australia, in Canberra. Eight are in my own private collection. Now, not only are none of these paintings signed, but, though understandably alike, none is a direct copy of another. If they were popular, therefore, why were they not signed? This may possibly be explained through Garneray's own memoirs, which tell of the Purser of the *Prothée* who claimed one in four of his paintings and paid for the other three at a price he *said* he received from the dealers ashore; of Abraham Curtis, the crooked Portsea dealer who handled his pictures after he had been transferred to the *Vengeance* and of the strange Portsmouth dealer who kept Garneray out of sight during his time at Bishops Waltham. All these men knew they were on to a good thing and would have been in no hurry to divulge the exact source of their artistic merchandise. They may have applied any one of a number of names to the frame tablets.

However, why Daniel Turner? Daniel Turner was a late eighteenth century landscape painter, who disappeared from view after his last Royal Academy exhibit in 1801 – five years before Louis Garneray's capture, and years before he was set up to paint in oils on the *Prothée*. Nevertheless, I think I know where the 'Turner' rumour started. Two of the paintings in my collection carry on their frames, old tablets which read:

FRENCH PRISON HULKS IN
PORTSMOUTH HARBOUR
HOPPEY TURNER

Who was 'Hoppey'? – possibly a dealer-thought-up alternative to Garneray, who knows? It is not even likely that Hoppey was an assistant in Louis Garneray's prison-ship 'studio' – if the master's name was kept dark, why use the genuine name of another prisoner?

There is, therefore, little more to say to the doubters, except that all these paintings appear to come from the same palette, all are old and date long before a great interest in prisoner of war work had materialised. The subject matter is not of the cheeriest, and as I have already theorised, it is unlikely that all fourteen 'copies' would have incorporated noticeable differences in each case.

1. S. Redgrave: *Dicionary Of Artists of the English School.* 1878.

2. E.H.H. Archibald: *Dictionary of Sea Painters.* 1980.

3. E. Edwards: *Anecdotes of Painters.* 1808.

4. E.H.H. Archibald: *Dictionary of Sea Painters.* 1980.

A rare box, the inside of the lid decorated with masonic symbols.

Chapter Eight

Part One

The Freemason Prisoners of War

We join in union not to tyrannise
But to alleviate all human thrall –
Granting what man to man too oft denies,
And prone to harmonize the hearts of all.

And thus, while in this grand old isle of ours
The glow of genial nature still expands.
The tie of life's Freemasonry secures
The love of many friends in many lands.

The Bard of Hawick Lodge[1]

I FIRST BECAME AWARE THAT FOREIGN FREEMASON PRISONERS OF WAR may once have practised their craft in Britain, some years ago, when I received in the morning post some packages of miscellaneous 'prisoner of war memorabilia'. The contents included a French Masonic Certificate, a document of marriage and a mason's apron – three fascinating relics.

Delighted with this surprising glimpse into an unexpected aspect of prisoner of war life, I approached the headquarters of Masonry in England, Freemasons Hall, in London. As I am not a member of the Fraternity, I approached it with some trepidation – only to be met with friendly interest and helpful assistance, which guided me towards the Masonic Lodge of Research in Leicester – and the work of John T. Thorp.

During the 1890s, John Thomas Thorp had begun to gather together odds and ends of information from other Masonic writers, which intimated that the founding of prisoner of war Lodges might have been more widespread than had previously been suspected. By the first year of the following century, he had published a little volume which listed twenty-six French Lodges – some dating as far back as the Seven Years' War.[2] Over the next thirty years, until his death in 1932, John Thorp added another twenty-four names to that list together with a wealth of little discoveries, which may have been lost forever without his untiring efforts.

I was, therefore, introduced to yet another, and rare, category of prisoner of war work: Masonic Certificates and Demits, Seals, Masonic Jewels and other relics. Only the most serendipitous of collectors can ever hope to include even a few specimens from this specialized field amongst their finds. Most of the Certificates from the Thorp collection are now in Leicester and few of the appliqué 'jewels of a specific type, made by the prisoners,' are likely to be seen outside official Masonic collections.

The craft of Freemasonry was popular with the officers of both the British and the continental armies and navies, throughout the whole period covered by this book. It was, therefore, to be expected that the prisoners taken by each nation would include a considerable number of the Fraternity – some of high degree.

The captive Mason, whether French or British, must have blessed the day he pledged his oaths, when he found that his foreign Brethren not only accepted him, but would often go to great lengths to render him assistance. Sometimes, on either side of the Channel, this brotherly help went dangerously far, some might consider even to the point of national disloyalty, and was, understandably, carefully watched by the authorities in charge of prisoners of war.

It may seem surprising that the captured enemy should have been welcomed in this way, but welcomed he certainly was, as the minutes of Lodges in the parole towns of England, Scotland, Wales and France could attest. That the paroled visitor to an English local Lodge might even be admitted as a member, is amply verified by documentary evidence. The earliest of references to French prisoners of war members of the craft being active in the British Isles, goes back to mid-eighteenth century. Entries in the records of the ANTIENT BOYNE LODGE, No.84 BANDON for 1746 and the following year, mention nine French officers who were admitted to the Lodge as Joining Members.

Thirty years later a Cornish Lodge recorded, 'at St Ives, March 18th 1778, the following seven Brethren......... being Prisoners of War, this evening favoured our Lodge with a visit. On the 22nd April, they proposed themselves to become members of the Lodge which was unanimously agreed to.'[3]

The first French Lodge, actually formed and worked by French prisoners in this country, was established, though not properly constituted, in 1756, in the first year of the Seven Years' War. The founder members were naval officers whose vessels had been taken some time before the outbreak of war. The captured ships were taken to Nova Scotia, where the paroled officers were introduced to a Masonic Lodge in Halifax, the capital. On arrival in England in 1756, they were paroled to Basingstoke, where they set up a Lodge and duly informed the Grand Lodge of All England. On finding that the sum required to have their Lodge properly constituted was way beyond their pocket – or possibly thinking it an unjustified expense, as they had no way of knowing how long, or how short, would be its existence – they nevertheless continued working their Lodge and making Masons. After two years in the town, some of these Masons were included in a transfer to Petersfield, where they lost no time in setting up a second Lodge. In the following year, 1759, they were again transferred, this time to Leeds, as were the prisoners who had been left behind in Basingstoke, and there they celebrated their reunion by establishing yet another Lodge in Leeds, which flourished until the Treaty of Paris, in 1763.

Only a few months before the end of the Seven Years' War, a warrant was issued by the Grand Lodge of All England to a group of paroled officers, 'enabling them and others to open and continue to hold a Lodge at the Sign of the Punchbowl in Stonegate in the City of York and to make new Brethren as from time to time occasion might require, prohibiting nevertheless them and their successors from making anyone a Brother who shall be a subject of Great Britain or Ireland.'

There is only one other record of a prisoner-Lodge being established during that particular war, and this time we know the name which the parolees gave to it – LA CONSOLANTE MAÇONNE. This name, 'The Consoling Mason' is typical of the names chosen by the many other Lodges which were later founded during the Revolutionary and Napoleonic Wars; descriptive as it is of a society formed by men in unhappy circumstances and far from home.

The 'Consoling Mason' was formed in Launceston in 1762, but the following extract from the records of the Grand Lodge of England, shows that there were Masons among the prisoners in that town who made themselves known before that date. It also shows the great consideration which the French Freemason might well expect through his membership of the Craft:

> 'A letter to the Grand Master Elect, dated 22nd April [1757], from Bro. N. de Court, late Commander of the French merchant ship *St James,* captured the 29th Oct. by His Majesty's ship *Windsor,* and now a prisoner of war at Launceston in Cornwall, wishing his Lordship could procure his liberty to return to Bordeaux and promising all good offices to Brethren prisoners in France, and praying relief: was read and spoke to: when it being observed that no cartel was yet settled with the French King, it might not be possible to relieve our Bro. otherwise than by money.
>
> 'Ordered, that the Treasurer do pay 20 guineas to the order of Wm. Pye, Esq., Prov. G. Master of Cornwall, to be applied to the relief of Bro. de Court in case, on enquiry, he shall find him worthy of assistance.'

At the time of the foundation of the French Lodge in 1762, there was no English Lodge at Launceston, which may account for the fact that *'The Consoling Mason'* admitted Englishmen as well as French, and issued Certificates in two languages. When an English Lodge THE CORNUMBIAN, made its appearance in 1767, it is probable that its creation owed something to English initiates of the French Lodge. The coastal inhabitants of Cornwall who had suffered the depredations of the French privateers over the years, had little reason to show goodwill towards the captives, but E.S.Vincent, in his book on Freemasonry in Cornwall[4], says:

> 'The people of Launceston gained a somewhat dubious notoriety for their tolerance towards the prisoners in their midst. Parish records show that there were a number of marriages, and evidence of assistance and connivance at escape were all too frequent. A request for a Charter to form a Lodge was submitted to Grand Lodge in 1809, (long after the original French Lodge had ceased to exist) but was refused on the grounds that the population was far too friendly to the French.'

Even after taking into consideration the small number of our captive countrymen held in France, against the many thousands of foreign captives held in this country, it is still surprising to find that only one British prisoner of war Lodge is known to have operated in France; whilst some fifty Lodges set up by the French in Great Britain have been traced. The solitary instance of a British prisoner-Lodge in France is that which was held by officers of the 9th Regiment of Foot, who were imprisoned in the fortress of Valenciennes from 1805 until their release in 1814.

Many regiments at that time, both British and French, had their own military Lodges, and that of the 9th Foot, 183 ANTIENTS, had been founded in 1803, when its members were free men. Two years later, part of the Regiment including the headquarters staff was captured when their transport vessel was wrecked off the French coast, and the Lodge was reborn at Valenciennes. The Brothers held their meetings regularly until the end of the war and the minutes of those meetings are still preserved.

Maybe the large number of prisoner-Lodges in Britain is just another example of the greater adaptability of the Frenchman and of his efforts to make the best of his captivity, or perhaps it was made more difficult for the British officers to set up a secret society in their *cautionnement* in France. Whereas the continentals were settled in relatively unguarded parole towns in this country, often pleasantly situated, where, if they respected their word of honour, they were treated with consideration by the residents and often welcomed into local society, the prisoners of the French were not so lucky. British officers who gave their word of honour were usually sent to fortified towns, such as Verdun or Valenciennes, where it was easier for their captors to keep an eagle eye on them. However, this in itself is not explanation enough, for, as we shall see, a number of French Lodges were held within closed prisoner of war depots in this country, and, even more remarkably, on some of the prison hulks!

The deep feeling of brotherhood between Masons from opposite sides of the Channel, even in time of war, caused both Governments to be apprehensive of any prisoner of war activities which tended to attract groups or encourage fraternisation between residents and prisoners. Their suspicions were directed not only to masonic brotherhoods; for all types of club and even theatrical performances came under the watchful eye of the authorities. There was often good reason for concern.

With the breakdown of exchange agreements between the two countries as the wars progressed, many French officers, with the prospect of long years of captivity looming before them, put freedom before honour and broke their parole. The Agents for the prisoners of war in this country were warned to keep close observation on Lodges in particular as being 'institutions for the fomentation *sub rosa* of agitation and disaffection', but it would seem that they made no great effort to suppress them – other than when made necessary by parole-breaking and escapes. The French authorities were far more cautious in matters of security – and perhaps in the long run they were the wiser.

During the last years of the Napoleonic Wars there was always the possibility of a general uprising of the prisoners of war in Britain. In fact there had been rumours and false alarms over most of the war years, even as far back as the War of Independence, when the exploits of John Paul Jones on the English and Scottish coasts had inspired the captive American privateers to give serious thought to the idea of revolt.

Now, thirty or more years later, the prime mover towards this end was a very senior French officer, General Simon. The General, who had been captured by Napier at the Battle of Busaco in 1810, though heroic enough in battle, was one of the least honourable and most troublesome prisoners ever to fall into British hands. Despite having pledged his *parole d'honneur*, he escaped more than once and had set up French escape agencies in London and elsewhere. He was a constant problem to the Government and Transport Office, who treated his high rank with more respect and consideration than, in his case, it deserved. The problem of General Simon was only solved when, in May, 1814, he was exchanged for the English Major-General Coke; 'it being evidently considered' said Francis Abell, 'that he could do less harm fighting against Britain than he did as a prisoner'.

There was a lot of truth in this supposition. Whilst on parole at Odiham in Hampshire, the General laid elaborate plans to provoke a revolution in the depots and parole towns throughout the land. His idea was to set up a pseudo-Masonic society, with 'Lodges' in every parole town in England, sworn to spread hatred of the English and prove even greater loyalty to Napoleon Bonaparte.

This society he called the SECRET ORDER OF THE LION and equipped it with many of the trappings of Freemasonry: Secrets, Oaths, Rituals, Badges, Signs and Passwords. This parent 'Lodge', which was intended to be the progenitor of a hundred others, did indeed operate for a short while in Odiham, its meetings being held in the same Masonic Hall as the genuine prisoner of war Lodge, DES ENFANTS DE MARS ET NEPTUNE, which already operated in that Hampshire town. This was an excellent cover-up, but somehow its existence and objectives were discovered before its branches could be established to any dangerous extent.

However, whatever the obvious dangers, and in spite of the official view, the prisoner who was a Mason was sure of a friend in the enemy camp. The value of this contact with kindly-disposed men in a strange and feared land must have been tremendous, particularly to the newly-captured and apprehensive soldier or sailor who had doubtless been warned of the terrible treatment he would receive at the hands of the British, if he was careless enough to get caught. Furthermore, the advantages were not always one-sided. On occasion, the introduction of new, even though foreign, blood was welcome and beneficial to the Lodge concerned. Vernon's *'Freemasonry'* states that the meetings of the Scottish ST JOHN'S LODGE at Hawick, fell off from 1802 and that each succeeding year saw it ever more thinly attended, but 'an impetus to the working and attendance was given about the year 1812 by the affiliation and initiation of several of the French prisoners of war who were billeted in the town, and from that time to the close of the war the attendance and the prosperity of the Lodge was in striking contrast to what it had been previously.' These 'Frenchmen' were, in fact, fourteen Germans and a Swiss, for it was not at all unusual at that time for all continental captives to be referred to as 'French'.

An interesting little pamphlet, *'French Prisoners of War in the Border Towns'*, tells of a typical instance where a local Lodge was 'enlivened' by the presence of its foreign visitors. It lists the names of eight Germans who were admitted to the Lauder ST LUKE'S LODGE, in January 1813. It goes on to say that 'after the Lodge had passed from labour to refreshment, the foreign installations used to delight the company of Brother masons with impromptu accounts of their war-like adventures and experiences.'

The Minute Books of Lodges all over the British Isles, and letters of appreciation from the prisoners themselves, attest to the fact that British members of the Fraternity did everything they could to help their prisoner-Brethren. Some may think too much, but the kindly feelings towards men they might reasonably be expected to have regarded with patriotic dislike and certainly with distrust, are typified by the following report:

> 'On the anniversary of St Andrew, 1810, we observe the Lodge was favoured with a visit from some French officers (prisoners of war) resident in Kelso. The Right-Worshipful, in addressing them, expressed the wishes of himself and the Brethren to do everything in their power to promote their comfort and happiness, after which he proposed the health of the Brethren who were strangers in a foreign land, which was drunk with enthusiastic applause...there is frequent mention of their appearance at the meetings, when harmony was greatly increased by the polite manners and vocal powers of our French Brethren.'

Perhaps it is because I am not a member of the Fraternity, that I find almost incredible the lengths which some of the Masons and their Lodge members went to 'to promote the comfort and happiness' of captive enemy officers in this country. It should also be remarked that this was equally true in general of the attitude of the French Mason towards his British Brother.

We have already seen that it was not thought preposterous for a French officer to seriously request that Masonic influence should be employed to secure his release (even if only by early exchange). The amount of money voted towards his aid, twenty guineas, was at that time a tidy sum, roughly equivalent to the annual pay of a British able-seaman, and there are many more instances of generous and over-generous aid. For example, the Master of a Melrose Lodge – who was also a magistrate – released French Mason-prisoners from his local gaol, where they had been confined for some minor breach of parole, and lodged them in his own home.

The records contain many references to sums of money subscribed for the relief of foreign prisoners in need and, as many had to depend entirely on the small Government allowance, this type of generosity was well placed. It is also most probable that the following cry for help from a group of unhappy American officers on parole in Ashburton did not go unanswered.There was already a French Lodge in Ashburton, called DES AMIS RÉUNIS, but it would seem that the Americans did not apply for help through them, professing themselves to be 'Ancient York Masons':

'Ashburton, April 6th. 1814 of our Lord,
and in Masonry 5814.

To the Grand Master, Grand Wardens,
& Members of the Grand Lodge, London.

BRETHREN,
We the undersigned, being Ancient York Masons, take the liberty of addressing you with this Petition for our Relief, being American prisoners of war on parole at this place. We are allowed 10s.6d. per week for our support. In this place we cannot get lodgings for less than 3s. per week, and from that to 5s.per week. Meat is constantly from 9d. to 1s. per lb., and other necessaries in pro-portion. Judge, brethren, how we live, for none of us have any means of getting money. Our clothes are wearing out, and God knows how long we shall be kept here; many of us have been captured 9 or 10 months, as you will see opposite our signatures. We form a body in this place by ourselves for the purpose of lecturing each other once a week, and have had this in contemplation for some time, but have deferred making application until absolute want has made it necessary.
    'We therefore pray that you will take into consideration and provide some means for our relief. You will please address your letter to Edwin Buckannon.
    We humbly remain your pennyless brethren.

Edwin Buckannon	Archd Taylor, Junr
G.W.Burbank	Ezra Ober
Pierson Baldwin	Wm Smith
Wm Miller	James Lans
John Schers.'	

There is much evidence to show that the captive who had been a Mason in his own country, or was initiated into a Lodge here, had a great advantage over his non-mason fellow-prisoner. Yet one ex-prisoner, a French officer named Lardier, tells quite a different story. In his memoirs *'Histoire des Pontons d'Angleterre'* he says that:

'...in all the parole towns there were Masonic Lodges, either English or French; but instead of forming a bond of brotherhood between the two nations, the reunions became often a cause of dissension among the prisoners. Some refrained from any association with the English, and more than once they immediately quitted the building when English visitors presented themselves. Sometimes also during the meetings, conversation led to the discussion of matters which aroused fierce hatred between the two nationalities.'

This passage has the ring of truth about it, as far as his own experience guided his remarks, and it would be strange if there were not men of either nationality – whether members of the Brotherhood or not – who had passionate nationalistic feelings in time of war. However, it should be remembered that Lardier had experienced incarceration on the English hulks, which cannot have endeared him to this country generally; also he may have been making a generalisation out of his experience of a particular Lodge.
    The British Mason imprisoned in France enjoyed similar assistance and fraternal

welcome at the hands of his Continental Brothers, to that extended to his French counterpart in Britain. However, after the renewed hostilities in 1803, few French Lodges would have had the opportunity to greet British prisoner visitors, as almost all of the latter were confined in a very few fortress towns.

In 1807, the French Lodge at Verdun gave a banquet in honour of one of our paroled officers. The officer, Lieutenant Barker, R.N., had made a name for himself through two acts of heroism. On the first occasion he had saved a child from drowning, diving to the rescue although he was ill at that time. On another occasion he was on the spot when a gendarme fell into the Meuse. This second rescue caused a sensation and was widely publicised in newspapers and broadsheets; 'the public prints all highly panegyrized his humanity and courage'.[5]

Similar acts of bravery on the part of French prisoners in Britain had earned for the hero his freedom and repatriation to France – until so many people began to fall into rivers, at just the right moment for a French officer hero to spring to the rescue, that authorities became suspicious and rather less generous with their rewards.

Although fêted and applauded, Lieutenant Barker was neither released nor exchanged, which is a pity. Three years later, still a prisoner, he once again displayed his gallantry – this time with fatal results. He defended the good name of an English family in an argument with another British officer. The result was a duel and Lieutenant Barker was shot dead. Duelling between prisoners was a punishable offence in Britain, but Bonaparte saw no reason why our officers should be deprived of the privilege of killing one another.

Between 1803 and 1807 over one hundred British officers and *détenus* were admitted as members into the Lodge of Freemasons at Verdun, and this happy state of affairs would no doubt have continued, had not the brotherly assistance gone too far. It was then discovered that a British officer had escaped with the aid of some of his French Brethren.

General Wirion, the corrupt Commandant at Verdun, would doubtless have taken a perverse pleasure in penning the report which he sent to Paris on the 9th July, 1808. He was able to produce specific evidence that this was not a unique instance of French Masonic assistance in British prisoner escapes. He proposed that all Certificates held by British prisoners should be confiscated and forbade the Lodge from admitting prisoners of war in future. This would seem reasonable enough, but he later admitted that as the members of the Lodge were civilian citizens of Verdun he could not enforce his orders, or enter their Lodge![6] At the subsequent enquiry a French Mason openly stated under questioning that, had the prisoner appealed to him for help, he would have felt duty-bound, as an act of Brotherhood, to assist in his escape. That, of course, put an end to British affiliations into the Verdun Lodge.

Major General Lord Blayney, one of the only three British generals to be captured during the Napoleonic Wars (1799-1815), spent four years in captivity, first in Spain and then Verdun. During that time he was introduced to, but not into, French Lodges in both countries. He was captured in the south of Spain late in July 1810, during the Peninsular War (1808-1814) and, apart for one short period of discomfort, was allowed great freedom and, one might say, lived a life of luxury compared with less senior officer-prisoners captured with him. The French, proud of their noble captive, used the General as a willing showpiece during his leisurely, nine-month-long journey through Spain and France to Verdun: dining and wining with French officers of his own rank and attending endless balls, banquets and assemblies, theatrical performances, race-meetings and even a bull-fight. In his memoirs[7] he has left an account of his visit to a French Lodge in Madrid:

'One evening I received a visit from an officer of the *26th Chasseurs à Cheval* to request my company at a Masonic meeting. The forms of admission were very serious, but I went through them sufficiently well and received a warm welcome from the Brethren, particularly from Colonel Vial, commanding the *26th Chasseurs*, who was Master of the Lodge, and who invited me to dinner and supper the next day. [General Blayney was pleased to accept the invitation but, whilst he must have been appreciative of the hospitality, he was honest as to his opinion of the conduct of his fellow guests. In describing the supper, he says:] ...when the punch began to mount, each playing some ridiculous trick to divert the company; one making hideous grimaces; another taking off a priest in his robes by means of a towel on his fingers; a third made mice out of parings of apple. Indeed I must do the French justice to acknowledge that they far excel us in the art of making fools of themselves *pour passe le temps*.'

In the spring of 1813, at a time when General Blayney was comfortably settled in Verdun, with its clubs, casinos and race-meetings – at which, incidentally, his own horses competed in almost every race – his Lordship met with a very unpleasant and worrying surprise. It will be remembered that the French General Simon, had founded the bogus masonic lodge, the SECRET ORDER OF THE LION, at Odiham, intent on bringing about a general uprising of prisoners. The news of his solitary confinement and impending trial in England brought cries of retaliation from France.

One morning, the Lieutenant of Gendarmerie arrived with an order summoning the British General to wait immediately upon the Commandant of Verdun, who regretfully informed him of the contents of a letter, dated the 6th March, 1813, which he had received from the Minister of War in Paris. This stated that, in retaliation for General Simon's incarceration, Blayney was to be detained in the Citadel of Verdun and 'answer with his head for whatever the British Government might do to General Simon'. However, after six weeks of anxiety he was released to his previous comparative freedom, when it was learned that the charges against Simon had been dropped.

Another British officer who was captured in Spain, avoided joining General Blayney at Verdun only through the good offices of a French Freemason and the compassion of France's most senior general.

Charles James Napier, at that time a twenty-seven-year-old major, commanding the 52nd Regiment under Sir John Moore in Spain, was severely wounded and taken prisoner at the Battle of Corunna on the 16th January, 1809. Napier, who, many years, battles and adventures later, became a general and was knighted, never forgot his debt to a foreign Mason, which can be related here in his own words:

'Few Masons owe so much to Masonry as myself. I was once a prisoner, without hope of being exchanged, and expecting to be sent to Verdun; for at that time there was no exchange of prisoners; a man who was taken lost all chance of promotion, or even of seeing his friends again. In this state of despair, knowing that mine must believe me killed, I was casting about in thought how to communicate with them, when it came to my head that I was a Mason. Then I poked out a Brother, a French officer called Bontems, a very good name, and like a good and honourable Brother he managed to send a letter from me to England; no easy matter in those days. It was a very hazardous undertaking for a French officer, but my honest and good Brother did it for me, and within three months my family knew I lived.'

Napier had many influential family connections in Britain and, on learning of his situation, the Government sent a frigate under a flag of truce to Corunna to enquire as to his welfare. The cartel was received by the French Baron Clouet, who immediately reported to his commander, Marshal Ney. The Marshal, himself a Mason, said 'Let him see his friends and tell them he is well and well treated.' When Baron Clouet hesitated he was asked why he waited, and replied: 'He has an old mother, a widow and blind.' 'Has he,' said Ney, 'then let him go and tell her himself he is alive.'

It is said that Marshal Ney allowed twenty-five other badly wounded soldiers to accompany Napier on his return to England, making only one tongue-in-cheek condition: that they take with them all the English female camp-followers, 'as they made the French soldiers quarrelsome'![8]

There is reliable proof of the one-time existence of prisoner of war Lodges, set up and worked by the prisoners themselves, in at least half of the towns to which paroled officers were sent in Britain. It is possible, indeed probable, that Prisoners' Lodges were also established in most of the other *cautionnements*. It may be that someone reading these words will remember some old document, Certificate, Demit or letter, which could help to prove the existence of one of them – that would really make this chapter well worth writing!

Once the French or other continental Masons made up their minds to set up a Lodge of their own, they went about it with great thoroughness. Their officers were appointed in the correct manner; their bye-laws were properly drawn up and minute books were scrupulously kept of their regular meetings. A fair number of those minute books survive to this day. It is obvious that these Lodges were set up by men who had, to a great extent, resigned themselves to the possibility of a long period of captivity. There was nothing makeshift about them; many of the paroled officers had been well-to-do in their own countries and received regular financial assistance from home, so their Lodges were often well-equipped, with both furniture and regalia.

The French Ashby-de-la-Zouch Lodge, DE LA JUSTICE ET DE L'UNION was particularly well-appointed, and some of its furnishings are still in use today: a number of items were purchased from the departing prisoners when they left for home in 1814. Included in the purchases was a domed and curtained canopy for the Master's Chair, supported by two side pillars and decorated with paintings of the Sun, Moon and Stars. From this, it cannot be presumed that all prisoner of war Lodges were so well-equipped or prosperous. When the charity Box was passed round at the end of a meeting of DE ST JEROME ET L'ESPÉRANCE Lodge at Chesterfield, the collection amounted to 'one shilling and a farthing'!

However, prosperous or hard-pressed, the opening of a prisoner of war Lodge in a town must have been a great day for those foreign gentlemen fortunate enough to be accepted into it. It is recorded that the establishment of the VRAIS AMIS DE L'ORDRE, an earlier Lodge at Ashby-de-la-Zouch on the 27th December, 1808, was celebrated by a ball, at which the French officers presented to each lady guest two pairs of white gloves, 'one pair long and one pair short'.

Although many of these Lodges were worked without Warrant, they were usually properly constituted bodies, acknowledging the authority of the GRAND ORIENT OF FRANCE and in at least four cases permission to operate was obtained from the Grand Lodge of England. British Masons were welcomed as visitors into most of the French parole-town Lodges in Britain, but actual membership was usually restricted to the continental prisoner of war – the ceremonies being carried out according to French ritual and in their own tongue. There were, however, exceptions; Englishmen were admitted as members to DES ENFANTS DE MARS ET DE NEPTUNE at Abergavenny, DE LA CONSOLANTE MAÇONNE – founded at Launceston during the Seven Years' War – and DE LA PAIX DÉSIRÉE at Wincanton, a prisoner Lodge of which we have a good deal of information and will be discussing later.

Paroled prisoner Masons desiring to set up their own lodge in a parole town would have been faced with only two major difficulties – finding a suitable meeting place and then finding enough cash to rent it. The founding, however, of such an enterprise in an overcrowded depot, or aboard a jam-packed prison hulk, was quite another matter.

We know that prisoners managed to produce works of art and craft, often of great merit, in these unsuitable surroundings. We know, also, that clubs and schools existed, teaching everything from boxing and dancing to mathematics, and that theatrical performances took place, but no other prisoner of war activity required the privacy and special conditions needed for the proper conduct of Masonic activities – except, perhaps, the forgers and coiners! Yet there is no doubt that such Lodges did exist, most probably in every depot, if not on every hulk. The founder-members would have been privateer officers, merchant masters and mates, 'broke-paroles' and naval and military officers who had refused to give their *parole d'honneur* in the first place.

Much must have depended on the sympathetic understanding of the Agent or Commandant. Without their help, or the cooperation of British Masons among the staff or garrison, it would have been well-nigh impossible to secure a meeting place in which to conduct a Lodge with any sort of dignity or propriety. The prisoners' Lodge at Portchester Castle is a case in point. We know from Louis François Gille's *'Mémoires d'un Conscrit de 1808'*, that Portchester had one such sympathetic Agent, Commander William Patterson, who had allowed them to build a theatre within the Castle.

Gille says that the Lodge was worked with the full knowledge and assistance of the Commandant, who allowed them to meet 'for the celebration of their mysteries, in a vault which was quite secluded.' Gille himself wished to become a member, but had to wait because 'the slenderness of my resources compelled me to postpone that step until a more opportune time', but Gille was eventually initiated into the new Portchester Lodge on the 24th June, 1812.

With the end of the war, two years later, he was released and his membership of the Fraternity stood him in good stead. On the journey home, he made the acquaintance of an English doctor on board ship, who, on discovering that Gille was a Mason, offered to tide him over with a loan of money and did everything in his power to make the homeward voyage a happy one.

Quite apart from obvious advantages, such as Gille experienced, and the boon of the certainty of a friend in need in a foreign land, the society of like-minded men, and the relief from dull boredom, made the Lodge of much greater importance than a mere club. Most seem to have had a deep and genuine interest in Freemasonry, but, of course, not all. The restless Baron de Bonnefoux would, one feels, have joined anything that was going, wrote, however, 'truth compels me to declare that I soon tired of the mysteries and the ceremonies, so that after leaving Odiham there has never been any desire on my part to assist in their work'.

That Bonnifoux was not typical of the prisoner of war Mason is obvious when we consider the relics which help to prove the one-time existence of these old Lodges and illustrate this chapter. The prisoner-made Masonic Jewels are fine examples of appliqué work, and the Certificates and Demits are, in most cases, beautifully executed works of calligraphic decoration, or typographical designs for print. Furthermore, the wax Seals which were attached to the Certificates by coloured ribbon were produced from delicately cut dies. All these examples of prisoner of war craft bespeak a loving regard and deep interest in their Brotherhood. To me, at least, the Certificates and Demits are of particular interest. To find, whilst scanning the signatures on these old documents, a familiar name – Bazin, Maurer, Duchemin etc. – of one whose life or work has been discussed elsewhere in this book, has a fascination all its own.

It is to these Certificates that we owe much of our knowledge of the names and locations of the French prisoner Lodges. Scrutiny of the obverse reveals the name of each Certificate's rightful owner, its date, the name of the Lodge and its location. However, in many cases the reverse has been at least as informative for, when its bearer visited another Lodge, anywhere in the world, an endorsement was made to that effect, and such an endorsement has often been the first clue to the war-time existence of a hitherto unknown Lodge.

Although these documents are most often referred to as Certificates – and will be so called throughout this chapter – some were really more in the nature of Character References. J.T.Thorp, founder of the LEICESTER LODGE OF RESEARCH, has said that they should, with greater accuracy, be called 'Demits'. He explained that, whereas the Certificate proper bore witness to the fact that the Mason named belonged to the issuing Lodge and had attained a certain rank or degree, the Demit was, however, a far more personal document. The Demit – also called a Travelling or Clearance Certificate – besides giving the above information, attested to his good conduct, and was usually issued to a Brother who was leaving the area.

It was more than a formal credential signed by officials who might not have know him personally; the signatories were men amongst whom he had lived and worked; who recommended him 'to all Enlightened Men on the surface of the Globe' and required of them 'assistance, relief and consolation' should the need arise. The following is a translation which is typical of the text of a Demit Certificate of this kind:

TO THE GLORY OF THE GREAT ARCHITECT OF THE UNIVERSE.
From an Enlightened Place where Silence, Peace and
Unity reign.

To all Masons spread the whole World over
HEALTH   POWER   UNITY

We Master and Officers of the W. Lodge of St John under the name of **LA PAIX DÉSIRÉE**, regularly constituted and meeting at North Tawton, Devonshire, by the Numbers known alone to True Masons, declare, certify, and attest that our very dear brother, *Antoine Darnel*, naval Surgeon, native of Souillac, Dept. of Lot, is a member of our W. Lodge in the third symbolic degree.

That his conduct, his manners and assiduity in his work has endeared him to us and made him worthy of recommendation. We beg all Regular Masons of Lodges both in France or of foreign countries to recognise the said Brother *Darnel* in that capacity, to accord him the consideration to which he is entitled, and give him all the help he may need, as we should be pleased to do for them. In token of which we have given him the present Certificate.

Done and delivered at our Lodge at North Tawton
the 10th day of the first month 5810
Vulgar era, March 10th, 1810

Signed by us, countersigned by our Secretary, and furnished
with the Seal and Stamp of our Lodge, to have full effect
after comparison with the signature of the said Brother
which has been added in our presence.

Apart from the large number of parole town prisoner Lodges for which we have some evidence, there are records of a further five Lodges known to have definitely operated in the depots and another six on the prison hulks!

Two documents refer to Masonic Lodges in Millbay Prison at Plymouth, known as the Old Mill Prison when it housed prisoners during the Seven Years' War and the War of American Independence. One is a Certificate which was issued to Master Mason, Etienne Chiapella, a native of New Orleans, in 1810. The other is an interesting endorsement which proves that the Lodge was active at least one year earlier. This endorsement is inscribed on the reverse of a Certificate issued in 1779 by a French Lodge held at Port au Prince on the Island of San Domingo. It is a remarkable example of a Demit in use. Over the thirty years since its issue, its owner had visited many Lodges in many parts of the world, as other endorsements show; but the relevant one reads: 'Inspected at the Lodge of DES AMIS RÉUNIS held at the Mill Prison, Plymouth, the 4th day of the 4th month of the year of the True Light 5809; in open Lodge.

The signature which appears below the endorsement is that of Guillaume Brousse, Master of the Millbay Lodge. For some reason Brousse was released from Millbay at the order of the Transport Board, but in 1811 he was captured for a second time, whilst serving as a surgeon on board a privateer. This time he was worse off than before and was sent to the prison hulk *Hector* at Plymouth. From there he petitioned the Grand Lodge, listing his services to 'subjects of His Britannic Majesty' and entreating that they obtain his liberty. From this it would appear that it was well within the possibility of the influence of the Grand Lodge to secure his release from the hulk, and that their reply to his petition would suggest that their reluctance in this case was based more on the technical standing of the AMIS RÉUNIS than on their inability to help.

They considered his plea, but, 'it not appearing that the Petitioner did ever belong to any Lodge Authority or Connexion with our R.W. Grand Lodge, nor can it be presumed that a Lodge Constituted in this Kingdom in a way we cannot recognise – that our interference in such cases could not be had, the Application was Rejected.'

Privacy and silence must have been the scarcest of luxuries in the crowded prison depots, but to the men confined to the prison ships it could have seemed only an unrealisable dream. From all the facts we know of these soul-destroying craft, the idea of a Masonic Lodge in such an unpleasant environment would seem a great deal more than improbable. On most of these vessels a sleeping place with any elbow room could only be obtained by purchase from another prisoner who put cash before comfort. Imagine, then, the difficulty of finding a secluded corner for secret meetings. Yet it is provably certain that Lodges did exist on hulks at Portsmouth, Plymouth and Chatham; definite proof of six having so far been discovered – on the *Canada, Sampson, Nassau, Bienfaisant, Guildford* and the *St Isidore.*

We are not left to imagine the conditions under which Masonic meetings were held in these improbable surroundings. A. Lardier, whose comments on the parole town Lodges have already been mentioned, visited the Lodge which had been formed on the *Guildford* hulk at Portsmouth and has left a fascinating account of that visit:

'The occupants of the demi-prison, aware that we [Lardier and two French Naval Officers] were "Children of the True Light", invited us to visit their Temple, and at the first opportunity afforded us we accepted the invitation. After traversing the whole length of the lowest deck (faux-pont), we came to a trap-door; this was raised, and we descended into the darkness down a short ladder, rotten and shaky, and continued a few paces forward from its foot, led by the hand of our conductor.

'After giving the pass-words, signs and grips, we were permitted to enter the Temple. Although less than the ordinary stature of men we were obliged to bend almost double, so limited was the space between floor and the roof. This Chamber, a place, according to Masonic phraseology, "strong and enlightened, where silence, peace and harmony reign", was in reality lighted by only a piece of candle inserted in the neck of an old beer-bottle, which, set before the Master's chair, made so much smoke that only a feeble glimmering ray of light was visible.

'The Master's chair was a dilapidated bench, with only three legs remaining, upon which he did his best to maintain an equilibrium. The high dignitary who presided was no less than a Sovereign Prince Rose Croix, was the only one present to have a seat, modest as it was. The rest of us, members of the Lodge as well as visitors, were requested to sit down upon the floor just as we were able, like tailors or Turks. There was a "ceremony" – the unsuitability of the place and the meagre resources of the Lodge rendered any physical examination and much of the ritual impossible; but this deficiency was more than made up for by an examination in morals.

'The candidate was rigorously interrogated; he was questioned at great length upon his principles, and more especially upon his patriotism. His replies were satisfactory, and he received "The Light." The shabbiness of the place and the poorness of all the accessories were, however, soon eclipsed and forgotten by the noble sentiments of philanthropy and affection for one's native land, which distinguished the two short, but stirring addresses delivered at the close of the meeting by the W. Master and the Chaplain. These can be best judged by a few words from the peroration of the former, which I give here word for word, for after the meeting I requested from the W. Master a copy of his discourse, which I have carefully preserved as a souvenir of my short stay on the *Guildford* hulk.

The Master concluded his Address to the Neophite with these words:

'"Oh France, happy country, abode of all the arts, abode of felicity and glory, one of thy children cannot close these labours without expressing his grief, and rendering homage to thee. My heart is not captive, it is still free and faithful, it lifts itself out of this place of bondage, and speeds to the land which gave it birth; it swells with joy and pride in contemplation of thy victories and thy laurels. May the glory of thy many triumphs never fade; may the hero who now guides our destinies be able to add the last and only jewel which is wanting in thy crown, by utterly destroying that odious rival, which dares to contend with thee for the mastery of the world."

'The meeting closed, as all Masonic meetings do, by a voluntary offering, the amount of which, added to that of the previous meetings, was devoted to the relief of those prisoners on the hulk who were suffering punishment, being closely confined [in the Black Hole] and deprived of their full rations. Thus these poor fellows, lulling for a moment the consciousness of their misery, found these informal meetings the means of bearing up against their misfortunes, by sharing generous sentiments, and practising, as far as their slender means would permit, the noblest of all the virtues, Charity and Brotherly Love.'

If it is surprising to learn that Masonic Lodges were held on the prison hulks at all, it is truly amazing that one should have operated on board the ill-famed *Sampson* hulk at Chatham, probably the most feared of all the prison ships, with more than its fair share of *mauvais sujets*: 'broke-paroles', tough privateers and perpetual offenders. The Lodge was called, appropriately enough, DE L'ESPÉRANCE, or 'Hope', which must have been the only thing left to a prisoner who found himself on board that terrible vessel. The ESPÉRANCE is recorded on the reverse of a Demit issued by a prisoners' Lodge DE LA PAIX at Thame in Oxfordshire; an endorsement which ends with the words, 'Done on the *Sampson*, on the River Medway at Chatham in England. 1812.'

A truly remarkable relic of this prison ship Lodge, is a copy of the Bye-laws of the Lodge DE L'ESPÉRANCE, which is recorded in the memoirs of Jacques Broquan, who was himself a prisoner of war for seven years and a member of the Lodge.

BYE-LAWS OF THE LODGE DE L'ESPÉRANCE

Act 1. This W. Lodge is established on the prison-ship *SAMPSON* on the Medway, near Chatham, in England, under the name of DE L'ESPÉRANCE by the unanimous resolution of the Founders, on the 18th day of the 2nd month, 5811.

2. The Lodge is composed solely of Brethren actually residing on the ship, because of the difficulties of communicating with other ships in the Roads.

3. It recognises as members those only who have been received by them or affiliated.

4. Every member of the Lodge bonds himself, having signed them, to a faithful observance of these rules; to keep inviolate the secrets and mysteries of the Order, and never reveal what has taken place in the Lodge – not even to absent members – if a strict request for silence has been made by those present. Not to be concerned during the meetings of the Lodge, either directly or indirectly, with matters of politics or religion. To practise benevolence and assist the unfortunate, as far as means will allow. To exercise always in the Lodge the virtues of amenity and docility, with the principle of equality, which are essential to unity. To allow no conversation contrary to good manners. To harbour no unfriendliness towards the Brethren. To refer all Masonic matters to the Lodge for decision. Never to converse about the Order in the presence of those who do not belong to it; to be very circumspect, and not to preserve papers which might disclose any of our secrets. Never to assemble as a Masonic Committee without express permission from the Lodge. Finally. Not to assist in carrying on an irregular Lodge, to have no Masonic intercourse with irregular Masons, and if compelled to leave the Lodge, to endeavour to join some other regular Lodge as soon as possible.

The Lodge on board the Plymouth Hulk *St Isidore*, named DE LA CONSOLATION DES AMIS, was active as early as 1801, but a Certificate issued in that year and a record of the visit of one of its members to another prisoner-Lodge, is the only evidence we have of its having existed.

Of the Lodge on board the *Nassau* at Chatham, the proof is limited to an endorsement which records its name as DE LA BONNE HARMONIE, and the conferring of higher degrees. Similarly, little more is known of the Lodge on her sister hulk, the *Canada*, than that it was called DE LA PERSÉVÉRANCE.

However, the scarcity of documentary evidence pertaining to the three last-named hulks, is more than made up for by the records of the DE LA RÉUNION, held on the *Bienfaisant* at Plymouth. Many interesting details regarding this Lodge were found in the works of the French Masonic historian, H. de Loucelles[9] and, preserved in the library of a Lodge in France, is the complete Minute Book of DE LA RÉUNION. It opens with the first inaugural meeting on the *Bienfaisant* in 1804, and continues as an unbroken record, until its affairs were wound up at a last meeting in 1809. The prime founder of this prison hulk Lodge was one, Barthelemi Le Corps, and of him Loucelles says:

'Soon after his arrival at Plymouth, oppressed with grief and subject to constant surveillance, Bro. Le Corps, overcoming every obstacle and braving the physical and mental suffering inseparable from his captivity, and animated too by a deep desire to employ the period of his imprisonment in the practice of Masonry, succeeded in getting together, from among his fellow captives, enough Brethren to form a Lodge.'

On the 18th June, 1804, Le Corps and eight other prisoners held their first meeting in the *Bienfaisant* and he was appointed the first Worshipful Master of the new Lodge. It was decided that regular meetings would take place on Sundays and special ones as occasion demanded. The Minutes note a number of occasions during the next few years when, for a variety of reasons, they were deprived of their meeting place. At the best of times the space was so restrictive that they often had to refuse new affiliations for sheer lack of room.

It would seem that the RÉUNION experienced less difficulty in communicating with the outside world, than did the Lodge on the *Sampson* at Chatham. A two-way correspondence was carried on between the *Bienfaisant* and Millbay Prison at Plymouth, and also with the ENFANTS DE MARS at the parole town of Tiverton.

This, and the fact that visitors from British Lodges, from Millbay Prison and even one – a Felix Desert – from the *Isidore* hulk, are mentioned in the Minutes, would suggest an excellent relationship between the Lodge and the British staff; for although letters could have been smuggled in return for bribes, visitors could have come aboard (or allowed out of their own prison) only with the knowledge and approval of the officers of the guard.

Barthelemi Le Corps did a good job. Apart from the welcome relief from boredom and idleness which the working of the Lodge afforded its members, the non-Mason prisoners of the hulk had good reason to be thankful for its being. The proceeds of the Charity Box, which was passed round at each assembly, was distributed among the poor and needy of the prisoners, whether they were Freemasons or not.

The regularity of its meetings and the conscientiousness with which the RÉUNION was conducted – over five, long, uncomfortable years – is a testimony to the courage and spirit of men who, one feels, would not have allowed the horrible conditions of their confinement to get the better of them, however long the war was to last.

On the 25th May,1809, the *Bienfaisant* was cleared of all captives and the Masons, who knew that this was about to take place, had held their last meeting on the hulk four days earlier, at which it was resolved:

> 'The meetings of the W. Lodge of St John, under the distinctive title of *Réunion*, established on board the prison-ship *Bienfaisant* on June 18, 1804, being terminated in consequence of the removal of its members, we hereby resolve that the books containing the Minutes and List of members be packed up, sealed with the seal of the Lodge; and that the W. Master be requested to take charge of them, and on his arrival in France to deposit them in the archives of his mother-Lodge, the W. Lodge of *AMÉNITÉ* of Havre.'

The register listed ninety-six men, twenty-nine of whom were absent members, fifty were naval officers, twenty-four merchant captains, six were medical officers, and the remainder included a number of military men.

There was an air of gaiety aboard the grim old hulk when it was announced that the prison ship was to be cleared, for rumour had spread among the captives that they were all to be exchanged for British prisoners of war held in France. However, their dreams were short-lived and they merely exchanged one type of prison for another – many of them ending up in Dartmoor Depot, the specially built prisoner of war depot in Devon, which opened its doors to its first captive on the very day that the *Bienfaisant* was cleared – the 25th May, 1809.

Thus, it was more than three years later – on the 27th December, 1812 – that Le Corps was exchanged and finally delivered his precious bundle to his home Lodge in France.

More than a hundred years later, J. T. Thorp requested that the records of the Lodge **AMÉNITÉ** should be searched for study of the *Bienfaisant* papers. One can imagine the disappointment of this dedicated researcher, when he was told that they had been unearthed but were 'so saturated and damaged by damp as to be quite illegible and useless'. Bro. Thorp ended his posthumously published book with the words: 'Alas! That there should have been such neglect.'

Just after his death, in March, 1932, another researcher, Bro. Lionel Vibert, again took up this matter with the French Lodge and found that John Thorp had been misled and that, though faded, every word was perfectly legible!

These documents are now preserved in the Library of the QUATUOR CORONATI Lodge.

However, that is not quite the end of the story of the Lodge DE LA RÉUNION. Neither was that last meeting on the prison ship the last to be held on behalf of the Lodge. There was one more, but this time in Dartmoor Prison. It took place only one month after the disillusioned members had left the hulk, and its object was to form a new Lodge under the same name in their new place of confinement.

That last Minute read:

'24th June, 1809. The Members of the regular Lodge LA RÉUNION, held on board the hulk *Bienfaisant* Floating prison at Plymouth, having re-assembled at Dartmoor, have opened a Lodge in the usual manner, with Le Corps as Master... '

The date tells us that Barthelemi Le Corps and his Masonic Brothers must have been amongst the first prisoners of war to enter the Prison on the Moor.

John T. Thorp recorded evidence of half a dozen prisoner of war Lodges in the Scottish Border Towns – Kelso, Lanark, Melrose, Peebles, Sanquhar and Selkirk, and mentioned other border towns where local Lodges welcomed masons among the paroled captives. Neither Francis Abell nor J. T. Thorp in his masonic researches mention Freemasonry in Biggar, but my own enquiries revealed that Biggar Museum Trust has a few relics of the parolees' stay, including a cocked hat left by one of the officers to the Tyler of the local Masonic Lodge and that it is still worn occasionally. This latter memento is of particular interest as it ties in with a reference to Freemasonry in a history of a local family published in 1867: *'Biggar and the House of Fleming',* by William Hunter. This small parole town had a very active Masonic Fraternity, THE BIGGAR LODGE OF FREE OPERATIVES, into which at least one foreign prisoner was accepted as a member, and Hunter's book tells of their keenness to set up their own Lodge:

'A number of French prisoners stationed at Biggar on their parole of honour, towards the close of the war with France, were Freemasons. In the beginning of 1813, they applied to the members of the Biggar Lodge [The Lodge of Free Operatives] for the use of their hall, the master's chair, the warden's tools, etc., in order that they might constitute a lodge of their own. This application was acceded to, and Brothers Elias Berger and Francis Renaudy became security for any damage that might be done. The French masons were here wont to practise their rites, which were somewhat different from those of Scottish brethren. One of their number, resident in Westraw, having died, was interred with Masonic honours, and a funeral lodge was held out of respect to his memory.

The Biggar Lodge had the honour of enrolling in its ranks one of these prisoners, a distinguished Polish nobleman and freemason, named Francois Mayskie, and received from him a fee of one guinea.'

MASONIC DATING

The dates on many Prisoner of War Masonic Certificates can be confusing for most Englishmen, particularly the non-mason. The addition of four thousand years to the Anno Domini date is common to all Freemasonry, based as it is on the fact that Archbishop Ussher (1581–1656) propounded that the world was created in the year

4004 B.C. precisely – though Masons ignore the odd four years.[10] Stephen Knight says that this would imply that 'Freemasonry is as old as Adam'![11] A further confusion arises with the interpretation of the months. For instance we would read:

Le 8e Jour du 12e Mois de l'An de la V∴ L∴ 5810' as: 'The 8th day of the 12th month of the year of the True Light 5810' or 'the 8th December 1810', but the French Masonic year commenced in March, so the actual AD date would be the 8th February 1811.[12]

'LA PAIX DESIRÉE' AT WINCANTON, AND LOUIS MICHEL DUCHEMIN.

I have decided to end this chapter with Louis Duchemin and the Prisoners' Lodge at Wincanton; partly because much more than usual is known of the life of this prisoner of war Mason; but partly, I must confess, through the collector's pride of possession – his Certificate, Masonic Apron and Certificate of Marriage to an English girl, are in my personal collection.

Prisoners of war were first paroled to Wincanton in 1804 and, from that year until early 1812, the town had a prisoner of war population which varied from three to four hundred parolees. Many of these paroled officers had been taken while serving in French vessels, or had been captured in the French colonies and, as one might expect, the majority of them were Frenchmen. However, Wincanton also had its share of Portuguese, Italian, German, and Spanish prisoners.

Every rank was represented; 'amongst them there were Generals, Captains, Lieutenants, Midshipmen, and officers of every grade,' and it would seem that the age range was equally wide. The General Census of 1811, noted the 'French Prisoners of War [at Wincanton], including boys of 10 years old.' These young lads would have been officers' servants, who were often allowed to share their masters' parole.

Except for those who could not overcome the depression, worry and resentment inseparable from captivity, parole life in this little Somerset town could be made quite pleasant, even if not exciting. The natives were friendly and in general made the enemy welcome; the landladies and shopkeepers being particularly pleased to profit from the business they brought with their presence. There were fairly frequent musical entertainments and some theatrical performances arranged by the histrionically and musically talented among them; and the larger rooms at some of the local inns were hired as meeting places and club rooms. On one occasion a room at the Swan Inn was used for the lying-in-state of a prominent prisoner-Freemason, whose burial was conducted with with a great deal of ceremony and attendance.

The French Lodge, LA PAIX DESIRÉE, was formed soon after the captured officers were settled into the town in 1804. It was certainly active by the 1st April,1806. A Certificate still survives which was issued to a French Merchant officer named Bernard Capdeville on that day, signed by no less than twenty-three fellow members.

At that time membership of the LA PAIX DESIRÉE, like most other prisoner-founded Lodges, was restricted to fellow prisoners of war exclusively, and Capdeville's Certificate is entirely in French. However, in 1810 the rules of the Lodge were amended to allow the admission of Englishmen, a practice which, as far as we know at present, was followed by only two other French Lodges – those at Abergavenny and Launceston.

From that time on, the form of LA PAIX DESIRÉE Certificates was changed so that the message could be read in both French and English This new Certificate was produced from an engraved plate, by a Wincanton printer named Clewett – a name of great importance in the life of Louis Duchemin.

Three of these bi-lingual Certificates are known to exist. One was issued to Benjamin Plummer, an English dealer in Masonic paraphernalia who, possibly for business reasons, was also a member of DES ENFANTS DE MARS ET DE NEPTUNE at

Abergavenny. The second was made out to another Englishman, Harry Cooper, a Wincanton auctioneer. The third, and the only one of the three to be issued to a paroled French prisoner of war, was that made out to Louis Michel Duchemin, '*Comptable Agent* in the Imperial Navy of France'.

Louis Michel Duchemin was born at Constances, in 1777. As a young lad he had joined the French Navy and we know a little of his life at sea. He was just nineteen when he was posted to a flute (a partly-armed warship, used as a transport vessel), the *L'Amiable*, where he first served as a *timonier*, or helmsman; but after a couple of months he was transferred to another flute, *La Prise*, and on this vessel Louis served for the next six years. In October, 1802, the Chief of the Fleet Administration at Brest had him posted as *Agent comptable* to the corvette *La Citoyenne* on the order of the Maritime Prefect. At the end of that year he was again transferred, this time to what was to be his last naval service ever, on board the corvette, *La Torche*. Duchemin was at St Domingo in 1804, and the document which proves this is the earliest evidence of his interest in Freemasonry – he was signatory to a Certificate issued in that year by the St Domingo Lodge, DE LA PARFAITE HARMONIE, to a Brother Achille Roy.

The corvette *La Torche* was captured by the British on the 16th August, 1805, and her officers and crew were sent to England. Louis was qualified to give his parole of honour and was sent to Wincanton, arriving there early in 1806. He could have lost little time in joining the French Lodge, for his signature appears on the Caperville Certificate dated the 1st April, 1806.

It is likely that he arrived in his parole town as dejected and apprehensive as any other captive, but from then on his story is a happy one. He had a quality about him which won him many friends in Wincanton, an English bride, and a new career in this country, where he was to spend the remaining fifty years of his life.

During the years that he spent in the town, Louis Duchemin seems not only to have met just about everybody of any importance, but to have made a universally good impression upon them. Miss Elizabeth Clewett, daughter of the printer of the bi-lingual Certificates for LA PAIX DESIRÉE, was particularly impressed – Elizabeth Clewett and Louis Michel Duchemin were married in the Parish Church at Wincanton, on the 4th February, 1808; the beginning of a very long and happy life together.

The extract from the Parish Register, which was transcribed in 1812, tells us that a fellow prisoner-mason, Deben Aine, was present at the ceremony. It also records the baptism of their daughter, Louisa Elizabeth, on 9th March, 1809.

It is interesting to note that among the signatures is that of George Messiter, who was Agent for the Prisoners of War on parole at Wincanton. In Messiter the parolees were blessed with the very best type of Parole Agent, who carried out his duties with great conscientiousness and consideration for their welfare. From the first years of captivity, the parolees appreciated his goodness and gave him little trouble or cause for concern; but, as the years dragged on with no sign of exchange or the war coming to an end, it is not surprising that some became impatient for freedom, and that escapes and attempted escape became ever more frequent. This, and the fears of a general uprising country-wide, led to Wincanton and many other southern towns being cleared of prisoners in February, 1812. The majority of them were transferred to new parole towns in Scotland, but Louis Duchemin was not among the departing officers. A petition was got up by the residents of Wincanton, requesting that he be allowed to stay in the town. The Agent, George Messiter, presented this to the Transport Board with successful result.

When the wars were over, the Duchemin family, now enlarged by the birth of a son, moved to the nearby city of Wells, where Louis, who had added to his income over the years by setting himself up as a language master, felt there would be more scope for his talents. Whilst in Wells he increased his already wide circle of British friends and when, in 1821, he applied for a teaching post in Birmingham, his references could not be bettered.

George Sweetman, in his pamphlet *'THE FRENCH IN WINCANTON'*, published in 1897, recorded the testimonial which accompanied his application. I reprint it here and make no excuse for including the rather lengthy list of signatories, as it shows the standing of many of those who held this one-time prisoner of war in such high regard:

'May the 29th, 1821.

We, the undersigned Inhabitants of the City of Wells and its vicinity, understanding that Monsr. L.M.Duchemin intends quitting this place, and establishing himself at Birmingham as a teacher of the French Language, take occasion hereby to certify that we have known him for six years and that his Talents and attention as an instructor, and his demeanour as an Inhabitant of this place, fully merit a Testimony of our Approbation.

J.Bishop of Rochester.	T.L.Surrage, Surgeon, Wincanton.
Roger Frankland, Canon of Wells.	Uh. Messiter, Bayford.
Thom. Woodhouse, Canon of Wells.	Edwd Dyne, Bruton, Somerset.
Bishop of Bath and Wells.	Thos. Bracher, Wincanton.
John Paine Tudway, M.P.	J.Radford, Curate of Wincanton.
J.L.Lovell.	Rich. Ring, Solicitor,Wincanton.
Wm. Melliar.	J.West, Surgeon, Shepton Mallet.
Hy. Hope, Banker.	T.Tidcomb, Grocer, Shep'n Mallet.
Steph. Davies, Mayor of Wells.	W. Perkins, Organist of Cathedral.
Edmond Broderip, Dean of Wells.	F.Nichols, Surgeon, Wells.
The Bishop of Gloucester.	John Lax.
Rev.W.P.Wickham, Shepton Mallet.	John Lax Jnr.
C.C.Clutterbuck, North Cadbury	Maurice Davies.
Henry Cook.'	

George Messiter, who by this time had known Louis for fifteen years, added his own testimonial:

'I the undersigned having been his Majesty's Agent, for the Prisoners of War on parole at this place during the late war, do certify that Monsr. L.M.Duchemin was resident for upwards of Six Years on his Parole of Honour in this Town, from the Time of the capture of the French frigate *La Torche* to the Removal of the Prisoners to Scotland, and that in consequence of his universal good conduct, he was excepted from the previous Order of Removal from this place with other prisoners of his Rank.

'Duchemin married whilst resident in this place into a Respectable Family, and having known him from 1806 to the present Time, I can with much Truth concur in the Testimonial of his Wells Friends.

G.Messiter.'

Louis Michel Duchemin got the job and spent the rest of his days in Birmingham. He died there in 1855, aged seventy-eight – and Elizabeth outlived him by only one week.

In 1894 the pamphleteer, George Sweetman, met the son of Elizabeth and Louis, who was visiting Wincanton, his father's old parole town.

C.F. Duchemin had followed his father's profession and was at that time the Local Secretary to Trinity College, London.

He brought with him, for George Sweetman's inspection Louis Michel Duchemin's Masonic Certificate and Masonic Apron and Marriage Certificate – which I have before me as I write. This Masonic Certificate is shown on page 250 (overleaf).

FRENCH PRISONER OF WAR MASONIC LODGES, 1746 to 1814

ON THE HULKS

CANADA	Chatham	'DE LA PERSÉVÉRANCE'	1813
SAMPSON	Chatham	'DE L'ÉSPERANCE'	1812
NASSAU	Chatham	'DE LA BONNE HARMONIE'	?
BIENFAISANT	Plymouth	'DE LA RÉUNION'	1810-12
ST ISIDORE	Plymouth	'DE LA CONSOLATION DES AMIS'	1801
GUILDFORD	Portsmouth	? ?	1811-12

IN THE PRISONS AND DEPOTS

DARTMOOR	Devonshire	'DE LA RÉUNION'	1810-14
MILLBAY	Plymouth	'DES AMIS RÉUNIS'	1809-11
PLYMOUTH DOCK	Plymouth	'LA CONSOLATION DES AMIS RÉUNIS	1800
PORTCHESTER Cas.	Hampshire	? ?	1812
STAPLETON	Bristol	'DE L'AMITIÉ'	1804?
VALLETFIELD	Midlothian	'DE L'INFORTUNE'	1813

IN THE PAROLE TOWNS : ENGLAND

ALRESFORD	Hampshire	'DE MARS ET NEPTUNE'	1813?
ASBURTON	Devon	'DES AMIS RÉUNIS'	1810-14
ASHBY-DE-LA-ZOUCH	Leics.	'DES VRAIS AMIS DE L'ORDRE'	1808-14
		'DE LA JUSTICE ET DE L'RÉUNION'	1814
BASINGSTOKE	Hampshire	? ?	1756
CHESTERFIELD	Derbyshire	'LOGE DE L'ÉSPÉRANCE'	1809-12
		'DE ST JEROME ET DE L'UNION'	1811
LAUNCESTON	Cornwall	'DE LA CONSOLANTE MAÇONNE'	1762-3
LEEDS	Yorkshire	? ?	1759-61
LEEK	Staffordshire	'L'AMITIÉ'	1810
		'DE LA RÉUNION DESIRÉE'	1811-13
LICHFIELD	Staffordshire	'ST JEAN EN BABYLONE'	1808-9
NORTHAMPTON	Northants.	'LA BONNE UNION'	1810-11
NORTH TAWTON	Devonshire	'DE LA PAIX DESIRÉE'	1810
ODIHAM	Hampshire	'DES ENFANTS DE MARS ET DE NEPTUNE'	1811
OKEHAMPTON	Devonshire	? ?	1810
OSWESTRY	Shropshire	'DES AMIS RÉUNIS'	1813
PETERSFIELD	Hampshire	? ?	1758
THAME	Oxfordshire	'DE LA PAIX'	1807
TIVERTON	Devonshire	'DES ENFANTS DE MARS'	1809-11
WANTAGE	Berkshire	'DES COEURS UNIS'	1810
WHITCHURCH	Shropshire	'DE LA TRIPLE UNION'	1813
WINCANTON	Somerset	'DE LA PAIX DESIRÉE'	1806-10
YORK	Yorkshire	? ?	1762

IN THE PAROLE TOWNS – SCOTLAND

KELSO	Roxburgh	? ?	1810-14
LANARK	Lanarkshire	'DES AMIS RÉUNIS DANS L'ADVERSITÉ'	1812
MELROSE	Roxburgh	'DE LA BIENFAISANT'	1813
PEEBLES	Peebleshire	? ?	1813
SANQUHAR	Dumfries	'DE LA PAIX DESIRÉE'	1812-13
SELKIRK	Selkirkshire	? ?	1813-14

IN THE PAROLE TOWNS – WALES

ABERGAVENNY	Monmouthshire	'DES ENFANTS DE MARS ET DE NEPTUNE'	1813-14
CHEPSTOW	Monmouthshire	?	?	?

FRENCH PRISONERS' LODGES OUTSIDE THE BRITISH ISLES

BERLIN	Germany	'DE LA FIDÉLITÉ'	1758
CABRERA	Balearic Isles	'DES MAÇONS CAPTIFS À BABYLONE'	1809-9
GIBRALTAR		'DES FRÈRES RÉUNIS'	1812
MAGDEBURG	Germany	'PARFAITE UNION'	1761
MALTA		'DES AMIS EN CAPTIVITÉ'	1811-20
VITTORIA	Spain	'DES INFORTUNES'	1813

The French prisoner of war Lodge in the Maltese parole village of Rabato, operated under the title of 'LES AMIS EN CAPTIVITÉ' – *Friends in Captivity*. The forty or so officer captives paroled there were received with great kindness by the Masons among their captors, who, one evening in 1811, invited them to a banquet at the English Lodge in Valetta. This was greatly appreciated by the French Brethren, but their attempt to reciprocate with a banquet at their own hall brought about a remarkable reaction from the local countryfolk.

Malta was suffering from a drought and cattle disease at that time, and the local priesthood instilled in the minds of the superstitious peasantry the idea that the island's troubles were 'solely caused by the evil practices of the Masons'. The Governor of Malta took the wise precaution of banning the banquet, but this was not good enough for the peasants, who were determined to carry out their raid on the hall. When the peasants had completed their vandalism, the priests entered the hall, sprinkling it with holy water until they were satisfied that it had been exorcised of evil spirits. It is not recorded how long the drought and disease lasted after the exorcism!

1. W. Fred Vernon: *Freemasonry in Roxburghshire and Selkirkshire,* page 206.

2. J. T. Thorp: *French Prisoner Lodges.* Leicester 1900.

3. W. L. Fox: *War Prisoners in Cornwall.*

4. E. S. Vincent: *A Record of Freemasonry in the Province of Cornwall 1751–1959.*

5. Edward Fraser: *Napoleon the Gaoler*: and the manuscript memoirs of Lt. R. H. James.

6. Lionel Vibert: *Masonry Among Prisoners of War.*

7. Lord Blayney: *A Narrative of a Forced Journey through Spain and France as a Prisoner of War in the years 1810–14.* Published 1814.

8. John Heron Lepper: *Freemasonry and the Sea.*

9. H. de Loucelles: *History of Freemasonry in Normandy. 1739–1875.*

10. Archbishop Ussher: *Annales Veteris et Novi Testamenti 1650.*

11. Stephen Knight: *The Brotherhood.*

12. W. Wonnercott: *Some Notes on French Prisoners' Lodges.*

Chapter Eight

Part Two

An English/American Officer
in France

'Part 14. It is equally agreed upon, that this same liberty shall extend to the persons on board the free ship, even if they should be enemies of either of the contracting parties, and they shall not be taken from the said free ships, at least if they are not soldiers, and actually in the enemy's service.'

Treaty between France and the United States: 8th Vendemaire, year 9.

SOON AFTER COMPLETING THE PREVIOUS CHAPTER, WHICH I IMAGINED had fairly covered the fascinating and seldom-mentioned study of the Freemason prisoner of war, I obtained from an American dealer in rare books, a small unbound journal, written by an English merchant officer who had spent a year and a half as a prisoner in France. I purchased it unread and was delighted to find, in the very first sentence of his preface, that it was dedicated to 'the fraternity of free and accepted Masons by a brother…and he deems it his duty to publish it in gratitude to French free masons, and the good of the order in general.'

Stephen Clubb was born in Suffolk in 1762, the penultimate year of the Seven Years' War, and began his apprenticeship as a mariner in his early teens. In 1787, with ten years of sea-time behind him, he was, by the age of twenty-five, Mate of a British vessel out of London. It was at about this time, that he was initiated into Freemasonry, as a member of Lodge No.66. called the 'Lodge of Sincerity' – and, during the whole period of his captivity some twenty years later, he was to have every good reason to bless the day of his initiation. In 1792, he married an American girl from Boston, Massachusetts, whose many virtues which endeared her to him included 'an inextinguishable love of her country', although, as we shall see, his own brand of patriotism was less impregnable.

We have some scant knowledge of his career over the next decade and a half. He tells us that he took command of a British merchantman in the Baltic trade which was later captured by the French; after which he bought into another vessel which was lost in a storm. Whether he was under-insured or uninsured, is not made clear, but Clubb must have been financially hard pressed after this latest stroke of ill fortune. He then applied for, and obtained, a Trinity House pilot's licence, which covered the North Sea and the Thames; an achievement which was to prove a disadvantage from the start of his captivity.

Stephen Clubb prospered for a few years until 1807, by which, time war in general, and in particular that between Denmark and Britain, had made serious inroads into much of that prosperity. The Clubbs now had one son, and Stephen determined that the three of them should leave England for good, and embark for America and his wife's hometown of Boston. Superficially, this would seem to have been a wise decision, as quite early in 1807 there was rumour of a fresh outbreak of trouble between England and Denmark, which in September culminated in the Bombardment of Copenhagen and a second war between the two countries. The Clubbs were by no means destitute, having cashed in on all their English assets in the spring of that year. They were well provided for with all the necessities for the long voyage, and would still have possessed sufficient capital to set themselves up in a ship-related business on the other side of the Atlantic.

It was not until October 1807 that they left Lowestoft in an American vessel called the *Triton*, but they made painfully slow progress. By December they had twice been driven into southern ports by storms and gales; first into Margate then Cowes. Whilst the vessel was lying off Margate, the American captain went ashore, returning with an English newspaper which bore devastating news for the emigrating family, containing as it did an announcement to the effect that their intended departure would be illegal: '...his Britannic majesty's proclamation forbidding British subjects leaving the kingdom, or sailing in any foreign ships or vessels, and commanding all those to come to England who might be settled abroad, under pain of being considered and treated as traitors to their country.'

There was some exaggeration in the above quotation, but Stephen Clubb must surely have known that the Common Law of England decreed that if one were born a British subject one died a British subject, whether or not they had been granted citizenship through naturalisation according to the laws of another country. In normal times it would have been impractical for Britain to attempt to enforce her nationality laws to the letter. Had it been possible, the country would have soon become overrun with hundreds of thousands of 'Americans' alone, quite apart from the unimaginable numbers of British merchant seamen serving in neutral vessels all over the world – but in time of war it was brought into action with a vengeance. In the early 1800s many Britishers still thought of Americans as renegades and rebels; and no Briton could ever have regarded the great American hero John Paul Jones as anything other than a pirate, and a traitor to the land of his birth. Only much later in the nineteenth century could a man legitimately and safely settle in a land of his choice. An extreme and interesting example of our nationality law in action took place after the Battle of Queenston in October 1812, when twenty-three 'Americans', born in the British Isles, were transported to England to face the capital charge of treason.

Stephen Clubb who, it would seem, could only accept a law, whether English, French or American, when it did not adversely affect him personally, read King George's proclamation with 'indignation, considering it as an arbitrary and oppressive measure, derogatory to the rights of nature...' He had much more to say on the subject in similar vein, and decided that whoever else it might apply to, it should not apply to him. He determined to go ahead with his plan to become an American, but frustration was added to frustration when, after the *Triton* was forced into the Isle of Wight by bad weather, he found that she was to be redirected to the West Indies.

The Clubbs transferred themselves, bag and baggage, on to another American vessel, the *Hyades of Saco*. On the the 31st December the *Hyades* left Cowes and sailed, they hoped, for America, with Stephen Clubb as pilot in the home waters and North Sea, and Second Mate for the rest of the voyage, in return for his family's passage to the States. For some reason known only to Clubb's way of thinking, he had complete faith in the Franco-American Treaty which heads this chapter – never thinking how he would stand according to English law, should he have the misfortune to be captured by the enemy whilst serving on a foreign ship and later be returned to Britain – or, for that matter, if he were to be discovered during one of the thousands of occasions when the Royal Navy exercised its hated right to stop and search neutral merchant shipping of whatever nationality, in its hunt for British subjects. Such worries seem not to have entered his head and, single-mindedly, he threw caution to the winds. Despite his previous disastrous experience as a result of inadequate insurance, he decided that as he was on an American ship carrying American cargo, he had no need to insure, recklessly theorising, 'where we trust our lives we will trust our property.'

Their voyage came to an abrupt end only a few hours after it began; it must have been one of the shortest departure-to-capture transitions on record! Clubb had left Cowes on the morning of the last day of 1807 and by the evening of the 1st January, 1808, he was a prisoner of the French in Calais. It had been intended that the *Hyades'* first port of call should be London but, by 2 p.m. on the 31st December, when Clubb had piloted the *Hyades* somewhere off Beachy Head, she was spotted and pursued by a small French privateer which, hoisting its colours, quickly overtook, captured and put a prize master and crew on board the American vessel.

When you read Stephen Clubb's journal, you may agree that he was gullible in the manner in which he dealt with his interrogators and fell an easy victim to the traps concealed in their questioning. Had he been less sure of himself and merely admitted to being a British passenger on his way to his wife's homeland, he may well have escaped eighteen months of unpleasant, though privileged, captivity; but he was soon lured into admitting that he was acting as a pilot and officer on the captured merchantman.

His wife was never at any time regarded, by the French or American authorities, as other than a voluntary prisoner. She was free to return to America at any time, and may well have been able to do more on behalf of the many badly treated American prisoners and her husband, had the latter encouraged her to do so. As it was, after the first night which she spent in a Calais hotel, Clubb arranged with his jailor for a rented bed to be set up in his cell for her to share! With typical self-pity, he described how much it pained him that his wife should find him 'a prisoner, betrayed and condemned, the victim of consummate hypocrisy and treachery, amongst obscure filth, damp and stench...the horrors of a jail, clanking of fetters, noise of wooden shoes, and sight of pale half famished wretches; their sighs and groans she could hear...' Stephen Clubb's wife is never referred to by her given name anywhere in the journal, as neither is their son, who is seldom mentioned at all. Clubb had little space to spare for anything outside his own predicament, and one is left to wonder how the youngster coped with a year and a half in France – a long time in a young boy's life – aware that his parent was, fairly or unfairly, held as a prisoner of war, for an indefinite period.

Mrs Clubb was free to go out from the jail at will, and frequently contacted authorities such as the American Consul, Le Veux, and the chief American representative, General Armstrong, by visit or by letter, bearing her husband's fervent plea that he was unfairly and illegally held captive by the French. The reply was always the same; that as a British subject they could not help him, and that he would have to await his arrival at a prisoner of war depot, where he could apply for parole, or petition the Emperor directly to regain his freedom. Filled with impotent rage, Clubb was convinced that he was the victim of a determination on everyone's part to condemn the *Hyades* and claim both ship and cargo as a legitimate prize. Mrs Clubb also sought help from the Freemasons, through M. Pigault, Master of the Calais 'Loge de St Louis des Amis Re-unis', who visited Clubb and promised him letters of recommendation addressed to the brethren of every Lodge at all stages of his journey to the great prisoner of war Depot at Arras, the best part of a hundred miles inland. M. Pigault was as good as his word and his recommendations were fulsome, even suggesting that Stephen Clubb may have himself given similar assistance to French prisoner of war Freemasons held captive in Britain.

After a fortnight in Calais, the Clubbs were told to prepare for their 'march' to Arras. For many prisoners of war it would have indeed been a literally foot-slogging march, sometimes for many times that distance before reaching a depot; but here again the Calais Masons came to their aid. Brother Pigault sent a *voiture* [a cart] to convey their luggage, often with themselves as passengers. They were also fortunate in that, unlike the experience of perhaps most other prisoners of war, particularly those who like them had been captured by privateers, their possessions remained unlooted by their captors.

All their goods had been kept stored at the hotel where they had spent their first night in Calais. When it was brought to the prison, it presented such a mountain of baggage, chests, trunks, packages and parcels – later estimated to weigh some nine hundredweights! – that Stephen Clubb had to hire a second wagon to accommodate the overflow.

And so the family set out on the first stage of their lengthy journey, escorted by a splendidly uniformed mounted gendarme. The first overnight stop was at Ardres, where they were invited to dine with an officer of Gendarmerie, but later had to conform to the local jailor's orders, that they must share a cell with two French deserters in the rather filthy town prison. Next day they arrived at a similar town prison in St Ormer, where they met an English merchant skipper, Captain Norfar, whom Clubb had last seen in Calais. His ship's company was under lock and key in the jail, but were allowed out long enough to unload the new arrival's baggage before being returned to their cells. Clubb considered this a fair exchange of labour, as he says he was pleased to reciprocate by acting as their interpreter – from the other side of the bars. Our hero and his wife, were allowed – at a price – to dine at the jailor's family table, their appetites overcoming their disgust at having to eat with certain of their fellow diners. Clubb tells the remarkable story of one of the latter, a condemned private in the French National Guard, who came to the table heavily fettered but unmanacled, although, at the end of a chain attached to his leg-irons, he carried a heavy iron bar which rested on his lap as he ate.

At every stage along the road to Arras – Ardres, St Ormer, Aire, Bithume – M. Rigault's demits, or letters of recommendation, were studied by the brethren of the local Lodges. Many of the fraternity visited their captive brother, assuring him of their goodwill and every reasonable assistance to speed him on his way to Arras, where, they hoped, he would be granted parole and perhaps his freedom.

On the 21st January, the Clubbs and their mounted guard who had escorted them all the way, arrived with their luggage-laden two-horse covered wagon at the Citadel of Arras. The gendarme conducted them to the reception bureau of the Depot, where they were interrogated by the receiving officer. During the questioning Colonel Duhamel, Commandant of the Depot arrived and, after listening to the Englishman's 'singular distressing story' – and after ascertaining by handshake that he was a member of the Masonic brotherhood – granted him immediate parole! The *voiture* was reloaded and they were driven to the *Hotel St Pol* in Arras, where the Commandant promised to visit them that same evening.

To the non-mason, this is all very puzzling and amazing. That this merchant officer, rather junior in rank at the time of his capture, who only just scraped into a category which might entitle him to the privilege of parole, should have received such preferential treatment would seem almost unbelievable; did we not know that much evidence exists which proves that such fraternal strength was not peculiar to French masonry. It would appear that the alleviation of much of what he called his 'sufferings', was entirely due to the Brotherhood, as he regarded all the non-mason French officials he had so far encountered as so many crooks, hell-bent on his destruction. Not yet an American, he was certainly no longer a patriotic Englishman. Smarting under what he probably took as the personal effrontery of King George III's nationality proclamation, which called on all subjects to be true to their country, he blamed the monarch himself for the terrible condition of 'common' prisoners of war in the Arras Depot, laying their 'extreme sufferings at the foot of his throne'. Some passages in the journal tell of the high mortality rate at Arras among the 'lower class' of prisoners: 'hundreds were carried out at the Paris gate [at Arras] feet foremost, starved to mere skeletons, 'til death, their wretches friend, came to their release.' The official French prisoner of war ration bore comparison with the English allowances; but, on either side of the Channel, so much depended upon the honesty of the provision contractors, who often cheated to a scandalous degree, delivering consignments short in both quantity and quality. However, it is unlikely that many, or even any, could have died from starvation caused by short supply alone and, however poor the quality, it is far more likely that gambling was as rife in the French as in the English depots, and that gambling and 'brokering' was really the prime cause of death in most cases.

After one night at the St Pol hotel, the family moved to rented accommodation in the Rue d'Amiens. Apart from a limit to his wanderings of no more than six miles from his lodging, (the paroled prisoner of war in Britain was restricted to only a *one* mile limit along the turnpike) and the inconvenience of attending muster twice daily, Clubb was a free man within the French town and its environs. After attending muster for a couple of days, he learned that brother Duhamel, the Commandant, had ordered that his attendance at these roll-calls should be suspended until further notice! So, from then on the days were spent in writing pleading letters to all and sundry, or roaming the pleasant countryside with its frequent festivities and pleasure gardens. In due season, he described the trees, walks, benches and facilities on the promenades of Arras, as 'handsome a place for recreation as I ever saw.' He particularly mentions such diversions as musical performances on Sundays – remembered with nostalgia by French parolees in Britain, particularly those sent to the Scottish Border parole towns, where the boredom of the dull, nothing-happening, Scottish Sabbaths, drove Frenchmen to distraction.

Clubb made regular visits to the Citadel, either to draw his prisoner of war allowance[1] or to speak with the comparatively few American captives in the closed prison. From the latter he learned that they had little hope of early release, as one group of 'Americans' who General Armstrong had recently liberated had later boasted by letter that they were in reality Englishmen. His Excellency had perhaps received a rap over the knuckles from the French or American governments, or both. So much for the hopes of the American-Englishman, Stephen Clubb!

The Rue d'Amiens, Arras, was to be the family's home for the following eighteen months. No matter how many letters Clubb wrote, no matter how much effort and influence his masonic friends could bring to bear, nothing concerning Americans, native or would-be, could ever succeed without the approval of the General, who was the most important American overseer of prisoners of war in France. If Stephen Clubb's journal can be accepted as unvarnished truth, then General Armstrong had much to answer for. That he may have found Stephen's case was untenable, was just a matter for his judgement; but that he had neglected to acknowledge or reply to any of his many letters and arguments, was inexcusable. Doubly so was the fact that he treated the petitions and submissions of American prisoners of war in a like cavalier fashion. Clubb had received the courtesy of replies to his letters from a number of French authorities, including the Minister for War and the Prefect Maritime, all of whom intimated that, despite the treaty, they could not act without the recommendation of the senior representative of the American flag. Of one thing we can be certain: the General was not a Freemason!

The breakthrough for the unhappy Clubbs began in the autumn of 1808. The Commandant of the Depot introduced them to a Mr Collet, an American resident in France, and most probably a mason, who, fully briefed by Clubb with the facts of his case and with encouragement from Duhamel, agreed to take a letter addressed to the General with him to Paris – and to do whatever else he could for him whilst in the capital. The General made no reply, but whilst in Paris Collet contacted the American prisoner of war Agent, Isaac Cox Barnet. For some insufficiently explained reason, Cox

Barnet took great personal interest in Clubb's 'singular' case. Over the next six months he entered into a busy correspondence with him, successfully appealing to the Minister of War on his behalf, and organising a petition to Napoleon himself! There is more than a hint that there was some strong criticism of Barnet's action in obtaining an Englishman's release, whilst twenty or thirty 'real' Americans remained prisoners in the Depot. Mention of this is made in the preface to the journal, and Isaac C. Barnet himself makes a point in one of his letters that no 'pecuniary consideration' was involved.

Stephen Clubb and his wife and son left Arras on the 22nd June, 1809 and made their way first to Paris, then to L'Orient where they embarked on the government vessel, *Mentor*, and resumed their long delayed passage to America. On arrival, he kept his word to the Americans he had left behind in Arras. He did deliver their letters and he did publish his journal within months of his arrival; but a last quote will show that he really did think that he deserved his good fortune, and that he had suffered at least as badly as any other of the prisoners of war in French hands:

> ' …that I would not only deliver their letters, but publish the sufferings I have experienced, as a specimen of theirs; for it would be impossible for me to recollect the wrongs and sufferings of each individual.'

****

Despite his frequent sermonizing, constant self-pity and exaggerations of his ill treatment and suffering, Stephen Clubb's journal is an interesting document, attesting as it does to the fact that the fellowship between free and captive Masons in France was as steadfast as it was known to have been in Britain. It also gives one pause to dream that, if groups of men from two nations which have been mortal enemies for centuries, can form themselves into an exclusive, dependable, brotherhood, even in times of hostility, could not the concept become widened and inclusive to a point where war became a thing of the past? But that, of course, is only a dream!

---

1. His wife, who was the only American woman in the town at the time, received the same allowance from the French Government as that allowed to other ladies whose husbands were paroled officer prisoners. Clubb was shocked that she had been given 'common prison bread', adding that he could sell it for no more than three francs a month!

Chapter Nine

The Gamblers and the Brokers

Wise leaders and overseers of large groups of men – whether in military or naval service, confined in civil prison or as prisoners of war – have always been aware of the many evils which may result from excessive gambling.

The great sixteenth century English explorer and navigator, Cabot, in the Ordinances which he laid down for the conduct of his crews during their voyage to Cathay (China), made special mention of gambling as an evil and a threat to discipline:

'No blaspheming of God, or detestable swearing be used in any ship, nor communication of ribaldry, filthy tales, or ungodly talk to be suffered in the company of any ship, neither dicing, carding, tabling nor other devilish games to be frequented, whereby ensueth not only poverty to the players, but also strife, variance, brawling, fighting and oftimes murder to the utter destruction of the parties, and provoking of God's most just wrath and sword of vengeance.'

SEBASTIAN CABOT. 1553.

OTHER CHAPTERS IN THIS VOLUME RELATE THE HISTORIES OF PRISONERS who overcame the wretchedness of their confinement, in prison ships or the depots and prisons ashore. These were men who made good use of any natural talents they possessed; who developed latent interests awakened in rebellion against unwelcomed idleness, and all those who occupied themselves in any way which made less burdensome the long hours, days and years of captivity. However they combated the soul-destroying boredom, whether teaching or learning, carving bone or plaiting straw, or merely performing menial tasks about their prisons, their efforts to create some sort of normal everyday life in such uncongenial surroundings can only be admired. True, these occupations often produced a monetary reward which helped to soften the austerity of their captive existence; but the mentally stabilising value of their industry was beyond all price.

This chapter has no such inspiring tales to tell. It deals with men who were beaten by their environment, their weakness and their folly; men who brought upon themselves a hardship and suffering far harsher than anything their captors could impose. It tells of losers and the hard bitten winners, and of the real villain of the piece, despicable beyond belief – the usurious 'broker' who trafficked in the vulnerability and desperation of his luckless fellow prisoners.

Gambling and the troubles which inevitably arose from it, created very real problems for the authorities of all nations who had prisoners of war under their care. At its worst it was as effectively ruinous to all classes of British captive held abroad as it was to all nationalities of prisoner in our hands. Drunkenness was perhaps the chief cause of trouble wherever the ordinary British prisoner was held – the incurable craving for alcohol led to fighting, disorderliness and general lowering of morals – but gambling ran it a close second as the reason for much of their discomfort and distress. Although seldom pursued to the disastrous extremes common to addicted Frenchmen, gambling among our soldiers and sailors in foreign depots went far enough to add an unnecessary suffering to the already considerable hardship of their captivity.

Wealthy British *détenus*, paroled officers of means, impoverished merchantmen, hard-up midshipmen and the rank and file in the closed prisons, large numbers fell under the spell of gambling's dangerous attractions. The *détenus*, civilian travellers detained as hostages by order of Napoleon in 1803, who, together with the majority of paroled British officers, were quartered at Verdun, included gambling facilities as one of the necessities in their plans for a home-from-home in that foreign fortress town.

Soon after their arrival at Verdun they established English-style clubs where members could meet privately. Here they could peruse and discuss the latest war-time news, garnered from the gazettes, news-sheets and pamphlets with which they kept themselves plentifully supplied. Here, too, they held their dances, extravagant dinners and, inevitably, card-parties and private gaming. The majority of these clubs were more or less exclusive, the membership – which sometimes included paroled officer prisoners of war – being selected by ballot. As the members were usually men of good financial standing and their gambling was amongst themselves, they had little harmful effect upon prisoners with less plentiful funds at their disposal. However, these private games were not allowed to continue for long.

The Governor of Verdun, General Wirion, an unscrupulous and avaricious character, who was not above intruding on these members-only sessions and participating in the games – safe in the knowledge that the British players dared not let him lose – later ordered that the Hazard tables should be closed down.

This suppression was based on no other motive than that he hated to see so much gold kept within the British family. With Wirion's blessing, professional gamblers came in to set up a French-run casino which was called 'The Bank', the proceeds from which would include a sizeable share for the General. With the establishment of this official gaming house every condition of prisoner was netted in – and the gambling excesses at Verdun became an international scandal. The Chevalier Lawrence, himself a British *détenu*, described the state of affairs at that time:

'A regular *Rouge et Noir* bank was soon afterwards established, which was open from one at noon to five, and from eight it continued all night. The sums of money lost by the English were considerable. Many lost a thousand pounds, others more.
'Not only men of fortune, but Lieutenants of the Navy, midshipmen, and masters of merchant vessels, were led astray by the temptation. Persons who never before touched a card in their lives, from want of occupation, from mere ennui, induced to risk half a crown, till the passion grew upon them, and then, to regain their losings, they plunged deeper and deeper into difficulties.
'Every night some drunken guests were decoyed by girls of pleasure, placed for that purpose; and to add to the infamy of those who were at the bottom of this nefarious institution, the following inscription In French was written in large letters:

THIS BANK IS KEPT FOR THE ENGLISH
THE FRENCH ARE FORBIDDEN TO PLAY AT IT

'Scenes took place in this house which would require the pencil of Hogarth to depict. Here the unwary spendthrift found an elegant supper, heating, wines, abandoned women – in short, every stimulant to vice.'

It would appear that the restriction against Frenchmen actually playing at the tables did not mean that they could not enter the establishment. Major-General Lord Blayney, Napoleon's most senior captive, remembered that gambling disputes between British officers often led to duels in which a number lost their lives. At that period Verdun had a *Pharo* bank and a *Rouge et Noir* table:

> '…to which every description of persons were admitted, where perfect equality reigned, and where our countrymen of the first rank might be seated alongside a ragged Jew, mud-covered peasant, or a *fille publique*. Here a great number of our young men were completely ruined, it being supposed that while it continued, £50,000 were lost by the prisoners each year. It was at last shut up in consequence of a general regulation limiting the number of licensed gaming-houses.'

The scandal of the gambling hell at Verdun was no secret to the authorities in England, but it was Napoleon, himself, who after Austerlitz (1805), sent an order through his War Office which closed it down. Too late, alas, for many British prisoners of war who had already gone too far.

Apart from the gaming houses there were any number of well-organised methods by which the officials of Verdun dipped into the pockets of the prisoners of war. Wily Wirion and his equally grasping second-in-command, the Lieutenant of Gendarmes, instituted a system of fines for small infringements of parole, some of which were difficult to avoid. Failure to attend one of the twice-daily musters could cost as much as five shillings. That such a fine was not designed to ensure that the prisoner would keep strictly to the muster rules, thus proving that he was still inside the walls of the fortress, is proved by the fact that, for a similar sum, he could have purchased permission to be absent from both that day's roll-calls. Such a high figure had the disappointing result of well-attended musters and the revenue was small, so later the fee was lowered and prisoners could avoid this monotonous routine for as little as one pound a month.

To keep out of trouble it was absolutely essential to keep on the right side of the gendarmes, who also had their own pocket-lining techniques. One of their favourite means of extortion was the organising of rigged lotteries – and it was luckier to lose than to win, when forced into a position where a ticket just had to be bought. The prizes were attractive enough:

> 'Horses, watches, trinkets, etc., that often had no existence, or if they had it made no difference, the winner being well assured that the consequence of insisting on receiving the object would be a visit to the 'Bitche'; as was the fate of a gentleman who won a horse in this manner from the Lieutenant of Gendarmerie, and did not say, as half a dozen others had, "*Monsieur, je vous prie de la garde comme un souvenir de l'amitie.*"'
> [Monsieur, I beg you to keep it as a souvenir of our friendship.]

If the horse had been a good one and the lottery fair, it would have been a very desirable acquisition, for race meetings were regularly held at Verdun.

As early as 1804, the British *détenus* and wealthy prisoners privileged by parole, had formed a jockey club and had their own racecourse in a converted meadow outside the walls of the fortress; 'hired and fitted up near the village of Charni, with distance posts, Stewards box, etc.' The British Race days were important social occasions, well attended by the French gentry of the Department, the French officers and families of the garrison, and prisoners who had signed out of the gate for a few hours or had purchased exemption from the muster. War and the restrictions of captivity may well have been forgotten for a while in the midst of such a colourful gathering; carriages arriving with the *détenus* and their fashionably dressed ladies, the uniforms of French and British officers of all ranks and the motley assortment of servants, vendors, tipsters and bookmakers. That these race meetings were grand, highly organised and well-conducted can be judged from the quality of the race-card produced.

A great deal of money would have changed hands on those days, the betting ranging from the few *sous* risked by hard-up junior officers to the heavy wagers of their wealthier countrymen – and it is a safe bet that there would be a large rake-off for the French officials if such a fancy privilege as a racecourse was to continue. It was said that, on a number of occasions, the start was delayed until General Wirion had received his 50 *louis,* and given permission for racing to commence.

Some of the really serious British punters went to a lot of trouble in their studies of racing form. General Blayney witnessed one of these researchers in action, and recalled: 'I once saw a friend of mine up to his middle in the river, with a Frenchman's coat and cocked hat on, and a fishing rod in one hand, while in the other he held a stop-watch to ascertain the fleetness of the horse going round the course. It is probable that these *ruses de guerre* would not be deemed admissible at Newmarket, but at Verdun the humour rendered them merely laughable, and as they were practised by each side, they were treated as quite fair, and none had the right to complain.'

Of course, gambling under such pleasant conditions was available only to the civilian hostage and the paroled prisoner. The rank and file of our servicemen in the depots abroad had recourse only to the dice-box and the deck of cards with which to enrich or ruin themselves. We hear of the habitual drinkers and gamblers in the French fortress prisons and of the British sailors in Denmark, imprisoned in the depot at Randers. After the bombardment of Copenhagen they gambled away their money, clothes and food until, penniless and hungry, they were reduced to begging aid from the kindly Danish countryfolk who visited their prison. The losers among their opposite numbers – the Danish and Norwegian inmates of the prison hulks at Chatham, were similarly driven to desperate measures when, often literally, they lost their shirts at the gaming tables. Many of these unhappy men cashed in their last saleable possession – the remnants of their self-respect – and committed a crime far worse in the eyes of their unaddicted fellow prisoners than robbery or murder. They escaped their debts by signing on as sailors in the service of Britain.

The Danish authorities were concerned enough to have warning notices posted up, reminding the prisoners of the dangers of gambling and of getting into the hands of extortionate money-lenders on board the hulks. They also warned of the action they would take if the gamblers did not mend their ways. In 1811, the Danish Consul, Jens Wolff, advised that those who persisted in their reckless gambling with food and clothing, should be punished by depriving them of their British and Danish prisoner of war allowances. The money should be put into a kitty and divided among better behaved brethren who would be more likely to put it to intelligent use. This was a very serious threat and probably did at least some good, but the incorrigibles were merely driven underground, or rather into darker depths and corners of the hulks – for the Danish Agent was still posting up prohibition notices two years later.

One officer prisoner of war who made his mark in Danish history, through adventurous acts of pioneering exploration and daring ambition, cursed the misfortune which led him into the society of the gaming fraternity. For the first half of his amazing life, Captain Jorgen Jorgensen exhibited a strength of character which one might have thought impervious to the influence of low-life swindlers and card-sharps. He was a man of great achievement – for a period he was King of Iceland, (coincident with being a paroled prisoner of war of the British!) – but capable of as great a folly once hooked by the gambling fever. In his writings he frequently referred with puzzled wonderment to his inability to conquer the addiction – and he did make many attempts.

Sentenced to the Chatham hulks in 1810, for five weeks he was confined in a London civil prison, awaiting transport to the Medway, and during that short time he met the gamesters whose intimacy, he said. 'steeped my future life in misery, in shades varied only by transient glimpses of anticipation and remorse'. If his first lessons in gaming were learned in the London prison he would certainly have graduated during his time on the Medway hulks. After his year on the prison ship, he was granted parole, first to Reading, then to London, and in his autobiography, unknown in this country until the end of the nineteenth century, he wrote of that time:

> ' …I was picked up in the metropolis by my acquaintances of Tothill Fields Prison, and was by them initiated into all the enticements and horrors of the gaming-table. For six months was I sunk in the wretched vortex of dissipation, until at last I found myself stripped of everything I had in the world, including a sixteenth share of a £20,000 prize in a State Lottery. Grave cause as I have seen to reprobate the vice of drunkenness during the manifold experiences of my chequered career, I am compelled to denounce gambling, though perhaps not so general, as a far more iniquitous and soul-absorbing propensity. The attacks of drunkenness are mainly in the first instance levelled at the body, but the demon of gambling lays siege at once to the citadel of the mind, and brings on the destruction of the body as a secondary consequence.
>
> 'When once this horrid vice has obtained possession of the heart, it absorbs and surmounts every other passion. The idea is ever present in the mind; it engrosses every thought. For ever expecting the vicissitude of success, the gamester goes on losing until all further hope of raising a stake is past.
>
> 'No cormorant or vampire ever contemplates the destruction of another so greedily as the gamester does that of his victim. They sit down together with the hope and determined savage purpose to devour each other, like the Irishman's two cats, till not a remnant of either be left. As for fair play or honesty, it is soon out of the question. The victim of the sharpers resolves upon reprisal by becoming himself a sharper… '

The above diatribe is not – like the 'holier-than-thou' advice of the ex-smoker – the preaching of a reformed character; for, much as he hated himself for his lack of will-power, Jorgensen never did conquer his demon.

Prisoners of war of whatever nationality and wherever they were confined, included in their number a high percentage of men who could not resist the temptation to try their luck at games of chance. However, none were so passionately or disastrously addicted as the French. The conditions aboard the hulks and in most of our depots made them ideal breeding grounds for gambling at its most vicious and the French were temperamentally suited to make certain it would thrive. Idleness, over-crowding, lack of privacy, shortage of clothing, meagre and monotonous provisions – often made even worse by the operations of crooked victuallers – all these things, and the miserable uncertainty of men imprisoned for the duration of wars which, it seemed, might well go on for ever, had their effect. It is natural that all but the strongest were infected with feelings of hopelessness which drove them towards any excitement or adventure which might, even temporarily, brighten the immediate horizon.

That conditions helped to create the evil is undeniable. Whilst no closed prison on land or afloat escaped the misery and degradation of gambling taken to extremes, there are few references to hard gaming among the paroled officers settled in towns and villages throughout this country. The parolees had their frequent card parties and doubtless there were real gamblers among them, but their comparative freedom, their higher hopes of exchange, and the opportunity to live a civilised everyday life during their captivity, kept them free from the excesses of their more closely confined countrymen.

It could be argued that the parolees were, in general, products of a better background than their fellows behind the stone or wooden walls of their prisons; officers and gentlemen whose education and intelligence held them aloof from folly or improvidence. This is not at all in keeping with the facts. Their equals in rank, education and social standing were to be found in the depots and the hulks and, as will be seen, were also among the naked and starving wretches who had staked and lost their all.

The French would bet on anything: dice, cards, dominoes, billiards, the athletic abilities of cockroaches, rats or flies, or the number of rolls in an officer's wig. When their money had gone, next would go their few possessions, followed by their bedding and, finally – the fatal step – their food and clothing.

A non-stop variety of games of chance went on by day and by night. Captain Vernon Harris, a nineteenth century Governor of Dartmoor, in a pamphlet which he published for private circulation, tells of the wagering and bookmaking that went on after the prisoners had retired to their hammocks for the night:

> 'When the lights were extinguished and the ship's lantern alone cast a glimmer through the long room, the rats were accustomed to show themselves in search of the rare crumbs to be found below hammocks. A specially tempting morsel having been placed in an open space, the arrival of the performers was anxiously looked for. They were all known by name, thus each player was able to select his champion for the evening. As soon as a certain number had gained the open space, a sudden whistle, given by a disinterested spectator, sent them back to their holes and the first to reach his hole was declared the winner.
>
> 'An old rat called 'Pere Ratapon' was a great favourite with the gamblers, for, though not so active as his younger brethren, he was always on the alert to get a good start when disturbed.'

This story of unconventional gambling which was comparatively harmless is amusing enough, but similar unusual methods were sometimes employed in serious contests where the outcome could only be tragic. When money and possessions had gone, men who had reached rock-bottom would draw single straws in what was a gamble with life. Each would draw with nerve-racking slowness, each fearful of the result; for the man who drew the shortest straw may well have lost his daily food for a week or a month. Sometimes the winner would use his double ration to replace lost covering for his scraggy frame, but more often he would already be in hock to a 'broker' and would use the food of his friend to reduce his debt. Or, certain that he was in for a run of good luck, would fritter it away on yet more wagers.

Louis Garneray was witness to a literally deadly game of cards on board the Portsmouth prison hulk *Vengeance*, towards the end of 1811. At that time Garneray was earning well as a painter and interpreter and decided to donate a little of his good fortune as a hand-out to the half-starved paupers who had left their luck at the roulette or hazard tables on the upper gun-deck. With this charitable intention in mind, he descended to the nauseous quarters of the down-and-outs, where a single game of cards was progressing with a seriousness and concentration unusual even in this abode of hardened gamblers. All the ragged occupants were crowded round the two men, Petit-Jean and Leroux, who were playing *écarte,* watching in fascinated silence as each card was turned. The stakes? The honour of killing an English guard named Linch, who had earned their hatred through his habit of striking and taunting the down-and-outs, simply because they were what they were. The first to obtain twenty points was to be declared the winner, and the game had reached a point where it seemed to them that Leroux was certain to be the executioner. Both players realised that the consequences for such a crime were inescapable, but when Leroux was asked how the prospect of the gallows affected him, he replied: 'I'd rather be shot, but one must take whatever comes. Lead? Hemp? It's much the same in the end. And before they turn you off they give you a good dinner, three courses, tea ad lib and a pint of beer. Come on, turn up the next card, everybody's waiting.'

From then on the run of the cards went in the opposite direction and it was Petit-Jean who finally stood up, shook hands with his friends, and bade them a dignified farewell. Five minutes later Master Linch lay dead with a knife through his heart and Petit-Jean was taken ashore for trial and his three course meal – and to honour his last gambling debt at the end of a rope. This act, cold-bloodedly conceived and carried out on the appropriately named *Vengeance*, was by no means unique. Neither was the method employed in the selection of the assassin.

A macabre lottery was held on board the ill-famed *Sampson* hulk at Gillingham, to decide who should murder the Master's Mate and the equally detested Sergeant of Marines. The winner – or loser, according to one's point of view – was Charles Manseraux, a man of strange conscience. He set off on his gruesome mission but, discovering that the sergeant was a married man with children, could not bring himself to commit the act. An admirable compassion, had he left it at that, but some twisted sense of 'honour' and loyalty to his task told him that someone must die in the sergeant's stead. For this slender reason he crept up behind the unlucky substitute, a young private of marines on fo'c'sle duty, and stabbed the poor fellow in the back. Manseraux and two of his accomplices in the gamble were tried at Maidstone Assizes for this senseless killing and were executed in 1813.

It is undeniable that the conditions in which great numbers – but by no means the majority – of prisoners lived or died in captivity, were truly shocking. The memoirs of ex-prisoners, with their bitter descriptions of shivering, starving, wretchedness, cannot easily be dismissed as the exaggerations of men smarting with resentment for wasted years of youth, spent in the hands of a hated enemy.

A review of these memoirs, and a study of the official recriminations between the two governments, show that descriptions were often accurate enough, but that the worst of the suffering could only be attributed to the folly and improvidence of the prisoners themselves, rather than to any calculated cruelty on the part of their captors. The man who had to depend on his prisoner of war allowance could at least survive as far as food was concerned, although he had not the faintest hope of getting fat. He might well be clothed in rags which would hardly protect him from the worst of winter weather – and for this he could blame his own government as much as the British. Their ceaseless wrangling as to who should clothe him still left him cold, whichever side won the paper argument. If he had any initiative there were a dozen or more different industries in which he could employ himself within the prison walls. However, all too often he fell an early victim to the snares laid out to deprive him of whatever little he had. The newly arrived prisoner, of whatever nationality, was sure of a warm welcome from the experienced syndicates of gamblers already established in all prison ships and depots. He would soon be befriended and introduced to the French-run 'Wheels of Fortune', *Rouge-et-noir*, *Alagalitie* or *Kaka* tables, or taken aside and persuaded into a 'friendly' game of billiards, dice or cards.

The Wheel of Fortune was innocent enough; a smooth board representing a clock face. It had numbers round its circle, or painted emblems or devices, and a revolving hand pivoted at its centre. For a halfpenny the player was dealt five cards with numbers or symbols, after which he twirled the pointer. If it stopped at a number or device corresponding with that on any one of his cards, he received his prize – a tuppenny white loaf. Most of the other games were more dangerous. Whatever the lure, even the Wheel, if the newcomer did not possess the strength to resist, his foot was set on the top of a very slippery slope indeed. If cards, then as likely as not the game would be *Vingt-et-un*, a beat-the-banker card game still popular with gamblers today: Pontoon was a British forces' corruption of the French abbreviation, *Vingt-un.*

For there to be losers, there had, of course to be winners but, in the long run, these were always the professionals – 'bankers' who owned the tables; the expert billiards players who fooled their victims with the odd deliberate mis-cue; the organisers of crooked lotteries and the sleight-of-hand merchants. The losers, whether fellow-Frenchmen or allies of another nation, could expect little sympathy – and even less charity – from the sharks who had relieved him of his cash. Neither could he expect them to grant a loan of part of it, against his future pay. Their attitude towards the would-be borrower was noted down by Benjamin Waterhouse, the 'Young Man of Massachusetts', who witnessed his fellow Americans being fleeced by the Frenchmen bankers on the prison hulk *Crown Prince*, at Chatham: 'Ah, *mon ami*. I am very sorry, very sorry indeed; it is *la fortune de guerre*. If you have lost your money you must win it back again; that is the fashion in my country – we no lend, that is not the fashion.'

Waterhouse described the manner in which the wily French gamblers lured the American sailors into games of chance – or of certainty, as far as the outcome was concerned:

> 'Their skill and address at these apparent games of hazard were far superior to the Americans. They seemed calculated for gamesters; their vivacity, their readiness, their ever-lasting professions of friendship were nicely adapted to inspire confidence in the unsuspecting American Jack Tar, who has no legerdemain about him. Most of the prisoners were in the way of earning a little money; but almost all of them were deprived of it by the French gamesters. Our people stood little chance with them, but were commonly stripped of every cent, whenever they set out seriously to play with them. How often I have seen a Frenchman capering, singing and grinning in consequence of stripping one of our sailors of all his money... the officers among them are the most adroit gamesters. We have all tried hard to respect them; but there is something in their conduct so much like swindling, that I hardly know what to say of them. When they knew we had received money for the work we have been allowed to perform, they were very attentive and complaisant and flattering... They would come around and say, "Ah. Boston fine town, very pretty – Cape Cod fine town, very fine. Town of Rhode Island superb. Bristol Ferry very pretty. General Washington *très grand homme*. General Madison *brave homme.*"
>
> 'With these expressions in broken English, they would accompany, with their monkey tricks, capering and grinning and patting us on the shoulder, with, "The Americans are brave men – fight like Frenchmen" and by their insinuating manners allure our men once more to their Wheels of Fortune and billiards tables, and sure as they did, so sure did they strip them of all of their money.'

The last thing to have lured Waterhouse himself, would have been the intended flattery of likening him to a Frenchman. His opinion of the American's continental ally can be gathered when he adds:

> 'Had not the French proved themselves to be very brave people, I should have doubted it by what I have observed of them aboard the prison ship. They would scold, quarrel and fight, by slapping each others chops with the flat of the hand, and cry like so many girls. I have often thought that one of our yankees, with his iron fist, could, by one blow, send monsieur into his nonentity. Perhaps such a man as Napoleon Bonaparte could make any nation courageous; but there is some difference between courage and bravery.'

That this rapid emptying of Yankee pockets by the French was not peculiar to the *Crown Prince* is made plain by two other Americans, Charles Andrews and 'Green Hand', who recorded their experiences in Dartmoor. Many of the Americans who arrived at Dartmoor had not been captured in action or at sea. They were men who were serving in the British Navy until the outbreak of hostilities with America in 1812. Those who refused to carry on and fight against their own country were immediately classed as prisoners of war and, unless their rank qualified them for parole, spent the remaining years of the war in a closed prison.

The greater number of this type of prisoner came into Dartmoor well breeched. Their back pay and any prize money they may have earned in the service of King George put them, in prison terms at least, in the class of men of means. To this sudden influx of wealth into the depot, was added the funds available to those well-to-do American privateers officers and owners who were not eligible for parole, either because their vessels were below the requisite tonnage or because they had jettisoned too many of their guns before surrendering.

The proprietors of the gaming tables had every reason to look forward to a record harvest that year, and they were not disappointed. 'Green Hand' says that gambling 'was the worst stain upon the body of the prisoners, and the only vice from which nineteen-twentieths did not keep themselves aloof.' Soon the bankers were able to 'window-dress' the tables before them with huge piles of silver coin; three-shilling pieces and half-crowns arranged in pyramids and towers designed to lure new players, whose hard-earned cash would shortly add height to this impressive display.

One Dartmoor American might well have been heard to murmur more than an ironical 'Easy come, Easy go!', at the end of his few days experience as a big-time gambler. This man had served in the British Navy for many years, not voluntarily but by way of a press-gang, and was also an experienced prisoner of war before he arrived at the depot. During his time at sea under the British flag, his vessel was captured and he became a prisoner of the French. After some time confined in a fortress depot, he became involved in a group escape attempt during which a French soldier was killed, and for this he spent a number of years below ground in a French dungeon. Rather surprisingly, he was later included in an exchange of prisoners and returned to England and service as a British Tar. But his luck was never in for long. Soon after his release from France, America was at war with Britain so he became a prisoner of the British, Dartmoor bound. By the time he arrived at Dartmoor he was a man with no money troubles. Apart from his prisoner of war allowances and the American Government allowance of tuppence-ha'penny a day for coffee and soap, there were sums due to him from a number of other sources. There was his back pay from the British Navy, his prize money from captured enemy ships, and in addition to this he was entitled to back pay for the whole of the period he had spent in the French depot and dungeon.

On a Monday he was handed the lump sum which represented his cash reward for so many years of hard-lived experience – the then considerable sum of £1,100. With such a fortune he could have lived in comparative luxury for the rest of the war and had money over at the end of it; but he headed straight for the gaming tables and, by the following Thursday, he could not raise the price of a cup of coffee. His case was not unique, except perhaps for the speed with which his fortune disappeared. There were many more who lost as much – and many more who lost far more than cash.

The persuasive charm exhibited by the proprietors of the tables towards the punter with cash, vanished with the latter's last losing stake. They created paupers in every prison, but their determination never to lend could have been a blessing in disguise. If, at this point, the empty-pocketed punter came to his senses, took notice of the misery around him, of the hundreds of down-and-outs who had pushed their luck even farther; if he cut his losses and made the best of his admittedly meagre allowances, then he still had a chance. However, few learned their lesson that easily. When the professionals had finished with him and the unhappy victim had watched his last penny being added to the bankers' hoard, he was then fit meat for the real vultures of the prison yards. These were the 'Brokers', the usurers who thrived on the desperation and suffering of their fellow captives. The usurer was the curse of all prisons. Robbery, murder, suicide and every sort of moral degradation could be traced back to his unfeeling greed. He traded in misery, his interest only in the loser who would sell his food, his clothing and his bed in order to rake up a few pennies to stake in a hopeless gamble to recoup his losses.

The activities of these vicious traders were at the roots of most prison evils. Their victims, with less than nothing left to lose, became rowdies and troublemakers who caused greater concern to the authorities than ever did the escapers, forgers or manufacturers of prohibited articles. The Agents and Commandants of the depots and hulks were forever penning reports to the Transport Office, which told of the difficulty of containing gambling within reasonable bounds, and of the terrible condition of the patrons of the 'brokers'.

The Transport Office, in turn, passed on this information and complaints to the Commissary for French Prisoners of War, in London. One such letter based on a complaint from Captain Woodriff, the Agent at Norman Cross Depot, is enough to tell the story. It was sent to Commissioner Otto, early in 1800, less than three years after the establishment of the Depot, and confirms that the 'broker's' only concern for his fellow prisoner was that he should survive long enough to settle his debt and perhaps create a new one:

> 'There are in those prisons some men, if they deserve that name, who possess money, with which they purchase daily at the market whatever is allowed to enter, and with those articles they also purchase some unfortunate and unthinking Fellow-prisoner his Rations of Bread for several days together, and frequently **both Bread and Beef** for a month, which he, the merchant, seizes upon daily, and sells it out again to some other unfortunate being, on the same usurious terms; allowing the former one half-pennyworth of potatoes daily to keep him alive: not content with this more than savage barbarity he purchases next his clothes, and bedding, and sees the miserable man lie naked on the planks, unless he will consent to allow him for one half-penny a night, to lie in his own hammock, and for which he makes him pay a further Deprivation of his Rations when his original debt is paid.'

The problem was indeed a serious one. Had the numbers been smaller it may have been possible to suppress gambling and the attendant usury to some extent but, in the great depots and even on the hulks, the hungry, sick and naked could be counted in their many hundreds. Many attempts were made to try to save them from themselves, but to no avail. Neither threat nor kindness had any lasting effect. Whenever they were reclothed and bedded – by official issue or from the proceeds of the many public subscriptions which were got up for their relief – the help was always abused by the majority. Within a few days the benefits would be in the hands of the 'brokers' and the cards, dice and billiards would be out for the table owners to make another killing.

Both the prisoner who sold his clothes and rations and the man who traded in them, were liable to punishment; but once again it was the ruined man who suffered most. The most probable punishment was that he would be put on two-thirds rations for a period, which meant that he would be in debt to the usurer for that much longer; for the ruthless 'broker' never released his grip until his debtor had paid up or died in the attempt.

There are, however, a few records of successful, though short-lived, suppressions of gambling and usury. The steadier among the Americans at Dartmoor rescued at least some of their reckless comrades, and the Danes on the hulks put a temporary stop to gaming on more than one occasion. The Danish prisoner, Jens Krog, noted in his diary for April, 1810, that all the French gaming tables on the prison ship, *Brave*, at Plymouth had been taken aft and broken up. However, gambling is never that easily put down. The toss of a coin and, as we have seen, the length of a straw or the speed of a rat, were as effective as any table.

By the following year the gamesters on the *Brave* had recovered from their loss and were evidently back in business. Krog was pleased to record that a loser, who in the circumstances might be described as spirited rather than unsportsmanlike – he had probably been taken in by an expert – had cut up the French billiards table, 'which was only bought a fortnight ago and cost them three pounds.'

The Danish Pastor Rosing also had some success on the Medway hulk, *Bahama*. One can imagine his sense of achievement when, after lecturing, preaching and appealing to their common-sense, he was surrounded by temporarily reformed gamblers, who made a great show of throwing all their decks of playing cards into the sea. So much for the Danes.

For the French there was no cure. The most depraved and down-and-out became a menace, not only to the authorities but to those of their fellow countrymen who had held on to their self-respect. Their filthy condition and vicious habits, their grubbing through the rubbish dumps for offal and scraps of food thrown out as too rotten even for the prison soup cauldrons, set them apart from all decent prisoners of war. Ostracised by their fellow captives, these poor wretches – for they can be pitied even though their suffering was largely self-inflicted – were forced into forming a class and society of their own, and were banished into lofts and corners of the prisons, where they could live according to their own squalid rules of conduct.

Within their segregated society a sort of communism reigned, as did every vice but the one beyond their reach – gluttony. All classes had their standards and regulations and not everyone was accepted into even this depraved society. The border-line case, who wanted to retain his shirt, or any possession whatsoever, would remain a drifter between the decent and the damned. Only when he had reached rock-bottom and was prepared to sleep naked on a stone floor or wooden deck was he admitted and recognised as a member of a class which had its own distinctive name, according to the place of imprisonment; *Les Kaiserlics*, *Les Misérables*, Rough Alleys and, as we shall see, other descriptive titles.

On the hulks, and in a number of the depots, members of the lowest strata of prisoner of war society were known as *Les Raffalés* – 'those under the weather' or 'the ship-wrecked'. At Portchester Castle they lived in the upper storey of the Tower, in complete nudity, the whole community possessing only a couple of suits of ragged clothing; reserved for the use of the scavengers who, by daily rota, rummaged through the daily waste.

There is no shortage of evidence of *Raffalés* on the hulks. When Louis Garneray first arrived as a prisoner on the *Prothée* hulk at Portsmouth, he soon learned of these men and their ways, from the old hands on board. Quartermaster Bertaud, who had experienced four different hulks in two years, told Garneray that on one of them the *Raffalés* numbered two hundred and that the *Prothée*, too, had its fair share. He described them as a 'mangy lot, with neither breeches, coat or shirt,' avoided by the other prisoners and quartered apart like wild animals. Some had a blanket with a hole cut in the centre, which they wore, poncho-like, at evening roll-call. Those who lacked even this small concession to decency, sometimes clubbed together to hire a covering, and presented on deck the pathetically comic spectacle of three men inside a single blanket. The hiring charge was a copper or two, paid in food from the next day's ration, before most of it was fed to the gaming tables or the grasping paw of the 'broker'.

Their destitution could not be exaggerated. They lived off the scraps thrown away by other prisoners such as potato peelings, cabbage stalks and fish heads. Even some of these disgusting items were used to pit as stakes in the gambling amongst themselves. Yet not all *Raffalès* were broken gamblers. It is amazing to learn that there were men of good education and family, who adopted this miserable way of life through perverse choice rather than by necessity. These were men of mystery to the other prisoners. One of them told Garneray, 'You'd never believe it, but there are people who actually *want* to join this tribe. But it is not that easy to get in. Anyone who wants to, begins by selling all his possessions and with the cash he is expected to treat all the *Raffalès* to a feast of bread and beer. Then he is given a large stone to serve as a pillow.'

The Baron de Bonnefoux, who was sent to the *Bahama* hulk at Chatham after breaking his parole at Odiham, saw how they spent their nights. They slept on the upper deck, packed side by side like sardines, to preserve body warmth and all facing in the same direction. At midnight the order was given, *'Par le flanc droit!'* and all turned to the right. At three in the morning came, *'Pare a virer!'* – 'prepare to tack' – and all rolled over to their left.

By day their time was spent in an endless search for anything which might be accepted as a gambling stake. The other prisoners kept well out of their way, for scrounging, stealing and extortion by intimidation was considered fair and normal, so long as the victim was not one of their brotherhood. Yet among themselves they lived according to some sort of code of honour. The rules were enforced by an elected 'Chief' or 'King', whose word was law, and woe betide the down-and-out who was brought before the court of rough justice over which he presided. The guilty offender was lucky if he got away with a mere flogging or beating; for if the offence was serious enough a sentence of death was not beyond his power.

One can imagine the roughness and toughness and brute strength of the character chosen to lead a community where 'a live rat was considered a gargantuan feast'. He alone among his naked subjects was clothed, clad, as befitted his position as their king, in a weird assortment of home-made 'regal' garments and attended by a drummer, whose beat announced his presence or called his people together.

It is harder to imagine that there could have been prisoners of a class even lower than the *Raffalès*, yet within their society there was one step even further down the hill. These were the men who had completely given up the fight against the ever-present louse and were considered lousy even by the standards of their well-bitten brethren. They were known as the *Manteaux Impériaux*, as the lice which adorned their roll-call ponchos were likened to the thousands of bees embroidered upon Napoleon's Imperial Mantle.

Many of the *Raffalès* of the hulks had been members of similar segregated groups ashore, where their unreformed character made it necessary to transfer them to the smaller and tougher prisons afloat. At Norman Cross in Huntingdonshire, they were known as *Les Misérables,* not only among their own kind and other prisoners of war, but in contemporary official documents and reports to the Transport Board. Soon after Norman Cross opened its gates in 1797, gambling and 'brokering' began to infect the depot. By the end of the eighteenth century many hundreds of victims of the passion could be picked out from the normal prisoners by their emaciated appearance and their lack of apparel. Their home at Norman Cross was the appropriately numbered Block 13, behind the hospital *casernes*. Whether the siting of their ill-smelling abode was fortuitous or the result of official strategy, it was certainly convenient. Illness and death were constant visitors to the inhabitants of the house with the unlucky number.

Unlike the *Raffalès* of the hulks, *Les Misérables* were not so much an organised society as a crowding together of rejected men. For one thing, many of them retained their hammocks – although most would have been able to enjoy this comfort only by renting from the 'broker'. Organised or not, their suffering was as great here as elsewhere, and the authorities were likewise at a loss. We have seen that reclothing was no answer – all stakeable articles disappeared in a few days. Sheer numbers in the great depots made it impossible to watch over each down-and-out to see that his daily ration was eaten rather than staked – and the punishments of detected usurers had no lasting effect.

All efforts to rehabilitate them within the depot failed. Their numbers were only kept down by the dispatching of batches of incorrigibles to the prison ships – or the inclusion of troublesome *Misérables* among invalids repatriated to a probably ungrateful France.

Winter was awaited with a dread almost as great in the hearts of the authorities and the depot hospital staff, as in those of the unprotected and undernourished inhabitants of Block 13. Cold and epidemics which periodically attacked the depots, carried off great numbers of these unclad and starving delinquents. Dr T. J. Walker, in his researches of the Norman Cross Depot, found among a tragic pile of death certificates a pencilled note, dated the 14th June, 1800. It was written by the depot surgeon for the attention of the Agent, and warned of the consequences if more of *Les Misérables* were not transferred or sent home before the worst of the winter weather struck the camp. It would seem that long experience and unappreciated help had killed any sympathy which he may once have had for his feckless patients. Perhaps he was less concerned with their continued existence than that they might die on his hands. Nevertheless, there was wisdom in his warning, as the next few months were to show. The note read:

> 'You see, my dear Sir, since our selection of the invalids, and the benefit of warm weather, we have had but one death in ten days.
> 'If another batch of these vagabonds, who by their conduct defy all the benefits the Benevolence of this country bestows upon them, were to be sent away in September next, we might expect a great benefit from it in the winter, for to a certainty all these blackguards will die in the winter.
> 'Compare sixty a week with one in ten days.'

Five months later, in November, 1800, his fears became a reality. A terrible epidemic, of what was probably enteric fever, struck Norman Cross. During the following six months 1,020 prisoners died, the heaviest mortality being among *Les Misérables*; many of whom breathed their last in their rented hammocks, before space could be found for them in the overcrowded Hospital Block. On hundreds of the certificates which recorded the fatalities of that terrible period, the entry 'Block 13' stands out like a death's-head. The cause of death beside the name was usually entered as 'Debility', often with the additional note: 'This prisoner had sold his Clothes and Rations.'

One might expect that the trail of illness and death left by winter and epidemics would have had a reforming influence on the survivors, but few who had taken the reckless gamble with existence itself had spirit enough to face the uphill struggle to self-respect. In the case of the French, gambling was perhaps more a disease than an addiction. Despite the human wreckage which disgraced the corners of all our prisons, and shrieked a warning to the newcomer, the ranks of the outcasts were never short of new membership.

The Treaty of Amiens in the Spring of 1802, brought a brief respite, when all the hulks and depots in Britain were cleared of most of their inmates; but within a few months of the recommencement of hostilities in May, 1803, it was as though they had never left and the tribes of the naked and starving down-and-outs were once again in evidence.

May, 1809, saw the opening of the great new depot of Dartmoor, specially built to cope with the ever-increasing numbers of prisoners of war flooding into this country. Moreover, by the end of that same year, gambling, 'brokering', poverty and segregation had created a deadbeat fraternity more organised and tougher than any of its predecessors. In Dartmoor the full-time gamblers and troublemakers were known as *Les Minables*, but this was a general term covering all who made gambling their way of life. The outcast losers were derisively named *Les Kaiserlics* by their luckier or more professional fellows, and by the non-playing prisoners in the depot. However, their chosen title and the name they gloried in was *Les Romains*. Their place of banishment was the cock-loft of each of the casernes within the depot and, in keeping with their name, they called their home *Le Capitole*.

The almost incredible tale of the 'Romans', as the British called them, was told by Basil Thomson, one time Governor of Dartmoor, in his history of that depot. I repeat it here, almost in his words, but omitting those passages where the story of *Les Romains* is so similar to that of their prototypes at Norman Cross and on the hulks as to be repetitious.

As the numbers in the cock-lofts grew, the 'Romans' began to feel a pride in their isolation and to persuade themselves that they had come to it by their own choice. In imitation of the floors below, where a *'Commissaire'* was chosen by public election and implicitly obeyed, they elected some genial, devil-may-care rascal to be their 'General', who held office only because he never attempted to enforce decency or order over his community. At the end of the first six months the number of admitted 'Romans' was about two hundred and fifty, and in later years it exceeded five hundred, although precise membership figures were always fluctuating. Like similar prison societies, the proceeds from the sale of their few possessions was used to purchase tobacco for the community. The communism was complete, among the whole five hundred there was no kind of private property.

In the *Capitole* itself, everyone lived in a state of nudity and slept naked on the concrete floor, except for the one hammock which was for the exclusive use of the 'General', who slept in the middle and allocated berths to his constituents. So a rough sort of discipline was maintained, for whereas a great number of men could have slept with a minimum of discomfort in three tiers of hammocks, the actual floor space was insufficient for much more than a third of that number of bodies placed side by side without indecent crowding.

At night the *Capitole* must have presented an extraordinary sight. The floor was carpeted with nude bodies all facing the same way, so closely packed together that it was impossible to get a foot between them. A turning routine was obeyed, similar to that described by Baron de Bonnefoux on the *Bahama* hulk. At nightfall the 'General' shouted, 'Fall in!' and the men ranged themselves in two lines facing one another. At a second word of command, alternate files took two paces to the front and rear and closed inward, and at the word *'Bas'* they all lay down on their right sides. At intervals during the night the 'General' would cry *'Pare a Viser'* (Attention.*), 'A Dieu, Va.'* and they would all turn over.

Pride was not a failing of which they could be accused. In all the alleys between the tiers of hammocks on the 'decent' floors below, there were always 'Romans' lurking. If a man was peeling potatoes a dozen of these derelicts would be round him in a moment to beg for the peel; they would form a ring round every mess bucket, like hungry dogs. They watched every eater in the hope that he would throw away a morsel of gristle, fighting over every scrap and bone.

Sometimes the continual state of starvation and cold was too much for the constitution of a 'Roman', and he would be carried off to the prison hospital to die, but generally the bodies of the 'Romans' acquired a toughness and resistance which seemed immune from epidemic diseases.

On the 15th, August, 1809, a few hundred 'Romans' obtained permission to pay a sort of state visit to No.6 Prison, which was something of a treat. At the head of the procession strode the 'General', clad in a sparkling uniform of blankets embroidered with straw which looked like gold lace at a distance. This straw-lacework would almost certainly have been very convincing and of excellent craftsmanship – (see illustrations in Chapter 4, THE STRAW WORKERS). Like the *Raffalès* they had a common store of filthy rags of clothing, which could be doled out for scavenging and on 'social' occasions, and also an odds-and-ends assortment of musical instruments. Behind the 'General' came the band: twenty grotesque vagabonds blowing flageolets and trumpets, and beating iron kettles and platters. The ragged battalion marched in column of fours along the grass between the grilles and the boundary walls wearing no more than a breech clout.

Thomson tells how all was going well and everyone was enjoying the occasion, when a rat chanced to run out from the cook-house. This was too much for them. Breaking rank, they chased the rat back into the kitchen, where the most agile cornered and caught it. After scuffling to keep possession from his neighbours, he tore it to pieces with his teeth and ate it raw. The rest, with whetted appetites, made matters worse by stealing the store of loaves and a general looting began. The guard was called out and the soldiers marched into the mêlée with fixed bayonets, but were immediately hemmed in by the almost naked men. They were soon disarmed and, amidst laughter and general merriment, were marched off towards the main gate, to shouts of *Vive l'Empereur.* At the gate they were met by Captain Cotgrave R.N., the Governor, who had hurried there at the head of strong reinforcements.

The 'General' halted his men and delivered a mock heroic speech to the Governor: 'Sir', he said, striking a theatrical pose, 'we are directing our steps to your house to hand over to your care our prisoners and their arms. This is only a little incidental joke as far as your soldiers are concerned, who are now docile as sheep. We now beg you to order double rations to be issued as a reward for our gallantry, and also to make good the breach we have just made in the provisions of our honourable hosts.'

Captain Cotgrave was a good and sensible enough officer not to exaggerate the seriousness of the occurrence; but nor did he issue double rations. The 'General' spent the next eight days in the cachot for his escapade – on reduced rations – and his troops were driven back to the *Capitole* with blows from the flats of muskets. For a long time after that the life of the soldiers was made miserable with banter and taunts, and they would bring their bayonets down to the charge whenever a prisoner feigned to approach them.

Just as amongst the dead-beat *Raffalès* there were men of education and substance, so, among the *Romains* there were young men of good family who received regular remittances from their friends in France. When the quarterly draft arrived the recipient would borrow clothes in which to collect the money from the Agent's office. Then he would return with cash in hand to the 'General', handing over £1 to be spent on tobacco and potatoes for the community. He might then take his leave, clothe himself in style and settle down once more on one of the other floors as a civilised human being. In most cases no more than a fortnight would pass before his fortune of twenty-five Louis or so, would have melted away at the gaming tables; clothes and bedding followed and the prodigal would slink back to his old associates, who would greet him with a boisterous welcome.

During the brief periods when the profligate was clothed and in his right mind, many efforts were made by normal prisoners to restrain him from ruin; but either the gambling or a natural distaste for restraint always proved too strong. It seems that no instance of permanent reclamation is recorded and yet it was often otherwise when the 'Romans' were restored to liberty. One would think that such men – who had become used to filth, vermin, hunger and nakedness – had permanently cut themselves off from civilised society, and that their story would probably end in the slums or stews of Paris. That that is not always the case is, perhaps, the strangest part of this social phenomenon. In August, 1846, one of the highest administrative posts under Louis-Philippe was filled by a man of great ability. Yet he, too, had been a 'Roman', and there must have been many in France who knew that the breast then plastered with decorations had once been bare to Dartmoor's icy winds.

In 1844 there was a successful merchant in Paris who used to boast to the point of boredom, with stories of the leading part he had taken in the internal affairs of the war prison at Dartmoor. By that date he had quite forgotten that his 'leading part' was an unerring nose for fish-offal in the garbage heaps!

As their numbers grew, from being objects of commiseration and pity, the 'Romans' came to be a threat and a terror to the captive community. Theft, pillage, stabbings and the darkest forms of vice were practised among them almost openly. Unwashed and swarming with vermin they stalked from prison to prison, begging, scavenging, quarrelling, pilfering from the provision carts and stoning anyone who interfered with them. A story has been told, and a horrible one, of what happened when the Dartmoor bakery burned down on the 8th October, 1812. It was arranged with one of the food contractors to send in bread from outside until the bakery could be restored. When it arrived it was so substandard that the prisoners refused to eat it, so the whole depot went without food for twenty-four hours.

The 'Romans' raked among the prison offal heaps as usual and when the two-horse garbage wagon came to remove the rubbish, they resented the carting away of their larder. In the course of the dispute with the driver, some of these famished wretches attacked the horses with knives, killed them and some began eating from the carcasses on the spot. The horror of this sickening spectacle was too much for the stomachs of the other prisoners, who helped to drive them off.

Occasionally the administration overcame their reluctance to help men who would not help themselves, and made an attempt to reclothe them. In April, 1813, fourteen who were entitled to a fresh issue of prison clothing were caught and scrubbed from head to foot in the bath house. Their filthy rags were confiscated and they were properly kitted out, but by the very next day they had sold every garment for gambling money, and they were to be seen back in the yards wearing only the threadbare blanket or poncho common to the tenants of the *Capitole.*

Another, and different, approach had been tried in 1812. All the 'Romans' were banished to No.4 Prison, and in order to keep them from annoying their fellow prisoners, walls were built which separated No.4 and its yard from the rest of the casernes. The idea was that if all who were destitute were put together, those who had clothes, bedding or food to sell would be unable to find purchasers. Although new hammocks and garments were contributed by charitable prisoners, as well as Government issues, they still somehow managed to sell them outside the bounds of No.4 Prison.

Serious crime in the depots could safely be left for the prisoners themselves to punish, but the inhuman traffic between gambler and 'broker' was the business of nobody but the persons who indulged in it – at least in the eyes of the captives. Unquestionably, the greatest evil which Captain Cosgrave had to face was the sale of rations. Sometimes the hopeless losers would sit down to starve or forestall their end by hanging themselves from the hammock stanchions, rather than be taken to the infirmary to die. In February, 1813, very much to their surprise, the Captain clapped a few of the most notorious of the food-buying 'brokers' into the Black Hole, and kept them there for ten days on two-thirds allowance. To their remonstrances, Captain Cosgrave made the following reply in the form of a notice:-

TO THE PRISONERS IN THE CACHOT
FOR PURCHASING PROVISIONS.

'The Orders to put you on short allowance from the Commissioners of His Majesty's Transport Board is for purchasing the provisions of your fellow prisoners, by which means numbers have died for want of food, and the hospital is filled with sick not likely to recover.

'The number of deaths occasioned by this inhuman practice occasions considerable expense to the Government, not only in coffins, but the hospital filled with these poor unhappy wretches so far reduced from want of food that they linger a considerable time in the hospital at the Government's expense, and then fall victim to the cruelty of those who have purchased their provisions to the disgrace of Christians and whatever nations they belong to. The testimony of your countrymen and the surgeons prove the fact.'

But it was all to no purpose and in the following month we find him appealing to the whole body of prisoners in Dartmoor:

NOTICE TO THE PRISONERS IN GENERAL

'The infamous and horrible practice of a certain number of prisoners who buy the provisions of some evil-conducted and unfortunate of their fellow-countrymen, thereby tearing away from them the only means of existence they possess, forces me to forewarn the whole of the prisoners that on the first appearance of a recurrence of this odious and abominable practice I shall, without any exception, prevent any person from keeping shops in the prison, and will stop the market.

'As it would be entirely against my wishes and inclination to have recourse to these violent measures, I strongly request of all well-conducted of the prisoners to use all their exertions to put a stop thereto.'

Therefore, there were short closures of the markets from time to time, but the Governor was faced with even more troubles after the Americans were added to the prison population on the Moor. In July, 1813, the 'Romans' attacked their Yankee allies, and so began moves which led to their extradition from their Capitole later in that year. Immediately after the attack, they were still further isolated by being confined to a small yard on the southern side of No.4.

For more than four years they had skulked about the yards by day, exposed to the damp fogs of summer and the icy winds of winter, and had huddled at night upon a wet and filthy stone floor. They had subsisted half-starved upon garbage until the wind seemed to blow through their skeletal ribs; had ignored every elemental law of sanitation and hygiene. And yet, strange to relate, every succeeding epidemic passed them by (how different from the *Misérables* at Norman Cross) and it was notorious throughout the prison that sickness – other than through starvation – was almost unknown among the 'Romans'.

By the time General Stevenson and Mr Hawker held their inquiry on the occurrences in 1813, the scandal of the 'Romans' and their way of life was so great that the principal recommendation of the Commission was 'that the prisoners calling themselves "Romans" should be removed and compelled to live like human beings in some place where they could be kept under strict surveillance. Therefore, on the 16th October, 1813, a scarecrow battalion of four hundred and thirty-six 'Romans' was mustered at the main gate, decently clothed, and marched under a strong escort to a prison hulk at Plymouth, where they were controlled by rigid discipline until the peace.

We have learned, then, that Prison No.4. at Dartmoor was walled around and isolated, not only in an attempt to protect its inhabitants from their own self-destroying habits, but for the sake of well-conducted prisoners in other parts of the depot, who might be troubled or contaminated by the contact. It says something of the regard which the Admiralty felt for our captive transatlantic cousins that, when the first Americans arrived at Dartmoor early in 1813, No.4. should have been chosen as a fit place to house them.

At that time some nine hundred 'Romans' were quartered in the upper floors of the isolated prison, and the Americans were shocked and resentful when they saw the type of men whose prison they were expected to share. This antipathy was a two-sided feeling, and the association lasted only a few months, ending in the Romano-American feud which made it absolutely necessary to separate the two peoples.

However, as time went by and the numbers of American prisoners in Dartmoor increased, a sort of natural selection provided them with an analogue of *Les Romains*, made up of men of their own nationality. Once again, gaming was at the bottom of it, but any American who lost the respect of his companions, through violence, crime or filthy habits, was shouldered out and dubbed a 'Rough Alley'. The society of the 'Rough Alleys' was less organised than the French 'Romans' and never quite reached the depths of depravity achieved by the Frenchmen. It has been said that whilst the 'Romans' lived like beasts, they were not fierce beasts, and that the 'Rough Alleys', less bestial in their habits, revelled more in crime and violence.

The name given to, or chosen by, this trouble-seeking band of American dead-beats is interesting in itself: the American memoirist, Josiah Cobb, called them 'Rough Alleys', whilst his countryman, Waterhouse, styles them 'Rough Allies'. A. J. Rhodes, in his *'Dartmoor Prison'* suggests that the name may have come from an earlier form of the present-day 'Rough houses'. Francis Abell wrote of the 'inmates of the Rough Alleys', as though they took their name from their habitat. However, remembering that most of the Americans had been prisoners on the hulks before being transferred to Dartmoor, I am of the opinion that the phonetic similarity of the French *'Raffalès'* and the American 'Rough Alleys' is too close to be coincidental.

I am less sure of another of my pet theories: the possibility that the name *'Raffalès'* itself may have derived from that of one of our earliest hulks, the old *San Rafael* at Plymouth, on which both French and Americans prisoners were confined during the War of Independence.

When the Americans were allowed into the other yards of the prison, they found the French professionals waiting for them. Every form of gambling, from 'penny sweat-cloth' to the more sophisticated tables run by the continental sharks, took its toll among the Yankee sailor-pigeons. Gambling certainly became an addiction with a great many Americans, but another addiction as great or greater, led many down the road to 'Rough Alley' membership, their craving for tobacco. Many a 'Rough Alley' would sell his shirt or beef ration to a Frenchman, in order to purchase a plug of chewing-tobacco.

Benjamin Waterhouse, who arrived at Dartmoor from the hulks towards the end of the war, was distressed to find that many of his compatriots had sunk so low. He says:

'In my opinion, they are as great villains as could be collected in the United States. They seem to have little principle and as little humanity, and many of them are given to every vice. I am wearied out with such lawless conduct.

'The Rough Alleys organised themselves into a company of plunderers. I have seen them run from their sleeping berths, in which they spend nearly their whole time, and plunder the little shop-keepers [who traded in the inner markets] and secret them in their beds. These gangs or mobs of robbers were a scandal to the American character, and strongly reprobated by every man of honour in the prisons.'

Although their loot, once converted into cash, would soon disappear into the coffers of the casino proprietors, it is obvious that the 'Rough Alleys' were more a gang of thugs and criminals. Unlike the desperate and weak-willed losers, to be found in all the depots and hulks, who were driven into pauper societies – *Les Misérables*, *Les Kaiserlics* or any of the other groups known under the general term *Les Minables* – the 'brokers' must have found the 'Rough Alleys' harder customers to deal with.

At the first sign of trouble in the depot, the 'Rough Alleys' would rouse themselves from their normal lethargy and hurry to the spot. Every fight or quarrel they claimed as their own and joined in enthusiastically, even when they were not connected with it, or even knowing its cause. The first to spot discord of any sort would raise the cry 'Keno!' which brought his companions scurrying from their beds, or interrupted their pokings through the garbage heaps. Soon a mob of dirty, ragged, toughs, shouting 'Keno!' as their war-cry, would be rushing towards the scene of disorder, each eager to land the first blow.

The 'KENO' adopted by the 'Rough Alleys' as their watchword and alarm call, was the name of the most popular, and least vicious, of all the gambling games within the prisons. Not all games of chance were ruinous and there were many prisoners who, whilst not total abstainers from all forms of gambling, kept their heads and only placed the occasional bet by way of entertainment and amusement.

It can be supposed that, then as now, almost everyone would have enjoyed the occasional flutter and, in moderation, it would have provided a little hope and excitement in the not very hopeful or exciting world of the prisoner of war camp. The prisoner who knew when to stop, but invested a few pence in the possibility of proving to himself that his luck was not completely dead, would at least be displaying a streak of optimism which could only do him good.

Americans in this category of punter usually patronised the Keno tables, where a numbers game was played in much the same way as Bingo is today, or the 'Housey-housey' of our servicemen in World War II. Joshua Cobb says it was the cause of the poverty of the Rough Alleys, but I doubt this, as the stakes were so small that only the man already on the brink could have suffered – and a hardened gambler would have found it a slow and feeble game when compared to the excitement of *Vingt-un* and the French-run tables. The Keno tables were set up to accommodate anything up to thirty players at a session and were open for play every evening of the week except Sunday. The Sabbath was observed by all decent American prisoners, as religiously as it would have been at home and, for them, gambling was definitely out on that day. Compared with most games involving stakes, it would take a great deal of time and patience to go broke at Keno. The numbered cards were one penny each and the callers took great pride in their individual techniques for calling the numbers, which tended to lengthen out each session.

There was little scope for sharp practice and although any game can be rigged, it is probable that these were run straight. All the stakes went into a kitty which, after the caller – who was usually the proprietor of the table – had taken his percentage, went to the lucky player who had the Keno, or winning card. The game was so popular that the tables were usually crowded long before play commenced. Play seldom started before darkness had fallen, and by then the scene had taken on something of the atmosphere of the fairground. The proprietors, who did quite well for themselves from the aggregation of small rake-offs from each game, ploughed back some of their profits into the business in the form of an abundance of candlelight to illuminate their pitches.

The games went on all night, the hoarse caller seldom crying his last number before dawn broke. Many a prisoner preferred to while away the night in this fashion, whether as player or spectator, rather than face the foetid atmosphere of his overcrowded sleeping place. Also, the wandering sellers of 'hot plum gudgeons' and drinks who peddled their wares from table to table could be counted on to work a night shift.

The most patronised table in the whole of Dartmoor was that which was established in the cock-loft of No.5. Prison. It was run by an extraordinary character who never failed to entertain his patrons with his rhyming calls, which he boasted never to repeat twice over. His antics and his comical appearance also added to the fun. His eyebrows were so long and bushy, that it was said that his eyes could only be detected when, for a brief instant at the end of each game, he raised his brows to reveal a twinkle as he raked in his share of the kitty.

It may be true that the caller never repeated one of his sets of rhymes – but we can do so here. In 1813, the 'Green Hand' jotted it down, and noted how, enjoining silence before he would commence his calls, he would plunge his hand into the bag and withdraw the first number, displaying it to the players with a wide sweep of his hand, to show that there was no deceit. There is such a familiar ring about his calling, that it would not be surprising to find 'Legs Eleven', 'Top of the House' or 'Doctor's Orders', occurring in his lines:

NOW SILENCE, Gentles, let us be,
Nor wink, nor speak, nor cough, not any:
Naught can ye win – no not a baubee,
Who thinks aloud – no not a penny.

Watch. We begin with **Thirty-four** -
Fegs. **Forty-six** is summat more.
If **Seventeen's** a number low,
Lower still is number **Two.**

Egad. Look sharp. for **Ninety-eight**
Is high, yet **Seven** will set it straight.
Don't hold your breaths. 'tis **forty-nine** –
Thirty is a choice of mine.

Says **Sixty** 'I'll a courting go'
Said **Sixteen**, 'Yes – you don't, I know.'

That skulking **Six** poked out his nose,
Quick slipped by **Ten**, and said 'Here goes.'
It's **Twelve** o'clock, ah me, O, whew.
Here's **Fifteen** sits all in a stew.

Can **Ninety-nine** on nothing stand?
About as much as **Eleven** can bend.

'O, wath's th' mather?' said **Twenty-six**,
Lisped **Eight**, 'I'm in a thorry fixth'

'What **Sixty-four** are you about?'
'Me says **Nineteen**, 'Coming out.'
Says **Thirty-three** 'I'se crooked legs.'
Says **Eighty-five**, 'I has no pegs.'

Here's **Fifty-four**, drunk as a Jew
Hiccups **Thirteen,** 'and so are you.'
This game is long – **Fourteen** is tired –
Grey **Ninety** says, 'You vas not hired.'

Pshaw. Let that wriggling crooked **Three**
Just take **One** look, stand straight like me.
Pray, how can you **Four** eat gum elas-
Tic? much, says **Nine**, as you would gas.

By gulping **Twenty** times, and then –
Just try you **Fifty** gulps again.
Twins. **Twenty-two**, or I'm no sin-
Ner – **Sixty-six** looks very prim.

Old square toes, **Fourty-four** can't come
It over **Twenty-five** I vum.
Handcuffs and cramps. Here's **Eighty-eight** -
'Fie, shame.' cries **Five**, 'These crooks I hate.'

Old **Hundred** is a round one, ye know,
But rounder still is **Naught**, that's *KENO!*

Gambling and its attendant suffering was never successfully controlled by governors, commissioners, agents or government orders anywhere in the country, at least not for long. It only ended with the end of wars, when prisoners both good and bad, returned to their homelands. As we have seen, some who had been regarded as untouchables and had lived off the rubbish and waste of their war-time home, made good in later years, achieving prosperity and even positions of honour. However, these must have been exceptional men, for no man who had known the life of a *Raffale, Misérable, Romain, Kaiserlic* or 'Rough Alley', could have survived without some permanent scar, however deeply hidden. Also, what of the professional gamblers who had lived so well at the expense and pain of their unlucky brothers?

We can bet that the 'brokers' did well for themselves. However, it is strange to relate that, whereas many prisoners who had conscientiously engaged themselves in some sort of industry or profitable craft, often took out with them what would have been small fortunes by the values of the times, few of the pros had much money at the time of their release. Perhaps the explanation is, after all, a simple one. During their successful careers in the small worlds of the prisons, the professional gamesters had wanted for nothing which money could buy within its walls – or brought in from the outside. We read eye-witness accounts of the gambling lords sitting down to banquets of goose, perch and sucking-pig and fine wines, supplied by the market caterers. Meals which cost three shillings a head – enough to keep a frugal captive for a couple of weeks – whilst many of their victims in the darker corners of the depots starved to the point of death.

Money so easily come by was probably as recklessly spent and, confident in their nefarious skills, they could look forward to the bigger world outside – where even bigger fish were waiting to be hooked.

NOTES:

Woodes Rogers : *A Cruising Voyage Round the World.*

Nov. 12.[1709]   Yesterday Afternoon, all our Ships Company sign'd the before-mention'd Agreement, finally to settle Plunder. At the same time we sign'd another Agreement, to prevent gaming and wagering: some of our Crews having already lost most of their Clothes, and what else they could make away with. To prevent those loose and dissolute Courses, we sign'd both Agreements as follows.

The Agreement to Prevent Gaming as follows.

'WE the Ship's Company belonging to the Ship *Duke* now in the South Seas, being Adventurers so far to improve our Fortunes in a private Man of War, under the Command of Capt. Woodes Rogers, who has a lawful Commission from his Royal Highness Prince George of Denmark, and considering the apparent Hazard of our Lives in these Remote parts; do mutually agree to prevent the growing Evil now arising amongst us, occasion'd by frequent Gaming, Wagering, and abetting at others Gaming, so that some by chance might thus too slightly get Possession of what his Fellow-Adventurers have dangerously and painfully earn'd. To prevent this intolerable Abuse, we shall forebear and utterly detest all Practices of this kind for the future during the whole Voyage, till our safe Arrival in Great Britain, where good Laws of this kind take place, and designing effectually to confirm this our Desire and Agreement.

'We do jointly remit all sort of Notes of Hand, Contracts, Bills or Obligations of any kind whatsoever, that shall any ways pass, directly or indirectly, sign'd by either of us after the Date hereof, provided that the Sum in each Note be for Gaming, Wagering or Abetting any way whatsoever by any of us; and to prevent our being misled for the future, all manner of Obligations of this kind, and for this Consideration, shall be wholly invalid, and unlawful here, and in Great Britain or Ireland; And thoroughly to secure this Method, we farther jointly agree, that no Debt from this Time forward shall be lawfully contracted from Man to Man amongst us, unless by the Commanders Attestation, and enter'd on the Ship's Book, it shall appear done publickly and justly to prevent each others Frauds being coniv'd at amongst us; and that none of us may fraudulently do ill things of this kind for the future, and make a Pretence at Ignorance. We have all publickly and voluntarily set out Hands, desiring the true Intent and Meaning hereof may take place without the least Evasion, it being (as we very well know) for our common Interest and publick good, that not one of us employ'd on this dangerous and remote Undertaking, might be so unhappy to arrive at this wish'd for Country and Habitation poor and dejected: And being thoroughly sensible of the Necessity of this Agreement, we have set our Hands.

Sign'd by
all the Officers and Men in each Ship in sight of California, Nov.11. 1709.'

'THE JOURNAL OF JOSEPH VALPEY Jnr OF SALEM.'

This simple, badly spelled, but charming little anti-gambling poem is taken from Valpey's unbound, pocket-sized, *'Journal'*, which was treasured by his family and published as a limited edition of 300 copies by a descendant in 1922.

The American Joseph Valpey, was captured when the 11-gun privateer *Herald* struck to two British frigates, the *Armide* and the *Endymion* in August 1814. Joseph was one of the 'one Hundred and twenty Brisk young Men' who set out 'for to try our Luck and fortune' in the *Herald*, and the four-month cruise which preceded their capture was indeed fortunate, taking almost twenty prizes – English, Irish, Portuguese, Russian and Spanish. The prisoners arrived in England in October, and Joseph's entry in his journal is a fine example of his prose style, completely devoid of punctuation and an indiscriminate use of capital letters:

' …on the thirty first of October we was Landed in plymouth and Marched to dartmoor it being about sixteen Miles in the Country and the Roads Exceeding bad and the Most was Without shoes and stockings and the Soldiers pricking us up with there Bayonets thus we poor half Starv'd prisoners was Marched in Rain from seven in the Morning until half past Eight in the Evening without having one Morsel to eat cast into a dark Cold and Wet Prison'

THE FRUITS OF GAMBLING'S

1

Come fellow prisoner's one and all
To reason lend an ear
To keep up Gambling as you do
Your ruined men its clear

2

For reason first should Beasley hear*
How we the money use'd
Hed say the prisoner's was to Blame
they that the state abused

3

The money that's sent was for intent
To help us in this place
In stead of which you all must see
It clothes you in disgrace

4

For should you ask for any more
As each man ought to do
Then would your Injured Country say
No money more for you

5

For reason why when i advance
To you this trifling sum
You keep up gambling Night and day
Which hurts you every one

6

Yet a few it help's – a little while
But mark his Latter end
His Bank get's broke, his dunnage sold
This Man's without a Friend

7

Then stealing next is there intent
Which often time's you see
Then be seized up like any dog
And flogged he must be

8

This story's told when he gets home
Unto his Friend's or wife
This man's dispised by them – he Loved
Therefore he cannot value Life

9

To now avoid those Ill's I'v stated
From Gambling now refrain
Then you'll be helped and respected
Should you ever get home again

---

* Reuben Beasley was the Agent for the American P.O.Ws in England, who issued their allowances.

Chapter Ten

The Entertainers

'Our fiddler did in triumph fetch
His fiddle from aboard a ketch
Called the *Portsmouth*, and did play
Oft times to pass the time away.
On forecastle we dance the Hay;
Sometimes dance nothing, only hop about,
It for good dancing passes 'mongst the rout;
Yet on my word I have seen sailors
More nimble dance than any taylors.'

J. Balthorpe: *The Straights Voyage* 1671.

WHEREVER GREAT NUMBERS OF MEN ARE PLUCKED FROM THEIR natural environment and herded together in time of war – whether serving in armies or navies, or captured and in enemy hands – there will always be found some with sufficient enthusiasm and organising ability, who will get together to arrange the entertainment of their fellows.

Spectator sports such as football in some form or another, cricket[1] and other easy-to-organise ball games were common to every depot, however small; and wrestling and trials of strength were as fascinating for the onlooker as they were good for the participants. Singing and dancing, even without female partners, were of great importance in the free sailor's hard shipboard life, with the hornpipes and sea-shanties which lightened his work, and would have followed him into his hard life as a captive.

Music and the theatre have always had their place in the life of almost everyone, but the importance of such pleasures and distractions is increased beyond all measure when the performer or spectator is a prisoner of war. The production of a play or concert provides an outlet for a whole variety of talents and, for the audience, a brief but welcome respite from the contemplation of the misery of prison life.

It is to be expected that officers on parole, comparatively free men and often also free from money worries, would have made good provision for their own entertainment and amusement, but what is not generally known is that the inmates of the closed prisons had their groups of entertainers and that there were prisoner-built theatres within the walls of many of the depots. Of greater surprise is the fact that plays were performed, and theatres or stages existed. In that most unlikely of places – the prison hulk.

Whilst it is probable that from earliest times, war prisoners, wherever they were confined, would have arranged group diversions of one sort or another, the earliest reference I have found to an actual prisoner of war theatre, appears in *'Liverpool from 1775 to 1800'*, by Richard Brook. It tells us that 'among the amusements, some of the French prisoners here confined, performed plays in a small theatre contrived for that purpose within the walls, and in some instances they raised in a single night £50 for admission money.' Unless the '50' was a misprint for '5'– or there was more than one performance a day – I doubt that the box-office took as much as he says, even on a good night. The price of a ticket would not have been more than one shilling at the most, which means that their 'small' theatre would have had to house – apart from guards, 'compliment-aries', the players themselves and back-room boys – at least one thousand paying customers.

It might be supposed that these prisoner of war productions would have been amateurish, rough-and-ready affairs, akin to the 'sods' operas'[2] of our own Royal Navy, but this was by no means always the case. Among the thousands of conscripted foreign captives who flooded into the depots, there could be found a hundred and one different trades and professions. Musicians and actors, singers and dancers, writers, painters and carpenters, amateur or professional impresarios – in fact, all the know-how and talent necessary to put on a good show – and some of their shows were very good indeed. In one case, at least, the quality of management, decor and performance, excited the interest and patronage of the local civilian theatre-goers – and the indignation and complaint of the local British theatre managers. This prisoner of war theatre was established at the Portchester Castle Depot.

Two French prisoners of war, once confined at Portchester, have each left details and descriptions of that theatre in their memoirs. These men, Louis François Gille and St Aubin, must have found Portchester Castle a luxury after their previous experiences as captives. Both had been captured at Baylen and then sent to the ill-famed prison-island at Cabrera; Gille having previously spent some time on the horribly over-crowded No.27 hulk at Cadiz. Other prisoners at Portchester Castle at that time, 1810, had also arrived there from the Isle de Leon and Cabrera, where some of them had attempted to introduce a little brightness into the misery of those truly dreadful prison islands, by arranging and performing in amateur dramatic shows. Now, in Portchester Castle, they formed themselves into a professional group of actors and technicians. All that was needed was some sort of venue for their productions. They were extremely lucky in having as their Prisoner of War Agent, Commander William Patterson, who listened sympathetically when they requested facilities to build a theatre of their own. He fully approved the scheme and obtained for them the necessary permissions and materials to go ahead.

There was no shortage of expertise; among the company were a number of men who had had professional experience of the theatre in pre-war civilian life: There was M. Carre, who had held an important position in the Theatre Feydau, in Paris, and M. Corret of the Conservatoire, who now took charge of the orchestra of four violins, three clarinets, two horns, a cornet and an octave. Besides these executives there were, of course, any number of men who were available to help with the construction and decoration. The approved site was the lowest floor of the old Castle Keep, which had, with good reason, been empty for some time. It had, at one time, been used to house prisoners, but proved a lethally unhealthy spot and after an alarming number of prisoners had died there, its use as a place of confinement was discontinued. Under the direction of Carre, the prisoners soon converted this miserable hole into a playhouse capable of holding an audience of about three hundred people. There was adequate seating and they also added the refinement of a row of theatre boxes, some of which were reserved for the use of British visitors.

St Aubin names some of the Portchester Castle productions. There were comedies: 'Deux Gendres'; 'Les Folies Amoureuses'; 'Défiance et Malice'; 'La Tyran Domestique'. There were also tragedies: 'Mahomet'; 'Zaire'; 'Les Templiers'; and a play which St Aubin himself wrote, called 'L'Heureuse Étourderie'. These enterprising captives also staged concerts and vaudevilles – and even had a go at opera. When the original music was either unavailable or too expensive for their budget, Corret composed their own or re-composed the originals from memory. Among the most successful of the Portchester presentations was their version of 'The Barber of Seville'. Not Rossini's opera (which was not produced until 1816), but the play of that same name on which it was based, by the French playwright Pierre Augustin Beaumarchais. The play, with its twelve-piece backing orchestra, was said to have taken £12 on the opening night. From the outset the Portchester Castle Theatrical Company was a great success and soon gained popularity with visitors from Portsmouth and other towns in the area – a popularity which was later to bring about its downfall.

Louis François Gille, in his *'Memoirs d'un Conscrit de 1808'*, said that some new plays were sent from Paris and that the whole thing was such a success that many British theatre-goers from Portsmouth preferred the Castle productions to the offerings of the theatres in that town. He describes Carre's greatest triumph – his *'Féerie'* – for which Carre painted a backcloth view of Paris, which was generally considered a masterpiece. The word got round that the show was excellent and the seats reserved for the British visitors were always full. One British officer took his whole regiment, by special arrangement, to see the performance. This must have been a bonanza for the box-office; the tickets were one shilling each. The Portsmouth newspapers gave the show laudatory write-ups, and even suggested that the directors of the Portsmouth Theatre should pay a visit to the Castle to see how a theatre should be run. After searching through a few hundred yellowed news-sheets, I found the article which Gille mentions. The management of the local theatres took up the suggestion and came to see the show. After the performance they were very complimentary to both actors and organisers, but when, soon after, a Government Order arrived instructing that the prison theatre should be closed, it was quite natural that the managers should be blamed.

Both Gille and St Aubin state that the managers were the complainants, and perhaps they were, for they certainly lost some revenue to the unexpected foreign competition. However, it is more probable that the reason given in the Order was the true one: that a security risk was involved and that the uncontrolled association of prisoners and public would probably lead to escapes. Once again the ever-helpful Commander Patterson came to the aid of his captive charges and the prison theatre was given a conditional reprieve – it was allowed to continue as long as no British civilians were admitted. The box-office receipts were never the same again.

It is easy, at this distance in time, to feel over-sympathetic towards these men who had put on such a brave show in more senses than one, and had helped to brighten not only their own dull lives, but those of their fellow captives; but the ban on excessive intimacy between the prisoners of war and the civilian population was plain common-sense. One prisoner had already escaped dressed as an Englishman, and there are a number of instances where theatricals played an important part in escape plans. The French writer, Catel, tells an amusing story of an ingenious escape from Dartmoor, which owed its successful outcome to a prison stage performance. A play was specially written by the prison playwrights and entitled *'Le Capitaine Calonne et sa Dame'*. The main characters were based on a British Officer and his wife, and were carefully written up to appeal to their vanity. After reading the script, the couple were so flattered that they assisted with the production and fell in with the suggestion that they should lend the prisoner-actors the Captain's spare uniform, his wife supplying a gown and accessories for the 'lady'. The curtain was raised to a full house and the first two acts were very well received; but towards the end of the second act the 'Captain' and his 'Lady' had left the prison by the main gate, saluted by the sentries as they passed through. The story goes, that when the real Captain and his wife tried to leave, they experienced some difficulty at the gate, as they had already been booked out. The two prisoners got clear away and some days later they sent a parcel from Tavistock, which contained the borrowed costumes and a letter of thanks addressed to the Captain.

A Captain Havas, captured with the privateer vessel *Furet*, used an illicit visit to Portchester Castle theatre as a means to spy out the land, prior to making his successful getaway to France. He was at that time, 1809, a prisoner on the *San Antonio* hulk at

Portsmouth, having been transferred from the *Crown* prison ship following an attempted escape with the famous French escape-expert, Tom Souville. Havas had an attractive personality and a good knowledge of the English language, which helped him to get on well with the English officers. He became very friendly with the Commander of the *San Antonio*, who appointed him French teacher and interpreter aboard the vessel, but he cultivated a more intimate friendship with the Commander's wife – *'belle tout point, blonde, grande, svelte et gracieuse'*. This lady, who was either very stupid or had nerves of steel, took Havas ashore to Portchester Castle, where Racine's *'Phèdre'* was being performed. After the show they took a stroll through the countryside, the lady no doubt enjoying the company of her handsome and interesting companion – and he noting details of the local topography, which he afterwards employed to good effect.

Norman Cross Depot in Huntingdonshire had its theatre and Dartmoor in Devon more than one. The first theatre at Dartmoor was opened by the French, but towards the end of the Napoleonic War the Americans had not only playhouses, but a dancing school, a boxing academy and a glee club. The American prisoner, Josiah Cobb – better known as the 'Green Hand', whom Francis Abell calls the 'Greenhorn' – who spent five months in Dartmoor towards the very end of its period as a prisoner of war depot, has left a number of glimpses of life in the depot, and often mentions the entertainers. He tells us that the forthcoming attractions were promulgated by prisoner-announcers, or 'town-criers', who went round shouting the news, some in improvised verse. We even know the name of at least one of them, Old Davis, who, for the penny he charged for his services, made the rounds of the prison yards, blowing his bosun's pipe and delivering his extemporised lines. Better still, his announcement of a particular prize-fight was noted down, so we can hear him now:

'Know ye all, short or tall, great or small!
That Bob Starr and Shott Morgan
Are to settle the difference that is between them
Tomorrow morning at half past nine o'clock,
At the ball-alley, the usual place for these affairs!

And as Bob is a rare one,
And Shott is a dare one,
And the box is a fair one,
Great sport is expected.
So now come and see,
This chicamaree –

And know it is me! Old Davis! afflicted,
Who is crying this notice;
Although a little rounded in the shoulders,
Yet he's a r-r-r-ready old dog!'

The American theatre was set up behind canvas screens in the yard of No.5 *Caserne* and Josiah Cobb arrived there at a time when they were preparing for their next dramatic offering. The 'leading lady' was a seaman prisoner known as Blowsy or Blowsy Bet. Unlike another French 'heroine', Pierre Cheri, whom we shall meet later in this chapter, this little fellow was not chosen to play female roles through any beauty of countenance – a sabre cut across the American's cheek had put paid to at least half of any good looks he may once have possessed. Blowsy's chief qualification as female lead was the length of his hair, which he had sworn to let grow until he was released from captivity. Now he was arranging his long hair to hide the disfigured side of his face and making sure his trousers did not show below his skirts.

It would seem that they took their acting seriously, for Blowsy Bet was berating his leading man for making a right mess of the last performance, muffing his lines and making himself ridiculous before the audience. 'You lie, you lubberly cow, begging pardon for blaspheming,' replied the stage lover to his 'lady', 'I was applauded the whole time'. 'Green Hand' also remembered the treasurer, who looked after the ticket-office:

> '...who is known to be a little tricky at times; but yet a good-hearted joker, who lends his help behind the scenes, often takes a part when short-handed, can repair worn-out scenery, is handy with the brush, and has more than once, rather than the play should not proceed, or the [prisoner] public be disappointed, appeared in petticoats; yet withal, never making any extra charge in his salary account, for his multitudinous duties, meliorating, in no small degree, his slight delinquence in the ticket-office.'

There was yet another theatrical company in Dartmoor Depot. These shows took place in No.4 *Caserne*, which housed all the black prisoners after they had been separated from their white fellow Americans. This separation came about as the result of a petition drawn up by the latter and presented to the Transport Office. Here, in the cock-loft of No.4, the negro actors staged twice-weekly performances of heavy dramas and tragedies – and besides the theatre they had, like their white fellow-countrymen, schools of dancing, fencing and boxing. All this in one of the toughest and vilest parts of the prison. So any prisoner who had not lost his last penny at the gaming tables which abounded alongside these less dangerous diversions, might easily afford an evening at any of a whole variety of entertainments, whether he be continental or white or black American.

Benjamin Waterhouse, 'the Young Man of Massachusetts', when writing his memoirs in 1815, had vivid memories of the theatre in No.4 *Caserne*. He tells us that the gateways and sentry-boxes were plastered over with playbills, announcing:

'**OTHELLO**, for the first time, by Mr Robinson – **DESDEMONA**, by Mr Jones.'

He spent a lot of time at these performances, not because he appreciated the sincerity with which they approached such a difficult challenge, but to have a belly-laugh at their expense. Waterhouse was scurrilous in the extreme when speaking of his black fellows-in-arms, and I shall quote only those parts of his account which touch on their acting ability, or in his opinion, lack of it:-

> 'These blacks have been desirous of having their prison the centre of amusement. They act plays twice a week, and as far as close imitation of what they have seen and heard, and broad grimace, they are admirable, but they are, half the time, ignorant of the meaning of the words they utter...
>
> 'I seldom failed to attend these exhibitions, and must confess that I never before or since, or perhaps ever shall, laugh so heartily as at these troglodite dramas. Their acting was assuredly the most diverting beyond all comparison or example I ever saw. They would cut so many negroish capers in tragedy, grin and distort their countenances in such a variety of inhuman expressions, while they kept their bodies either stiff as so many stakes, or in a monkeyish wriggle and ever and anon such a baboon stare at Desdemona, whose face, neck and hands were covered with chalk and red paint, to make him look like a beautiful white lady was altogether, considering that they themselves were very serious, the most ludicrous exhibition of two-legged ridiculousness I ever witnessed.

'In the midst of my loud applause, I could not, when my sore side would allow me to articulate, help exclaiming – O! Shakespeare! Shakespeare! – O! Garrick! Garrick! – what would I not give (a despised American prisoner) could I raise you from the dead, that you might see the black consequences of your own transcendent geniuses. When Garrick rubbed himself over with burnt cork to make himself look like a Moor, or with lamp-black to resemble Mungo, it did pretty well; but for a negro man to cover his forehead, neck and hands with chalk, and his cheeks with vermilion, to make him look like an English or American beauty, was too much. Had I been going up the ladder to be hanged, I should still have laughed at this sight...'

Another, but less acerbic, Dartmoor theatre critic, Benjamin Frederick Browne, had memories of both the theatres, and took home with him two 1815 playbills which announced the forthcoming attractions at each. One was for the 'white' theatre in *Caserne* No.5, where Blowsy Bess and company often made their appearances; and the other proclaimed the offerings of the 'black' theatre in *Caserne* No.4:-

THE DARTMOOR THESPIAN COMPANY
respectfully announce that there will be a performance
at the Theatre No.5.
this evening, December 29th when will be presented
the admired Comedy of
THE HEIR AT LAW.
[here followed the cast of characters]
together with the favourite afterpiece of
RAISING THE WIND
On account of the reception of the happy news of the
TREATY OF PEACE
the theatre will be Splendidly Illuminated.

Benjamin Browne said that, although the performances in No.5. were generally considered of a higher order than those in the cock-loft, the scenery, decoration, costumes and props were nowhere near so good. There was good reason for this. Over the years, the French had put a great deal of work into their theatrical decor and properties, and skilful artists and craftsmen were more easily found among the French than among the Americans. When the French began to leave the depot, shortly after the Yankee prisoners started to arrive, the negroes got in first and snapped up all the paraphernalia of the French theatre – and the white Americans were thrown onto their own devices, and had to start from scratch. The plays performed in Theatre No.5 were 'sometimes tragical, but more generally what were called genteel comedies. Some of the performers, it was thought, exhibited a talent for the drama, which, if it had been fostered by cultivation, would have made them highly respectable, if not eminent anywhere.'

THE AMATEUR DRAMATIC COMPANY
will give a performance this evening, Feb. 3, at
Theatre No. 4.
When will be presented Home's celebrated Tragedy of
DOUGLASS
Together with the admired Pantomime of
HARLEQUIN REVIVED
Doors open at 5 o'clock –
Performance to commence at 6.
Admission, seats 6d., rear 4d.

Occasionally a white actor would play a part in one of the No.4. productions, but all parts were usually taken by American negroes, using white make-up where necessary; with young lads taking the female roles and, according to Benjamin Browne, when properly painted, they did the thing well enough. However, he could not forget once witnessing 'a tall strapping negro, over six feet high, painted white, murdering the part of Juliet to the Romeo of another tall dark-skin.'

The visitors to No.4. Theatre appreciated the pantomimes more than any other type of show and it seems that the black actors had a gift for it. It is recorded, however, that during a performance of the *'Harlequin Revived'*, featured on their playbill, something went wrong with the complicated French scenery, which could have turned pantomime into tragedy. The scene was one which called for a great storm and thunder, and a bolt of lightning was to strike Harlequin dead. Columbine was to have descended and resuscitated him with a touch from her magic wand. The cloud was made of cloth and suspended by cords, and the lightning was manufactured from a small amount of gunpowder and combustible cotton. The great moment came, the lightning struck – but in the wrong place. It burned through the cords which held the cloud and Columbine crashed on to the stage and Harlequin below. Both survived!

Not all Dartmoor thespians were captives; there were enthusiastic actors among the garrison troops. An Irish regular regiment, which after its return from active service in Spain, had replaced one of the County Militias which had served its term with the Dartmoor garrison, charged sixpence a head admission to their shows, which were staged in the No.6 *Caserne* at the Moor.

Doubtless, sufficient research would reveal the existence of 'theatres' wherever prisoners were confined. Many would have been no more than platforms for stages, or screened-off corners of depot yards; but others would have had playhouses to the standard of Dartmoor, Portchester or Liverpool. The Agent or Commandant of a depot, hulk or *cautionnement*, who wisely assisted his charges in the organisation of any form of activity which would occupy their minds, and provide some interest as an alternative to gambling and the constant planning of escapes, made everyone's life a little easier – including his own. In the world of free sailors, Horatio Nelson was one such wise commander, who encouraged anyone who could provide entertainment for his crews, and it is said that some owed their promotion, at least in part, to their ability to stage theatricals for their fellows.

It is pleasant to encounter, amidst the hate and complaint which pervade the memoirs of many prisoners of war, the occasional appreciative reference to British officials who, whilst they could not afford to be soft, were at least fair. We have already seen that Commander Patterson, the Agent at Portchester, was such a man and there were others like him. For a prisoner who had spent time aboard a prison hulk to have had a good word to say of any of its officers, would indicate more than fair treatment; but it would seem from Louis Garneray's memoirs, that when the Portsmouth based hulk, *Vengeance*, was put under the command of a Lieutenant Edwards, the whole atmosphere of prison ship life took on a change for the better. After being approached by a group of actor-prisoners ambitious to start up a theatrical company on board, this enlightened officer approved the conversion of an area at the end of the orlop deck for the purpose. It is perhaps not so surprising that naval or privateer captives should have considered the credibility of organising and operating a theatrical society on a prison hulk. Unlike the landsman or the soldier, the sailor had to take his distractions and amusements with him or go without.

In a very short time the group had built itself a playhouse of which they were justly proud. Garneray tells us of the ingenuity which went into its construction, and of the enthusiasm with which the normally bored and discontented captives set about the hard work involved. Odds and ends of clothing and any old rags available were used to create costumes; sail-cloth provided the backdrops and scrounged old waste timbers were skilfully converted into all manner of stage props. Two prisoners with some literary talent, were appointed playwrights and came up with a two-act comedy which they called *'The Adventures of a Sentimental Traveller'* and a five-act melodrama, *'The Corsair's Bride'*. Two full weeks were spent in preparation for the opening night, and as most of those taking part would normally have been busily engaged in profitable work of one sort or another – and therefore losing money – the business aspects of the venture were thoroughly looked into. The authors – a straw-worker and a slipper-maker – were given the choice of outright purchase of their work – 30 sous for the comedy, four francs for the melodrama – or a share in any profit after all expenses had been paid. All writers, captive or free, have great faith in the value of their labours, so they decided to share the risk. The first call on the receipts was to be the payment for lighting, scene painting and props, and then remuneration to the actors. Leading men and 'ladies' were to be paid one franc, other speaking parts ten sous, and those with only walking-on parts were to get four sous.

Garneray was in charge of the scenery and entered into the spirit of the thing with verve and generosity. As he was doing quite well for himself as a painter and was the paid official interpreter to the hulk, he waived his fee of twenty-five sous a performance for the five sets he had designed. He says, 'I was held to be a marvel of unselfishness and devotion, and was voted an honourable mention'. Likewise, the 'orchestra', a violinist and a flautist, gave its services free. The best-looking young lads were chosen for the female roles and the problem of dressing them was overcome by a carefully worded appeal to the ladies of Portsmouth, which the Commander circulated ashore. The response was overwhelming; garments and accessories of every description were sent on board. The company was able not only to dress its 'actresses' in style, but some months later and I cannot imagine a group of Americans taking acting this far – to form a *corps de ballet*!

At last the great day dawned and we hear of the tremendous excitement on board; of actors in a last-minute panic; of the boats coming alongside with visitors from Portsmouth, Southsea and Gosport and off-duty officers from neighbouring hulks. Lieutenant Edwards, who had reserved a pounds-worth of seats, arrived with his wife and relatives, and the curtain went up on time. The whole evening was an unqualified success and the *'Sentimental Traveller'* was received with much applause. The straw-worker-playwright was delighted, and was heard to remark that, perhaps after all, the English were somewhat misjudged, as they were obviously not without judgement and taste. Garneray adds that just a little appreciation and applause was enough to drive years of hate from the author's heart. *'The Corsair's Bride'* was equally well received and the 'leading lady', a young privateersman named Pierre Cheri, enjoyed a great personal success. It was said that he soon had half the British ladies in tears – in spite of the fact that many of them knew not a word of French. A sure sign of the evening's triumph was shown by the fact that, although it had been agreed beforehand that any prisoner who was dissatisfied with the show after the first act could demand his money back, the cashier did not have to return one sou.

That first night of the first presentation by the *Vengeance* Theatre must have been a happy and memorable one for most of the prisoners, but not for all. During the interval an application was made by *les Raffalès* – the down-and-outs of the hulk – to be admitted to see the show, but it was decided that, 'much as we would have wished to afford them a momentary relief from their suffering, we could not let a horde of half-naked savages enter the same theatre as our guests.' There was a tricky moment when, during the *'Corsair's Bride'*, fifty or more *Raffalès* began chanting vespers out on deck. A compromise was imperative: it was agreed that ten of their number should be admitted, that lots should be drawn and that the lucky ten should be decently clothed by the remainder. A quarter of an hour later, 'ten spectres clothed in heterogeneous rags made a quiet entry into the back of the stalls.'

The professional approach of the prison ship 'impresarios' of the *Vengeance* was no doubt exceptional for the hulks. The general standard was probably not very high – and not every Commander would have been as cooperative as Lieutenant Edwards. One French writer of the time spoke sourly of 'these prison representations wherein rough sailors with a few rags wrapped round them, mouth the intrigues and sentiments of our great poets in the style of the cabaret'; but bearing in mind the conditions in which they worked and overcame, one can only admire, and wonder at, the spirit of those men who took part, however poor the quality of their production.

There is a celebrated escape story connected with the theatre on the orlop deck of the *Vengeance* which, if true, would show a poor return for Lieutenant Edwards' kindly consideration. Whilst there is little reason to doubt the veracity of *'The Captain and his Lady'* escape from Dartmoor – successful escapes during World War II were based on equally improbable schemes – the following, though not impossible, sounds to me just a little too good to be completely true. You will remember that Pierre Cheri, the young privateersman, had achieved a personal success as the corsair's bride in the melodrama of that name. When the play was over, his acting ability, according to the story, was put to a tougher test. Pierre had signed on as a privateer only to earn enough money to marry his girl-friend Angelique, but his sea-going career was brought to a sudden end when his ship, the *Eclaire*, was captured in the Straits of Dover. He arrived on board the hulk, a lad of sixteen or seventeen, only a few weeks before the theatre was built, and was in such a state of deep despair that, after a few days, he attempted to commit suicide. His fellow-prisoners rallied round and did everything they could to cheer him up. After he had recovered from his self-inflicted stab wound, they managed to persuade him to take part in the forthcoming theatricals. He agreed, but on one condition – that the corsair's bride should be called Angelique and that he himself should play the part. It was said that when he appeared on stage there were murmurs of surprise and admiration, and that few real girls were ever prettier or more alluring.

Among the visiting audience was the English commandant of one of the neighbouring 'Danish' hulks who, believing that Pierre Cheri really was a girl, was immediately attracted and determined to meet this lovely creature. During the interval the captain made enquiries and was referred to Louis Garneray, the official interpreter on board, and offered him a guinea if he could arrange an introduction. From the Frenchman, the officer was given a story of how 'she' came to be aboard: that Angelique had chosen to share her fiancé's imprisonment on the hulk, but that he was now in irons in the Black Hole, or *Cachot*, as a punishment for trying to escape. The captain was assured that, as her lover had tried to get away without her, all feelings which she had once had for him were dead. They were introduced between acts and arrangements were made for them to meet after the performance. The show ended at nine o'clock; the deck was illuminated and the guards doubled to prevent any of the prisoners slipping ashore with the visitors – but Pierre Cheri left on the arm of the British captain.

This story from Garneray's *'Mes Pontons'* has been repeated with all seriousness by the Danish writer, Carl Roos, in his *'Prisonen Danske og Norske'*. Francis Abell, and others, tell us that the captain was so embarrassed by the whole affair that, in fear of ridicule, he allowed Pierre to escape. Whilst it is a fact that there were some women, a very few, who had joined their men on the hulks, it is hard to believe that the commandant of one of these vessels, experienced in the wiles of his own ingenious French and Danish captives, could have been so easily duped, or that he would not have first spoken with the officers of the *Vengeance*. If true, then Pierre must have been some 'girl' for the captain to have risked aiding a prisoner of war to escape.

The Danish and Norwegian prisoners on the hulks were generally better off than their French counterparts, both financially and in the quality of their accommodation. Their allowance was higher and, although no part of a hulk could be called a desirable place to live, they were allocated the best that was available – a gun-deck rather than the orlop deck. In these circumstances it is to be expected that there would have been areas set up for entertainment on most of those hulks reserved primarily for Scandinavians.

The small theatre on the 'Danish' hulk, *La Brave*, at Plymouth, was built by the prisoners, right aft on the upper gun deck. They decorated it well, made drapes, painted scenery and back-cloths and formed an orchestra of violins. The costumes and some props were supplied by the hulk's officers and their wives. Except when the stage was used for patriotic shows, of which they were particularly fond, they concentrated on comedies and the works by the Danish playwright Holberg, which were copied out by hand for the small group of actors.

The performances took place twice weekly and, on those days, the British guards retired to the upper deck – unless they were willing to expend the one penny admission to see the show. The commandant of the *Brave* was a regular patron, often accompanied by visitors from ashore who paid well for their tickets and seemed to have enjoyed the performances. On one occasion some titled ladies from nearby towns, who had particularly enjoyed some of the Danish shows, petitioned their friends and sent on board a packing case full of 'dresses, skirts, hats, stockings, shoes; in fact everything for the well-dressed lady'. The Danish prisoner, Federspiel, who often played female roles, wrote of the difference that this made to their theatrical possibilities; 'we didn't make a lot of money, but we had a lot of fun, most of our profit we used to improve our theatre which, in the end, became a good one'.

The diaries and memoirs of Danes who had spent years of confinement on British prison ships spoke surprisingly often of some happy hours in the long days of their imprisonment, brought about by the efforts of the thespians to entertain them. Comparative happiness, of course, but invaluable breaks in the long tedious waiting for freedom. We read of parties, plays and dancing on the Chatham hulks, but it would seem that the birthdays of King Frederick and his Queen were the high days of celebration for their captive subjects. The serious minded and humourless Jens Krog, whose diaries have already given us so much information and detail regarding the life of the Scandinavian prisoner of war in British hands, considered most of the efforts of the entertainers frivolous and trivial in times of war, and felt that the Royal anniversaries were the only cause for celebration whilst they were held captive.

In 1809, Krog was on board the *Panther*, and his diary entry for the 28th January, reads:

> 'Today was our King's birthday. It was remembered by all honourable Danish prisoners on this ship. Some of us who had money bought drinks with which we proposed a toast to our King and all the Royal Family and the welfare of our country. In the evening we held a dance in which fifty young people took part, which lasted until the morning of the following day.'

On the same day one year later, Jens Krog was on the *Brave,* and went into great detail in his journal:

> 'The upper deck was illuminated and took on the aspect of a ballroom. At one end the prisoners had erected a loyal set-piece, in the centre of which the scenic artists had painted the King's name surmounted by the Danish crown and the slogan, "Long Live the King". To the right was the figure of Peace, blowing a trumpet and holding an olive branch: on the left, the figure of Justice with sword and scales.'

Krog recorded in his diary a song which some of his fellows had composed for that day and of which they were very proud (it probably sounds a lot better in Danish!):

1

All Brothers, let us be happy,
On this our King's Birthday,
We'll sing a song to honour him,
And make our prison gay.

2

We did not hire a writer,
To help us with this lay,
But with our pens we wrote it
To celebrate this day.

3

With happiness we sing it,
And the British hear us sing,
Today they'll know we're happy
And that we love our King.

4

We love our King and Country,
And though in prison penned
We're not afraid for Dan or Norg,
For Frederick is our Friend.

5

We honour Law and Justice,
And we this promise place,
The Flag of our Mother-Country,
We never shall disgrace.

6

We don't know how to flatter,
Nor insincere can be,
The Dane and the Norwegian
From hypocrisy is free.

The music, dancing and singing went on all night, to the annoyance of the ship's officers who lost some sleep; but the only punishment was that the prisoners were kept below decks until a later hour on the following day. On the Royal birthdays all the hulks with Danes and Norwegians aboard were brightly illuminated, which must have proved expensive and a genuine sacrifice – and, I should imagine, the great fire risk must have put strain on the hulks' officers and staff. It is surprising to learn that the French on the neighbouring hulks, who were by no means so well-off, nevertheless supported their ally by illuminating their ships on those days, but to a lesser degree.

Hans Peter Dam, a Danish prisoner who had spent some time on the *Bahama* hulk at Chatham, wrote an interesting little book called *'Den i engelst Fangenskab vaerende Somand'* – 'The Danish Prisoner in an English Prison' – on his return to Denmark. This also tells of the celebrations on the hulks in January, 1810. These began at noon with all prisoners on board, some five hundred men, giving three cheers for Frederick, which were echoed by the inmates of the nearby *Irresistible.* They then went below to carry on with the festivities and await the main event of the day – the theatrical offering on the upper gun deck.

The little theatre was well equipped with quite elaborate sets. The main back-cloth was similar to that described by Krog on the *Brave*, except that the King's name, supported by Mars and Bellona, was shown in what Hans Dam describes as a 'transparency', which probably means that it was painted in reverse on the back of a thin material and lit from behind by candles or flares. Another, and very different, variation of decor was that the back-cloth carried a slogan which read:

HAVE FEAR BRITONS!
DEPART & SEEK REFUGE FROM REVENGE!

This bit of bravado probably caused the organisers some uneasiness, for as they had found it necessary to borrow a number of things from their captors, items essential to the show, they had felt duty-bound to invite the officers and their wives, and waited with apprehension their reaction to this militant welcome.

If the prisoner-audience had expected – and perhaps half-hoped for any violent reaction from the visitors when they read the insulting slogan, they were in for a disappointment. The Commander and his guests, who had been allocated the best seats, far from taking offence, applauded as enthusiastically as the prisoners. The humourless Jens Krog, who could never understand this aspect of the British character, concluded that only because of our natural arrogance and feelings of superiority could we possibly shrug off, or smile at, such taunts and insults.

About the last thing the visitors could have expected to encounter on one of the ill-famed prison hulks would have been a ballet performed by captive sailors; but it may be remembered that Louis Garneray has told us that the French on the *Vengeance* at Portsmouth had formed a corps-de-ballet with the aid of clothes donated by the ladies of that town. Unless taken as burlesque, Hans Dam's description of just such a show on that evening could conjure up an embarrassing picture of rough, tough, soldiers and sailors lumbering around on the stage. However, we know that they were performed and viewed with all seriousness, for a fair number of the prisoners were young lads – some as young as ten years of age. So the curtain was raised on a ballet danced by sixteen performers; eight dressed in white shirts, scarves and trousers, with red handkerchieves on their sleeves. The other eight were dressed as girls, also in white. with flowers in their hair and scarves round their waists.

The second act was a comedy by Herman van Unna and this was followed by a parade in keeping with their intense patriotic feelings on that day. The backdrop this time displayed the figures of Mars, Justice and Fortune, and before it was a representation of a black marble altar. The actors entered two by two bearing Danish banners, flags, shields and the emblems of France. Specially composed patriotic songs were sung, during which flowers were placed on the national altar. Hans Dam says that this moment in the show was so moving that many of the prisoners were in tears. It is interesting to compare the national differences between the dour seriousness of the Northerners on these occasions, and the high spirited and riotous enthusiasm with which American prisoners, on the hulks, in Dartmoor and elsewhere, celebrated the 'Fourth of July', or the vivacious French, on Napoleon's birthday.

After the last act, a musical masquerade in which some thirty actors sang songs descriptive of their various costumes, all who had bought tickets to the *Bahama* show were entitled to a drink and a sandwich at the bar. However, the beer must have been well watered down to go round, for Dam, writing many years later, recalled how disappointingly weak it was.

The sets described above were no doubt typical of the remembered scenery of the Danish theatres at that time.

There are other records of prison ship festivities, on the *Buckingham*, and on the hospital hulk *Fyen* at Chatham. They all follow the pattern of those aboard the *Panther*, *Brave*, and the *Bahama*, except that we learn that the day often began with speeches made in condemnation of Danish and Norwegian prisoners who had so far forgotten their loyalty as to have entered the service of the British. One Danish prisoner, Jens Rasmussen, reminiscing as an old man, spoke of the hellish conditions and misery of the prison hulks, but also told of the memorable breaks when theatricals brightened their day: '…for we were young and healthy then and shared many a good laugh between us, which helped a lot. We danced and sang with each other and certainly created a lot of noise.'

The Scandinavians were not alone in their enthusiasm for observing national anniversaries. Birth dates of national heroes were always the excuse for patriotic fervour in the depots, prison hulks and parole towns all over this country. The French loyally hailed the birthday of Napoleon, as no doubt they had hailed, with equal fervour, King Louis before him. George Washington's birthday, on the 22nd February, was celebrated in grand style by the Americans wherever they were confined. In Dartmoor a great procession was formed, led by a band made up of anyone who could play any sort of instrument. One can imagine the ear-splitting din as fifes, flutes, bugles, trumpets, drums, clarinets and violins in great number, unrehearsed and played with varying degrees of skill, struck up, and thousands of other prisoners joined in to the strains of *'Yankee-Doodle', 'Hail Columbia'* and the *'Washington March'*.

These nationalistic demonstrations were usually taken in good part, even with tolerant amusement, by the British officers of the hulks and the garrisons guarding the depots, but this was not always so. Sometimes they were taken too far, and excitement and boisterousness had to be brought under control, particularly when captives were confined outside of this country and nearer their homes. The American Thomas Dring, who was less given to exaggeration than some who, like him, had suffered extreme hardship, wrote of a jubilation which ended in tragedy. Dring, who had been captured when the American privateer *Chance* was taken by HMS *Belisarius* in May, 1782, was one of its sixty-five crew confined on the British prison ship *Jersey* moored off New York. The *Jersey* was a disease-ridden and verminous floating hell and, as Dring puts it, 'many a one was crushed down beneath that sickness of heart'. Nevertheless, they decided to celebrate the Fourth of July. Thirteen national flags were displayed on the boom, they sang the choruses of patriotic songs and were generally having a good time, with occasional outbursts of loud cheering and hurrahs. After a while this got on the nerves of the Scottish guards, who pulled down and trampled the flags and drove the prisoners below at bayonet point and closed down the gratings. When the singing, cheering and chanting did not cease as darkness fell, the gratings were opened up, 'and the guards descended among us, with lanterns and drawn cutlasses in their hands. The poor helpless prisoners retreated from the hatchways, as far as their crowded situation would permit'. Many of the nearest were wounded, possibly unintentionally, in the crush, and on the morning of the 5th of July, eight or ten corpses were found below – twice the normal daily mortality rate on that truly dreadful vessel.

So far we have discussed organised entertainment and the prisoner of war playhouses, where both talented and would-be actors, musicians and all those with an interest in any of the back-up occupations which make up the world of the theatre, got together to beguile their fellows. However, there was – and always has been – another class of entertainer; the individual who, often uninvited, puts himself forward to divert his companions. Such men are the 'characters' to be found in every army, navy and workplace – and they come in great variety. There is the man with a 'voice'; the joker; the comic; the raconteur, whose anecdotes are sometimes the narrations of a born story-teller; and the 'exaggerator' whose romanticising entertains as he builds himself a dream-persona, on stories so often retold that he, too, has come to believe them, with himself as the hero – and then, there is the downright bore. In the restricted world of the ocean-going vessel, the barracks or the prison camp, these individuals could 'break the ice', entertain, please or annoy their auditors, but whether welcome or not, they enlivened their otherwise monotonous surroundings.

There was, however, yet another 'character', with all the imagination of the exaggerator and romanticiser, who did not set out to enlighten the cut-off life of his fellow prisoners. This was the spreader, often inventor, of unsubstantiated rumours, who set about his reports with sadistic enjoyment as he saw men worked up into a frenzy of anger or despair at his 'news'. One such was an American on the *Crown Prince* prison ship at Chatham. His fellow captives had heard that Baltimore had been burnt to the ground; that New York was taken, that the Newfoundland fisheries were to be closed to Marblehead men; that New England had declared for the British and a hundred and one other worrying yarns masquerading as reported truths.

> 'Suchlike stories were told to us, oft times, so circumstantially that we all believed them. When discovered to be false, they were called *'galley news'*, or *'galley packets'*. These mischievous characters are continually sporting with our feelings; and secretly laughing at the uneasiness they occasion. There is one man who has got the name of 'Lying Bob'; who is remarkable for the fertility of his invention; there is so much apparent correctness in all he advances, that we often believe his sly rodomantades [empty bluster or bragging]. He mentions and describes the man who informed him, states little particulars, and states circumstances, so closely connected with acknowledged facts, that the most cautious and incredulous are often taken in by him. He is a constitutional liar; and the fellow has such a plausible mode of lying, and wears throughout such a fixed and solemn phiz, that his news has been circulated by us all.'[3]

In all the prisoner of war establishments, the captives were divided into 'messes', usually each of six men. Even such small groups were likely to be made up of men of disparate dispositions, and it was sheer good luck – or the natural authority of a strong character among them – if harmony was to reign in any degree. Josiah Cobb, whose keen observation of his own and adjoining messes provided him with material for a fascinating memoir, said that the surnames of men were soon forgotten within the mess – replaced by nicknames, sobriquets earned in many interesting ways.[4] There was 'Little Nap', 'the Doctor', 'Josh-the-Tiger', 'Irish Pat', 'Black Tom', 'the Professor' and Cobb, himself we know as 'the Greenhand'. From time to time a nearby group would join to form a double-mess, and from this we hear of 'Capstan Jack', 'Chaw-Tobacco Pete', 'Six-penny Bob', 'Well-Bred Jim' and others.

The mess table was their 'social board', where each man sat before his carefully weighed-out ration and ate in an atmosphere of badinage, chit-chat and sometimes argument. Josiah says that, with so little to do with slow-passing time, they sometimes sat for hours, 'joking, laughing singing and quizzing each other – none letting the opportunity pass when he could turn the joke… to pin it on his neighbour'. These were the hours when the story-teller, the comic or the singer came into his important own – and at this point Black Tom emerges from the colourful characters listed above. In appearance the most unlikely of entertainers, Black Tom, so called from his swarthy complexion and unusually sullen and taciturn disposition, was ever ready to sing at the drop of a hat; but his sombre countenance did not change or brighten as he sang.

His *magnum opus,* and always the first he would deliver, was 'Black Tom's Own', the theme of which was the life, love and adventures of a bold buccaneer. Tom always insisted that once he had started, he would 'sing the song, the whole song, and nothing but the song'. Perhaps it could only have been enjoyed or tolerated in its entirety by a captive audience, as it comprised thirty-five verses (plus a third as many choruses) – of which, I hasten to add, only the first, fifth, twenty-first and twenty-ninth will be set down here! Cobb assures us that no matter how often Black Tom's rendition was repeated, a crowd would gather and stay from first verse to last, joining in with the choruses with great enthusiasm:

'BLACK TOM'S OWN'

'In the year fifty-four with a full top-sail breeze,
We were boxing about in dark Biscay's rough seas,
When we saw on our lee bow, a long, low, dark brig,
Which at once was pronounced a piccaroon rig;
And had not only wealth, but had one far more dear
To our captain, God bless him, who sang out with good cheer,
"Give me but the beauty, take the rest to your share:
Aloft lay, ye jollies, the brave ne'er despair."

CHORUS:
Crack sail on all, Blow high, blow low;
Let one and all, Sing yo-heave-yo;
Sing yo-heave-yo.

'On board of this brig, was the captain's first love,
Whose hard-hearted parents her tears could not move;
For this beautiful maid was intended to pillow
Her head by the side of an old Spanish fellow
Who had dollars more plenty than sense or good learning,
When we fell in his wake this bright July morning;
And our skipper roar'd out, "this dark old freebooter
Shall ne'er have the maid, to whom once I'm been suitor."
                                        Crack sail on all, &.

'We fired not a shot at this bold buccaneer,
On their own native planks, hand to hand without fear,
Did we fiercely contend for the deck of their craft,
O the joys of this maid were but equall'd by those
Of our captain, her lover, who'd conquered her foes,

When he gave out the word, with a heart-cheering grace –
"All hands now stand ready, to splice the main-brace."

Crack sail on all, &.

'Each and all of the crew shared the prize he had won.
Chiming in with the dance and the glee, and the song;
Toasting long happy life to that beautious prize,
Whom our captain had gain'd – and whose laughing blue eyes,
Told a tale of delight, I shall never forget,
Till I'm called aloft, the last judgement to meet,
As her white lilly hand softly laid on my arm,
Gently saying, "dear Tom, shield your captain from harm."

Crack sail on all, &.'

'Black Tom' had a few minor numbers in his repertoire for encores. The favourite among these was 'The Coquette', which owed its popularity more to 'Chaw-Tobacco Joe' than to Tom's vocal prowess. Joe himself could not sing – the huge chaw of tobacco always under his tongue would have made that impossible anyway – but he was a born comic and mime artist. He uttered not a sound as 'Black Tom' sang, but he not only entered into the meaning of each word and sentence, but showed every tantalizing look, sneering haughtiness, and scornful scowl of the coquette throughout the different stages of her career:

'THE COQUETTE'

'At sixteen, beaux were gay and plenty,
All were handsome, most were wealthy;
Smiling, smirking, lisping, pleasing
Bowing with their anxious teasing;
   This one's willing,
   That one's billing,
   Oh! How killing.
   You can't please me,
   You shan't please me
   Oh! Don't tease me,
With your faddle daddle talking,
I'm engaged, so pray be walking.

At six and twenty, things went different,
Offers now were much less frequent;
Few were praising, none were vying
To be foremost – not one dying.
   One amuses
   With excuses,
   He refuses,
   Now they flout me,
   Go without me,
   Laugh about me.
How provoking, thus to suffer –
Cruel, cruel, none to offer.
At thirty-six – gracious! How many
call me 'fusty, Mistress Granny' –
Hateful nothings, lack-brained donkeys,

> Graceless, grinning, two-legged monkeys.
> First they greet me,
> Then they twit me,
> All then quit me;
> They are glad now –
> 'Tis too bad now,
> To be made now,
> Game by such a set of fellows,
> Only fit to grace the gallows.'

These convivial get-togethers helped them to forget for a moment they were in captivity:

> ' ...for none could look on, without being more or less drawn to the excitement, by the enthusiasms displayed by the singers, Heavy, indeed, would the hours pass, when we had neither amusement and employment to engage our minds – bringing with them moroseness, and a wish to estrange oneself, even from his most intimate companions, more especially when our money ran short, compelling us to subsist upon our rations alone... '

Officers who had been given their parole and were most often quartered in pleasant English or Scottish towns or villages, had every opportunity to shape their captivity into a reasonable way of life. Their days need not have dragged by too wearily – days, that is, other than Sundays. An old Wincanton man, who well remembered the mainly French officer prisoners, told the pamphleteer, George Sweetman, in 1869:

> 'Sunday was to them the dullest day of the week, they did not know what to make of it. Accustomed as they had been at home to attend theatres, galas, fêtes and what not, to them the English Sunday was wearisome above all days of the week. Some of them, however, went to the parish church and helped with the instrumental part of the service, which a century ago was a more considerable portion than it now is... The majority were, in name at least, Roman Catholic; whatever they were, they spent Sunday in playing chess, draughts, cards, dominoes. Indeed almost anything to while the time away.'

Wincanton in Somerset, already had a small theatre when the first prisoners arrived in 1804/5, and Sweetman possessed one of its old playbills, dated the 5th February, 1790, which gave the names of the players and actors, and the admission prices – Pit: Two Shillings; Gallery: One Shilling (with an inviting footnote) 'A Good Fire will be kept in the Pit'. During the winter months the parolees produced twice-weekly operatic and theatrical performances. These were of a high standard and among the officers there were talented musicians who arranged regular concerts, which were well patronised by the people of the town. At about that same time, a company of strolling players came to Wincanton and stayed for a considerable length of time, converting an old nearby barn into a theatre. Therefore, all in all, the people of the Wincanton area had probably never been so well entertained theatrically before.

At Odiham, in Hampshire, the paroled officers had not only their own theatre but a Philharmonic Society, and many of the *cautionnements* could boast a prisoner of war Freemasons' Lodge. However, as with all other types of war imprisonment, much depended on the attitude of the Agent of any particular parole town, and not all encouraged or approved of group activities. Our old friend, Louis Garneray, who, after many years on prison hulks was finally paroled to Bishops Waltham, found much to complain of in that little Hampshire village. He says that on his second day as a paroled prisoner, his room-mate told him, 'whenever we have attempted to organise concerts or dramatic productions, the Transport Board has closed them down, on the grounds that they give rise to improper relations between the natives and their enemies. Do not rejoice yet at your release from the hulks. You have a lot to learn!'

It is true that the Transport Board did clamp down in a number of towns where the natives were much too friendly, where escapes had occurred or the Agent was lackadaisical; but group entertainments were seldom discouraged in well-conducted *cautionnement*s. Garneray was, perhaps, exaggerating but, after so long on the hulks, he should be allowed his moan. He escaped a few months later (but was recaptured) and, when writing his memoirs – *'Mes Pontons'* – he used the entertainment ban and other criticisms to excuse the breaking of his *parole d'honneur*.

All the Scottish parole towns had their clubs and meeting rooms, and not a few had their play-houses. The paroled officers were so well received by the Scottish borderfolk that one would imagine that if the Transport Office was going to be particularly vigilant, it would have been in these towns. However, I can find only one reference to really drastic action being taken in connection with organised entertainment. This was at Cupar, Scotland, where the interned officers were treated with such excessive hospitality – and the degree of fraternisation grew so extreme – that the authorities felt they had to act quickly. Therefore, when the officers in the town built a theatre at their own expense, for their own and the inhabitants' entertainment, their first performance was also their last; the French prisoners were suffered to play only once in their theatre, and then the rout came for them. Amidst loud and sincere lamentations from all concerned, the officers were summarily removed in a body, and deposited in a town at some distance from their former guardians. As a final *gage d'amitié* the owners of the theatre left it as a gift to the town of Cupar[5].

The parolees at Hawick had a club-house in the Kirkwynd where they had installed a billiards table, the first seen in that town. We know that the French had a passion for, and a skill at the game – billiard tables were to be found in depots, and even on prison hulks, wherever French prisoners were to be found – in fact, it is probable that the game of billiards was first introduced into Scotland by paroled French prisoners of war. The Hawick prisoners also presented small musical and dramatic shows in their club-house and charged a few pence for admission. However, this was small-time compared to the ambitious efforts of the officers at Kelso. There had been a theatre in Kelso for many years before the prisoners arrived in the town, situated in a close near the Horse Market. The performances took place on the first floor, the ground floor being used for the stabling of horses. Macbeth Forbes, in his booklet on the Scottish border towns, says that in those days:

> '...the drama was well patronised in the provinces by the county families and others, and first-rate actors like Charles Kemble, who were obliged by slow stage-coach travelling and bad roads to break their journeys at wayside towns, were only too pleased to swell their receipts by performing at such places for a night or two before resuming their way. This theatre the officers were desirous of getting into their own hands. They accordingly clubbed together and, as some had good means, they were able to secure it. Their great enemy during the long winter evenings was ennui, and here was an opportunity to combat it. As soon as they became lessees of the theatre they at once set to work to overhaul and decorate it.'

Until the beginning of this century some of this work was still to be seen, and it is only about sixty years ago that the carved and gilded woodwork and the fringes connected to the drop scenes were pulled down. Although the prisoners made transforming improvements to the playhouse itself, there was little space for dressing-rooms, and most of the actors preferred to dress in their own lodgings. This meant that they had to walk through the streets in costume and make-up, to the delight and amusement of the local youths and children, who lay in wait and made their progress as uncomfortable as possible.

Under this new management the Kelso theatre had a new lease of life. It was well supported by the local people, some travelling for miles to see each new production. There were memorable days when performances were patronised by the neighbouring aristocracy and nobility, such as the Duke and Duchess of Roxburgh. On these occasions the prisoners showed their appreciation of the honour paid them, by carpeting the street outside with scarlet cloth. When I visited Kelso some years ago, there was nothing left of what must have been the entertainment centre of the little town, but on the wall of a local inn, I found an old Kelso theatre poster.

One of the most interesting accounts of histrionically talented paroled prisoners of war can be found in the *'Memoirs of William and Robert Chambers'*. It is all the more worth recounting as it was written by one who had himself often visited the French prisoner theatre at the parole town of Peebles. William Chambers says:

'Billiards were indispensable, but something more was wanted. Without a theatre, life was felt to be unendurable. But how was a theatre to be secured? There was nothing of the kind in the place. The more eager of the prisoners managed to get out of the difficulty. There was an old disused ball-room. It was of rather confined dimensions and low in the roof, with a gallery at one end over the entrance, for the musicians. Walter Scott's mother, when a girl, had crossed Minchmoor, a dangerously high hill, in a chaise, from the adjacent county, to dance for a night in that little old ball-room.

'Now set aside as unfashionable, the room was at anyone's service, and came quite handily for the Frenchmen. They fitted it up with a stage at the inner end, and crossbenches to accommodate 120 persons, independently of perhaps twenty more in the gallery. The whole thing was neatly got up with scenery painted by M. Walther and M. Ragulski, the latter a young Pole. No license was required for the theatre, for it was altogether a private undertaking. Money was not taken at the door, and no tickets were sold. Admission was gained by complimentary tickets distributed chiefly among persons with whom the actors had established an intimacy.

'Among these favoured individuals was my father, who, carrying on a mercantile concern, occupied a prominent position. He felt a degree of compassion for the foreigners, constrained to live in exile, and, besides welcoming them to his house, gave them credit in articles of drapery of which they stood in need; and through which circumstance they soon assumed an improved appearance in costume.

'Introduced to the family circle, their society was agreeable, and in a sense instructive. Though with imperfect speech, a sort of half-English, half-French, they related interesting circumstances of their careers. How performances in French should have had any general attraction may seem to require explanation: There had grown up in the town, among young persons especially, a knowledge of familiar French phrases; so that what was said, accompanied by appropriate gestures, was pretty well guessed at. But, as greatly contributing to remove difficulties, a worthy man of obliging turn and genial humour, volunteered to act as interpreter. Moving in humble circumstances as hand-loom weaver, he had let lodgings to a French captain and his wife[6] and, from being for years in domestic intercourse with them, he became well acquainted with their language. William Hunter, for such was his name, besides being of ready wit, partook of a lively musical genius. I have heard him sing *'Malbrook s'en va t'en guerre'* with amazing correctness and vivacity. His services at the theatre were therefore of value to the natives in attendance.

'Seated in the centre of what we may call the pit, eyes were turned to him inquiringly when anything particularly funny was said requiring explanation, and for general use he whisperingly communicated the required interpretation. So, put up the joke, and the natives heartily joined in the laugh, though rather tardily. As for the French plays, which were performed with perfect propriety, they were to us not only amusing but educational. The remembrance of these dramatic efforts of the French prisoners of war has been through life a constant treat. It is curious for one to look back on pieces of Molière in circumstances so remarkable.'[7]

Another Scottish border town which was similarly culturally enriched as a result of being appointed a parole town or *cautionnement*, was Selkirk. Whilst in Selkirk I could not believe my luck when I found, by sheerest chance, a rare little pamphlet, *'The French Prisoners of War in Selkirk'*, which was, in fact, the reminiscences of Sous-lieutenant Adelbert J. Doisy de Villargennes of the 26th French Line Regiment.

Francis Abell relied much on this officer for his notes on Selkirk, and was pleased to quote him at length, as his memoirs 'reflect the brightest side of captivity in Britain'. He certainly made long-lasting and worthwhile friendships among the British military and townspeople during his time as a prisoner, and whether remarking on his parole at Portsmouth, Odiham and Selkirk, commenting on conditions at Forton Prison, where he went to visit a relative, or on the hulks – which he did not visit – he was invariably understanding of our treatment of prisoners of war. Whether he genuinely enjoyed a rose-coloured view of the conditions of the ordinary prisoner of war, as seen from his privileged position as a parolee, or was something of sycophant, it is difficult to decide from reading his reminiscences. However, they are certainly interestingly detailed and include particular reference to the manner in which the exiles spent their day.

Although only ninety-four officers were sent to Selkirk in 1811, and the number did not vary greatly from that figure over the following two and a half years, they quickly got down to work to create a corner of France in Scotland. Soon, they had a French-only club and café, complete with a billiard table which they had ordered from Edinburgh, hired a meadow which they could use for general recreation and football – and started to build a theatre.

They built their playhouse, the *Théâtre des Subtils*, with their own hands, converting a building called Lang's Barn into a theatre which could seat a paying audience of two hundred. They must have been a resourceful and talented bunch for, though so few in number, they had soon built up a popular repertoire, sufficiently large and varied to be able to put on a show on the Wednesdays of each week. On Saturday evenings their twenty-two man orchestra presented musical concerts which were well patronised by Scottish music-lovers from miles around. De Villargennes, speaking of the efforts which went into making the theatre a success, says, 'the costumes, especially those for the ladies, necessitated us to employ a high level of tailoring. Not one of us had been trained as a weaver, carpenter or tailor, or had an apprenticeship with a dressmaker. However, intelligence stimulated by good will can produce little miracles.'

It would appear that the parolees were 'omnivorous readers, with a penchant for History and Biography, but devouring all sorts of literature from the poetical to the statistical'. The Day Book of the Selkirk Subscription Library records that about ninety of the ninety-four French officers joined the Selkirk library, and that it was far more popular with the Frenchmen than with the local Scottish students.

With the end of the war and the Peace of 1814, the Selkirk-based officers packed their possessions and made ready for their homeward journey to France. They clubbed together to pay for the hire of carriages to convey them to the coast, and it was decided that a useful addition to the transport kitty might be realised by the sale of the structure, props and costumes of their theatre. A *roupe*, or auction, was arranged and a French officer appointed as auctioneer. It was expected that the sale would realise at least one hundred pounds, but, though well attended, the auctioneer could not push the bidders beyond the forty pound mark.

This figure they unanimously decided was unacceptable and, after a hasty meeting, adjourned the *roupe*, gathered together everything that was portable and carted it to the middle of their football field, where the lots were put up for sale for a second time.

The second auction was not much more successful than the first, as the canny Scots raised the bidding by only an additional two pounds. The proud, and now free, ex-parolees must have expected as much, and their object in moving their goods to the field soon became apparent, as they heaped all their theatrical gear – the product of thousands of man-hours of patient work and ingenuity – in the centre of the pitch. The inhabitants of Cupar, it will be recalled, were left a theatre as a token of appreciation by their foreign visitors; but all that the people of Selkirk received from their departing ex-prisoner-thespians was the production of one last great spectacular –

A FAREWELL BONFIRE !

1. Both games date back at least to the sixteenth century.

2. The 'Sods' Opera' was a lower-deck-only talent show, which took place on many naval vessels, usually on Friday evenings. The turns varied from comics, skilful performances on musical instruments to conjuring and recitations of unprintable verse; the singers from the operatic and 'Ave Maria' to the less talented and 'The Good Ship Venus'. The prizes were usually cartons of cigarettes, a couple of tots of illegally stored 'grog,' or a tin of 'pusser's' jam.

3. '*Journal of a Young Man of Massachusetts*' 1816.

4. Josh-the Tiger was derisively so called bcause of his extreme fear of ghosts or spirits. Little Nap, after going absent without leave in Italy, he returned saying he had been on a 'mission to the Nap-olese'. Well-bred Jim gained his nickname through his frequent assertion that a man's breeding can always be seen by 'the cut of his jib'. Every nickname had its story.

5. S. Keddie. *Three Generations – the Story of a Middle-Class Scottish Family*.

6. A number of the wives of French officers voluntarily shared their husband's captivity in the parole towns of Great Britain.

7. 'Memoirs of William and Robert Chambers'.

Chapter Eleven

The Forgers and the Coiners

'What one man can do, another can imitate.'

BEFORE 1725, THE PUNISHMENT FOR FORGERY IN ENGLAND HAD NEVER been severe, but in that year an Act was passed which added not only forgery itself, but the 'possession' or 'uttering' of forged bank notes, to the list of over two hundred offences already punishable by death. From time to time after that date people had been capitally punished for these offences, but it was not until the hasty introduction of Bank of England notes of small denomination in 1797, that forgery and its shocking punishment appeared on the national scene with a vengeance. Why, therefore, were those notes so hastily introduced in that year?

With Britain standing more or less alone, Spain and Holland having gone over to the enemy, and Austria about to make a separate peace; with the French Fleet refitting at Brest and our own Royal Navy in a mood of mutinous activity at Spithead and the Nore; and with rumours of a French invasion of Britain becoming more and more believable, British spirit was at a low ebb. A year before, in 1796, the Republican General Lazare Hoche, had led a large naval force and fifteen thousand troops to Bantry Bay, encouraged by the Society of United Irishmen who had called on France to release Ireland from British dominance: 'To subvert the tyranny of our execrable Government, to break the connection with England, the never-failing source of our political evils.......'[1] However, this Franco/Irish dream was subverted, not by our naval superiority, but by the power of the storms which split up the French fleet of seventeen ships of the line with attendant frigates and support vessels and drove them back to Brest.

Nevertheless, both the Government and the British public had every good reason to be on the qui vive and prepared for the worst; and when reports came in that a French force had landed at Fishguard in Pembrokeshire, apprehension turned to panic, particularly among the more affluent members of British society. The first report of suspected enemy activity in the area was sent post haste to the Home Secretary by an official of the

Swansea Custom House, who had been advised by the Master of a sloop that suspicious-looking vessels had been observed about six miles north of Lundy Island. The Admiralty and Plymouth were also informed.

The landings at Fishguard – which came to be remembered as 'The Last Invasion of Britain' began on Wednesday, the 22nd February, 1797, when four vessels were sighted off the Welsh coast (see *A History of Napoleonic and American Prisoners of War 1756-1816 – Hulk, Depot and Parole*, Chapter 4). Two were large 40-gun frigates, the *Vengeance* and the *Resistance*, one was a corvette and the other a 14-gun lugger, the *Vautour*, and all were flying the English Flag. From the outset to the end, there was something of the unbelievable – and comical – about this attack on Britain. It is said that Fishguard Fort, misled by the false colours, saluted the ensign with a blank round as the first ship entered – at which the French, misled by the blank shot, struck the British colours and hoisted the tricolour!

It is not hard to imagine the alarm and consternation ashore. What had been feared most was about to happen. Messengers were dispatched for military assistance, beacons were fired and those countrymen who did not make a dash inland, gallantly armed themselves with whatever weapon came to hand, from flint-lock to pitchfork. Later that day a force of some thirteen-hundred men were disembarked from the French ships, under the command of Colonel Tate, an American in the service of France, who had been given the rank of *Chef de Brigade* of the *Légion Noire* by General Hoche. As thousands of Welsh countryfolk watched from the cliffs and hill-tops, the intruders landed at Carreg Wastad Point, above Fishguard, and never before did such a rag-tag-and-bobtail invading party hit an enemy shore. There were some well-trained and tested military men and a few Irishmen among them, but the vast majority were galley-slaves and convicts, 'the most abandoned rogues', criminals cleared from their prisons; a ne'er-do-well brigade which France was only too pleased to dump upon British soil. Colonel Tate himself said: 'Saw the *Légion Noire* reviewed; about 1,800 men. They are the banditti intended for England and sad blackguards they are...' After the French squadron, under Commodore Jean Castagnier, had off-loaded Tate's ruffian army, it lay off Fishguard for no longer than was necessary to see the last man ashore, before sailing back to France.

Finding their landing unopposed, the invaders began to settle in, commandeering local inns, houses and farm buildings, whilst Tate and his officers set up a headquarters a little way inland. The local Militiamen, who were scattered and taken completely by surprise, began to reform themselves into some sort of defence force, and were joined by the Welshmen, with their strange assortment of weapons; but they were greatly relieved at the arrival of Lord Cawdor and a body of men including several hundred trained Militia.

From this point on the story sounds more like a comedy than an invasion. Legend (and some French and British contemporary accounts) has it that many hundreds of Pembrokeshire women had joined the assembly and that, in their round black felt Welsh hats and their long scarlet cloaks, from a distance they had all the appearance of red-coated soldiers. General Tate did, indeed, report back to France that he had been faced by a large force of redcoats, although the Militiamen were dressed in blue. It was said that Lord Cawdor marched his motley forces backwards and forwards over the hills, using the same people over again, thus giving the impression that he had a great army under his command. General Tate fell for the deception and surrendered without firing a shot!

One might well wonder what possible connection there could be between all this and the forgery of English and Scottish bank notes – not to mention prisoners of war – but that there was a very real connection will soon be shown. The possibility of a French invasion had inspired the Government to issue an Order in Council a year or two earlier, directing that an inventory be made of all farm stock near the coast and that all goods and cattle should be brought farther inland at the first sign of trouble. There was much basic wisdom in this Order, but at the very first sign of trouble, its immediate effect was to spread even greater panic and alarm. Farmers and businessmen sold out at whatever price they could get and, receiving paper money in payment for their goods and farm stock, rushed to the banks demanding that they keep their promise to pay up, and give solid cash in return for their notes.

Within a few days the run on the banks became overwhelming; the small West Country banks were the first to suffer and one after the other put up their shutters. This panic affected banks everywhere and the Bank of England, too, became seriously concerned at its rapidly dwindling reserves. The Government was no less concerned and, on the 27th of February, 1797, only four days after the Fishguard affair, an Order in Council – *The Restriction of Cash Payments Order* – was issued, which prohibited the Bank from honouring the promise inscribed on its paper money, and making payments in cash illegal. The Bank of England posted up notices which acquainted the public with the situation, at the same time attempting to reassure their customers that their money was perfectly safe in the Bank's hands:

BANK of ENGLAND
FEBRUARY 27th, 1797.

In consequence of an Order of His Majesty's Privy Council notified to the BANK last Night, Copy of which is hereunto annexed. The Governor, Deputy Governor, and the Directors of the BANK of ENGLAND, think it their Duty to inform the Proprietors of BANK STOCK, as well as the PUBLICK at large, that the general Concerns of the BANK are in the most affluent and prosperous Situation, and such as to preclude every Doubt as to the Security of its Notes.
FRANCIS MARIN, Secretary.

COPY of the Order of PRIVY COUNCIL
At the Council Chamber, Whitehall,
FEBRUARY 26th, 1797,
By the Lords of His Majesty's Most Honourable Privy Council
PRESENT
The Lord Chancellor, Lord President, Duke of Portland,
Marquis Cornwallis, Earl Spencer, Earl of Liverpool,
Lord Glenville, Mr Chancellor of the Exchequer.

UPON the Representation of the Chancellor of the Exchequer, stating that, from the Result of the Information which he has received, and of the Enquiries which it has been his Duty to make respecting the Effect of the unusual Demands for Specie, that have been made upon the Metropolis, in Consequence of ill-founded or exaggerated Alarms in different Parts of the Country, it appears that unless some Measure is immediately taken, there may be Reason to apprehend a Want of sufficient Supply of Cash to answer the Exigencies of the Publick Service: It is the unanimous Opinion, of the Board, that it is indispensably necessary for the Publick Service, that the Directors of the Bank of England, should forbear issuing any Cash in Payment until the Sense of Parliament can be taken on that Subject, and the proper Measures adopted thereupon, for maintaining the Means of Circulation, and supporting the Publick and Commercial Credit of the Kingdom at this important Conjuncture; and it is ordered that a Copy of this Minute be transmitted to the Directors of the Bank of England, and they are hereby required on the Grounds of Exigency of the Case to conform thereto until the Sense of Parliament can be taken as aforesaid.
(Signed) W. Fawkener.

The rush on the banks and the *Restriction of Cash Payments Order*, created an immediate need for small cash and new low-value notes: at that time the lowest paper currency was the five pound note and that had not been introduced until 1793. Although silver was the basis of this country's currency, it would have been uneconomical for the Mint to produce the vast quantity of coins required to satisfy even the first demand; as the intrinsic worth of the silver coinage of that time was greater than its face value – which not surprisingly would have led to a great deal of melting down and clipping of coins. Instead the requirement was catered for by the issue of Spanish dollars and pieces-of-eight which had been taken in vast quantities from captured Spanish ships. This Spanish silver, which was worth less than its nominal value, was first sent to the Tower of London, where the Royal Mint struck a small die of the head of King George the Third on to the neck of the King of Spain. These rather un-English, and generally detested, coins remained in circulation for almost twenty years. The public dislike for the Anglicised foreign coin is echoed in a contemporary published couplet:-

'The Bank to make its Spanish Dollars pass,
Struck the head of a Fool on the neck of an Ass'.

Similar make-shift methods had to be employed in the production of new low-value notes. An Act of 1777, which prohibited the printing of notes for sums less than £5, had first to be speedily amended. Then old worn plates, previously prepared and used for higher values, were quickly re-engraved and one pound and two pound notes were introduced for the very first time. With that introduction, forgery 'attained the dignity of a public industry'.

The engravers and printers were pushed into such a rush to produce the new one pound and two pound notes, that it is understandable that when they were ready for issue only eight days after the 'invasion' – on the 2nd March (700,000 were issued by the end of that month) – they should have fallen short of the Bank of England's normally high standards, and were therefore easily copied. In the following year, 1798, the hastily produced one and two pound notes were redesigned and new plates were engraved; but despite this and subsequent changes of detail and watermark, forgers everywhere found little difficulty in imitating these notes. At the end of 1800, the Directors of the Bank were informed that one in seven hundred of all banknotes offered for payment were forged; and in the following year, 540 false notes were proffered during the month of April alone.

It is probable that the money-making attractions of forging and coining will persist as long as currency exists in its present forms. In June 1995, an interesting newspaper article on modern forgery quoted a British Retail Consortium estimate that one British banknote in one hundred was a forgery. Despite modern technology, amazingly subtle watermarks, metal strips, holograms, etc., forgery has increased over the last two hundred years rather than diminish; bearing out the old dictum which heads this chapter – *'What one man can do, another can imitate'*.[2]

The flood of forgery which followed after the Cash Restriction Act and the issue of low-value notes, was not restricted to this country. Almost immediately great numbers of forged notes on the Bank of England made their appearance in France and other parts of the Continent. It is thought that these were printed by order of the French Government as quid (!) pro quo for British Governmental forgeries of *Assignats*, French paper money backed by the church lands which had been confiscated by the state in 1789 and was in use until 1796.

Every effort was made to prevent the smuggling of the French-forged English notes into this country. Notices were posted up, the Customs were alerted and bank

investigators, inspectors and 'searchers' were stationed at Dover and other ports where neutral shipping arrived, which may have first called in at French ports. Also, advertisements were regularly carried in continental newspapers warning readers that uttering of false banknotes in Britain was a capital offence. 'Official' forgery of enemy banknotes probably takes place during the course of most wars; but the record for wartime forgery of notes on a vast scale must surely be held by Germany in World War II. 'Operation Bernhard' was the code name for a forgery factory in Sachsenhausen Concentration Camp, which employed over a hundred Jewish prisoners, under the direction of Major Frederich Kruger. It is said that 'Operation Bernhard' produced more than £150,000,000 of false British paper money, most of it in 'fivers'.

From the beginning of the decade there had been only one execution for banknote forgery in England, but between 1797 and 1817, seven hundred and ten persons were convicted of the crime. Three hundred and thirteen paid with their lives by hanging and most of the remainder were transported to Botany Bay for fourteen years or life. Those who suffered these harsh punishments were usually the ignorant dupes of the actual forgers who employed them to distribute their fakes, or people who had themselves been duped but, though innocent, were nonetheless considered culpable.

Until 1793, and the introduction of the 'fiver', the lowest denomination of banknote was ten pounds, and few peasants or working-class people had ever come into contact with paper money at all; but now, with the introduction of the one and two pound notes, they were using non-specie currency for the first time. How these poor people, often illiterate, were expected to know the difference between a forgery and the real thing is puzzling, yet the punishment for the man who passed (uttered) or even possessed the false note, was the same as it was for the man who forged it – death or life as an exiled convict. However, in spite of barbaric punishment, the existence and availability of imitation banknotes proved a great temptation to some. Anyone who was willing to risk his neck or exile, could buy 'money' at a very cheap price. The going rate for 'two pound' forgeries in York was about thirteen shillings, whilst in Birmingham false 'oncers' could be bought for five shillings each. It is hardly necessary to mention that the forgers themselves were seldom apprehended.

The number of hangings and transportation for life, horrifying though it was, would certainly have been even greater if the laws had not been softened slightly in 1801. In that year an Act was introduced which differentiated between 'possessing' and 'uttering', and the penalty for the former was reduced to a mere fourteen years in Australia. It is very probable that many accused persons, some perhaps unknowingly in possession and proffering a false note, would have confessed to the lesser crime rather than risk their necks by standing trial for the greater. Yet transportation was not deterrent enough for some inveterate forgers and counterfeiters. Judith Kelly is a famous case in point. She was tried for possessing and uttering forged banknotes, which she carried in her Prayer Book, and was sentenced to death. Judith was a lucky lady, for not only was she reprieved and transported for life, but later pardoned and allowed to return to England. Lucky, but unappreciative of her luck, two days after her return from the Antipodes and with her Pardon still in her pocket, she was picked up for uttering false notes. This time she was hanged.[3]

At that time the office of Public Prosecutor had not yet been established, and all prosecutions connected with forgery of paper money had to be instigated by the bank concerned – and that bank was responsible for the costs incurred. For the latter reason, some of the smaller banks found these cases too expensive to pursue, but the Bank of England was unrelenting in its war on forgery – and the ghastly results of its successful prosecutions caused something of a public outcry. It was felt by many that the Bank of England did not make a great enough effort towards producing an 'inimitable' note, and that the simplicity of the engraving and the ease with which the issued notes could be copied by almost any competent engraver – or talented art student – was the main cause of such widespread forgery; resulting in so much suffering and loss of life. It should be said that the Bank did consider many hundreds of designs for 'inimitables', many of them very ingenious, but in every case the Bank's own engravers were able to copy them. It may be that the Bank officials and experts were too academic in their approach. Because their master-engravers could replicate the 'inimitables', it does not mean that all forgers could have copied the best of them convincingly. Therefore, whilst the search for design and technical perfection went on the public hangman was still kept busy. The Directors of the Bank of England came in for much public opprobrium over the years, the newspapers and periodicals attacking them from a number of angles; that it was their duty to find a solution to the unforgeable note; that the Bank was directly responsible for so many deaths resulting from their production of a poor quality product; and describing them, with some justice, as 'Grand purveyors to the Gibbet' and as 'Priests of the modern Moloch's bloodstained Altar'. Yet there was another and paradoxical complaint against them: that in many cases they could be accused of leniency! There were many cases where 'utterers' were induced to plead guilty to possession thereby escaping the gallows. The matter was discussed in Parliament where it was said 'that the Prince Regent will not approve of prisoners having been induced to plead guilty to uttering forged Bank Notes by an assurance, which compromises the Royal Prerogative', and Lord Sidmouth expressed his 'strong sense of impropriety of inducing a prisoner to confess the guilt of one offence by a threat of prosecuting for another'.

In 1801, trials were begun on an important change to the watermark, which made the imitation of the low-value notes much more difficult to achieve. The idea was that the straight 'laid lines' of the watermark should be replaced by wavy lines and, in large capital letters, the words 'ONE' or 'TWO' incorporated in the translucent design in the paper for the £1 and £2 notes. This innovation was put forward in 1799, by the Chaplain of Newgate Prison, the Revd B. Forde, who was rewarded with twenty-five guineas for his suggestion. He, in turn, had been tipped off and instructed as to the wisdom of such an additional security move by the forger, Charles Linsey, who was himself rewarded

with execution by hanging later in that same year.

The new notes with their new watermarks were put into production and issued in the spring of 1803 and an Act of Parliament made the making of paper with wavy lines illegal. Paper-makers were warned that no such watermarking could be employed without the Bank's specific permission; a prohibition which, I believe, is still in force today. The Act also stated that the penalty for possession of watermark moulds, or made or issued paper made from them, would be fourteen years transportation to the Antipodes. That a strict lookout was kept for holders of, or requests for, suspect watermarked paper, is shown by a report from a small Scottish Border town. It is the only reference which we have to a paroled officer-prisoner of war being possibly connected with a forgery offence. In February,1812, the Procurator Fiscal of Kelso, reported that an officer, on parole in that town, 'had bespoken of Archd. Rutherford, stationer there', paper of a type and quality which led to the suspicion that he wanted it for forgery. The paper was shown to the Banks, but nothing came of it.

Before proceeding to the real subject of this chapter – the prisoner of war as forger and coiner – it may be appropriate to end this preamble with the story of a 'Bank Note' which played at least some part in bringing about the abolition of capital punishment for forgery and other minor crimes. George Cruikshank, the artist and political cartoonist, was sickened and disturbed by the sight of a number of poor men and women hanging from gibbets outside Newgate Prison. It is improbable that any of them had been forgers themselves, but far more likely the utterers of the work of real crooks. Cruikshank, disgusted, decided to do something about it in his own way, and through his art. He took the risk of designing a 'Bank Note' – for there was a very real risk involved in producing anything which looked even remotely like paper money. The result was his famous 'Bank Restriction Note', which carried the message 'Specimen of a Bank Note – not to be imitated. Submitted to the Consideration of the Bank Directors and the Inspection of the Public.' It illustrated the horrible scene which he had witnessed and was designed to shock – and shock it did.

Britannia is shown as a female Moloch devouring a child, the Pound symbol is shown as a noosed rope: the vignette is made up of suffering transported prisoners and a

Death's Head, and the background shows transportation vessels bound for Botany Bay. The main panel depicts eleven men and women hanging from a gibbet below the words 'Bank Restriction'. The inscription read:

Bank Restriction
I Promise to Perform
During the Issue of Bank Notes
easily imitated and until the Resump-
tion of Cash Payments, or the Abolition
of the Punishment of Death,

For the Govr. and Compa: of the
BANK OF ENGLAND

J Ketch

Jack Ketch was the Public Executioner from 1663 until 1686. Ever since, his name has been synonymous with the word 'hangman'.

The publication of Cruikshank's Note added fuel to the already burning indignation of the public. It is said that when it was displayed in the window of William Hone, the bookseller, on Ludgate Hill, and copies offered for sale at one shilling each, crowds so blocked the street that carriages could not pass. This was in 1819, and Cruikshank later claimed that after the publication of his Bank Restriction Note, the Bank of England issued no more one pound notes,[4] and that ultimately the death penalty for forgery was abolished. He exaggerated slightly: for it was not until two years after the publication of his 'Note', in 1821, that the One Pound Note was discontinued, and the abolition of capital punishment for forgery did come about 'ultimately', but not until a decade later, in 1832. Even so, his brilliant idea and draughtsmanship were significant contributions towards the ending of a barbarous practice.

The Prisoner of War Forgers and Coiners.
The flood of forgery which followed the Restriction of Cash Payments and the introduction of the new low-value notes, was not composed entirely of the products of our own crooked craftsmen. Much more than a dribble came from foreign pens and plates – the work of the prisoner of war. I have found little evidence of bank note forgeries executed by war captives which predate 1797. Doubtless there were some, but prior to that date they seem to have concentrated their efforts in the production of false passports – an ever-in-demand escape accessory.

We have seen that even in a society of free men there were many, with sufficient talent and craftsmanship to have earned them an honest income, who succumbed to the temptation of the short-cut to wealth – in spite of the vicious penalties imposed on the convicted. We should not, then, be surprised to learn that, on all the hulks and in every depot, where all but the barest necessities had to be paid for, prisoners of war with the necessary skills applied them to the arts of forgery and counterfeiting.

The fact that these ingenious prisoners, usually Frenchmen, were able to set up, surreptitiously, the apparatus essential to this delicate art, shrieks of outside help, of bribed guards and Militiamen, or 'helpful' visitors to the prison markets. With so many of the countryfolk who visited the depot markets handling paper money for the first time in their lives, the quality of craftsmanship required would not, at first, have had to be of a very high standard to deceive. It is true that the crudity of some of their efforts could have deluded only the illiterate and the most unwary; but others were such skilful imitations that they could be detected only by expert scrutiny or soaking and observing the reaction of water and inks.

The shore-based prisoner, with more opportunity to contact visitors from the outside world, would have found it easier to acquire the requisite 'tools of the trade', but that their brothers on the hulks managed somehow is evidenced by the many records of their successes and their failures. In 1812, the Bank of England awarded a piece of silver plate, valued at sixty guineas, to Lieutenant Robert Tyte R.N., commander of the three-decker hulk, *Glory*, moored at Chatham. It was inscribed:

> *'Presented by the Governor, Deputy Governor and Directors of the Bank of England to Robert Tyte Esq. Commander of His Majesty's Ship* Glory *as a mark of their approbation of services rendered by him to the Public and the Bank in the detection of French Prisoners concerned in the fabrication and circulation of Forged Bank Notes.'*

One wonders whether he enjoyed his breakfast on the morning of the 9th April, 1812, when he found, tucked away in the corner of his newspaper, the news that:

> 'Fidel Rouelle, and François Adams, and Guillaume Leman, sentenced to death at Maidstone for forging a £1 note of the Bank of England, and being accessories to the same on board the *'Glory'*, in the Medway, were duly executed.'

In cases of forgery and murder the prisoner was tried under the civil law and the penalty was death, but although many were found guilty of the former offence, no prisoner of war was executed for forgery before 1810. This was owing 'to a doubt in the minds of judges whether prisoners of war were answerable to municipal tribunals for this sort of offence, which is not against the law of nations.'

A prisoner from the *San Raphael* hulk at Plymouth had similar doubts, and used them to good effect when brought before the court. He was charged with imitating a two pound note, which he had drawn with pen and Indian ink. He argued that as he was under the protection of no laws, he could not have broken any. His plea was accepted and he was acquitted; but not every court would have spared him. Among the first captives to suffer the full penalty of the law, were two French prisoners from the hulk *El Firme*, another Plymouth prison ship. Their names were Guller and Collas and some time in 1809 they decided to set themselves up as banknote fabricators. For reasons which only they could know, they felt that their object could be more easily achieved if they could contrive a transfer from the *El Firme* to a sister hulk, the *Généreux*.

Unfortunately for them, they brought into their scheme an apparently cooperative member of the hulk's staff, an unpleasant character who acted as the clerk to the captain of the *El Firme*. He agreed to fall in with their plans and give them all assistance in return for a good slice of the profits. However, he secretly informed the captain. The clerk then arranged their transfer, obtained for them the tools which they required – paper, inks, fine hair brushes and quills – and the two Frenchmen soon got down to work. With great skill and industry they produced false notes on the Bank of England, the Naval and Commercial Bank and an Oakhampton bank – cleverly imitating the perforated stamp necessary for the appearance of authenticity in the case of some of these notes, with tools made from polished halfpennies and sailmakers' needles.

When they had completed their little stack of 'money' and it was ready for distribution, they informed their English accomplice – who in turn informed the authorities. The two unhappy forgers, who had not gained one franc from their illicit labours were carted off for trial. Guller and Collas were executed at Exeter in 1810. This sad little story would, perhaps, have a more appropriate ending if we could but read of a third man dangling from the gallows.

Two years later, another two Frenchmen, named Dubois and Benry, also prisoners on a Plymouth based hulk, were sentenced to death for forgery. These two feared death far less than the dishonour of hanging; declaring they would die as 'soldiers not as dogs', they attempted to take their own lives by cutting their veins with pieces of broken glass. They were rescued in time but later the sentence was carried out and, with shouts of *'Vive l'Empereur!'*, they were made to die like dogs.

In all my reading and research I have found only few references to prisoners convicted in connection with forged paper money who were not Frenchmen. One of these rare examples was Robert Dolliver, an American who was convicted in 1812 for uttering false notes. His associates were three Frenchmen and one of our own Marines. All five were detected and sentenced to death. Dolliver had not been the luckiest of men. He had been forcibly enlisted to serve on a French ship when his own vessel was wrecked off the French coast. When the French ship was itself captured by an English warship, he found himself on board a fourth, and much worse, craft – a Chatham prison hulk. Now it seemed that he faced his last adventure, death by hanging; but this time his luck changed, if not completely, at least somewhat for the better. The Bank of England untypically recommended his reprieve and the sentence was reduced to one of transportation. His confederates were not so lucky. On the 18th, March, 1812, they were publicly executed 'in the presence of all the prisoners of war on board the prison-ships lying in the River Medway'.

The penmen and engravers did not limit themselves to the production of false money alone. All manner of documents were forged including 'Exchange Lists', but the greatest demand was for passports. For many prisoners their dream of freedom was the one thing which sustained them and made bearable the endless hours of miserable confinement. A passport was the key item in any well-planned escape.

During the Seven Years' War, in 1759, five prisoners on the *Royal Oak* hulk at Plymouth who had already obtained imitation passports and were ready to make their getaway, were suddenly arrested. Convinced that they had been betrayed by Jean Maneaux, one of their fellow-prisoners, they determined on revenge. Maneaux the informer was executed in a particularly gruesome manner. In April of that year they were all hanged at Exeter – not for forgery but for murder. At that time, in fact at any time before the 1790s, the incidence of Banknote forgery would have been rare indeed, for the obvious reason that there were no low-denomination notes to forge. No doubt the 'passport' purveyors made as much from their art as the later producers of false paper-money – as it would seem that these much in demand documents were often systematically produced, rather than the work of the lone craftsman. One such established manufactory became known at Winchester Depot in 1780, when two French prisoners betrayed their enterprising fellow countrymen. Craftily, they said how scared they were to say too much, but once sure that they would be rewarded, gave names and even offered to expose the method of production. They barely dodged death and undeservingly gained their freedom. The Winchester Agent informed the authorities:

'I have been obliged this afterrnoon, to take Honoré Martin and Apert out of the prison, that they may go away with the division of prisoners who are to be discharged to-morrow, several prisoners having this morning entered the chamber in which they sleep, with naked knives, declaring most resolutely they were determined to murder them, to prevent which their liberty was granted.'

Stapleton Depot near Bristol was another centre of forged passport production. It would appear that a French woman was deeply involved with the business of supplying these valuable documents to French would-be escapees. Madame Carpentier, who was ostensibly a dealer in legitimate merchandise, had a good deal of influence at the Transport Office through past services rendered to British prisoners in France; probably also in the form of false papers. That influence and the fact that she traded in coffee, tea, sugar and the like, would have gained her easy access to prison hulks and the depots. Although she operated from 46 Foley Street, near Regent Street, London, her connections were far and wide, and certainly touched upon Stapleton. Passports were particularly in demand in the early months of 1814, when officers were anxious to get to France to prove fidelity to the restored monarchy. It was at that time that a Mr Edward Prothero of Harley Street Bristol, informed the Transport Office of the wholesale forgery of passports at Stapleton, and that Madame Carpentier was involved in their distribution. The Treaty of Paris soon after, and her 'influence', probably saved her from punishment in this country.

That the prisoner-produced passports were at least as convincing as the prison-produced notes, is proved by the many records of their successful use in escapes from both shore-based depots and prisons afloat. Reproduction of banknotes, passports, coins and tokens became so widespread that public warning notices were posted up in all the depot markets, and an official was in attendance during market hours to inspect and sign all notes proffered by prisoners. Unless the official was changed very often, his signature would have soon become known to the penmen, and forgery would have been added to forgery. Every depot, and probably most of the hulks, had its forgers' den, and a fair sized volume could be filled with records and reports of trials of both prisoner forgers and their accomplices. The latter were most often the militiamen from the garrison guarding the depots. The rules against fraternisation were strict, but that guards were often involved in both the distribution of false notes and in aiding escapes, is shown by the precautions taken at depots like Dartmoor. There the battalion of militiamen was changed every eight weeks.

It would be cheering to believe that this flouting of the rules was based on a sympathetic feeling for fellow- (though foreign and enemy) servicemen who were having a hard time of it. The truth is less inspiring; most communications between British guard and foreign prisoner were carried out in the language of money – either for favours and privileges or assistance in escape attempts. One Roscommon Militiaman was particularly unlucky in his fraternisation. He accepted a very large bribe to help three Frenchmen to make their escape from Dartmoor, and was given his reward in paper money. The Frenchmen managed a successful getaway, but when the Irishman tried to turn his ill-gotten paper wealth into hard cash, he was arrested for uttering false notes. His was an absolutely hopeless case. The penalty for uttering was death, but had he admitted how he came by the Notes he would have been charged with abetting an escape. For this offence he could have been flogged to death. He said nothing and was hanged in 1812.

The Notes most often imitated were the low denomination issues of Bank of England currency, but local and provincial banks did not escape the prisoners' pens. The chief victims in the Dartmoor area were:

Grant, Burbey & Company, of Plymouth.
The Launceston and Totnes Bank.
The Tamar Bank.
The Plymouth Commercial Bank.
Harris, Langholme & Harris of Plymouth.

We have an account of the makers of prisoner of war artifacts in Dartmoor Depot, from the American prisoner Charles Andrews, which includes the activities of French master penmen. He says, 'They manufactured shoes, hats, hair and bone-work. They likewise, at one time, carried on a very lucrative branch of manufactory. They forged notes on the Bank of England, to the amount of one hundred and fifty thousand pounds sterling; and made so perfect an imitation that the cashier could not discover the forgery; and very much doubted the possibility of such forgery.' And I doubt it, too. Good, the most skilful of them undoubtedly were – but surely not that good.

Bank note production and coining were French specialities, but coining was not exclusive to that nation. Another American, Green Hand, told of a particularly gifted American coiner, who used lead clipped from the prison roof and hardened it with a mixture of his own devising to give it a 'ring'. He said that the finished coin 'would scorn at being compared to the present currency of these degenerate shin-plaster times, which in point of value, is no better than that of Tom Pepper's make'. Tom was nearly caught in the act on one nerve-racking occasion. A group of officials on a tour of inspection suddenly came upon his 'mint', just as he was about to cast. Panic, one would expect but, with 'impudent sang-froid', he asked them how would they like to buy some counterfeit coins, hot from the mould. They laughed, said they were not in the market for medals, and passed on.

There is evidence that prisoners of war as well as the British banks and public sometimes had reason to be concerned at the proliferation of false coinage in the depots. Charles Herbert, who spent more than two years in Old Mill Prison, at Plymouth as a

'rebel' prisoner during the War of American Independence, noted in his journal:

'11 December 1778. At this time, there is considerable bad money in prison, which was brought and handed in as change for good money, by some of the turnkeys or market people, and now that they begin to be suspicious of our going away soon, they will take no more of it, though it has passed in and out for several months, so that there is considerable laying upon our hands, which we are obliged to lose. Some in prison have several shillings and bad half pence.'

Two ex-Governors of Dartmoor mention coining in their histories of the prison. Captain Vernon Harris spoke of the ingenuity with which prisoners turned unpromising materials, such as waste paper, straw and odds and ends of wood, into saleable 'prisoner of war work'; but he went on to say:

'Some of the industries exercised were of a more doubtful character, as we find that the prisoners excelled in producing good imitations of the coins in use, notably the eighteen-penny and three-shilling pieces then current. Forged bank notes were also issued, and were disposed of by the less scrupulous among the soldiers.'

Governor Basil Thomson also recorded that, after the 'Dartmoor Massacre', on the 6th April, 1815, a story was current among the Americans that the soldiers who had fired on them from the walls, did so because they were 'smarting under a cheat', practised on them a few nights earlier when some Yankee prisoners paid them with base coin for smuggling liquor into their prison. Knowing the penalty for smuggling, the soldiers would have had no redress, but the accusation was probably just one of many engendered by natural bitterness and anger at the terrible events of that day.

Some of the French set about their counterfeiting of cash in an original way; they

'...carried on the coining of silver, to a very considerable advantage; they had men constantly employed outside the yard, to collect all the Spanish Dollars they could, and bring them into the prison from the market. Out of every Dollar they made eight smooth English shillings, equally as heavy, and passed as well as any in the kingdom'.

The counterfeiters employed as much skill and craftsmanship to achieve their illegal aims as any forger of banknotes. Their 'set up' was more difficult to hide, involving, as it usually did, a fire, moulds and the pots and crucibles of the trade, and if coins were to be 'struck' there was the consideration of noise. There are less detailed records of the methods used by coiners, mainly because their products were of smaller value individually than the lowest denomination of bank note – and of less concern to the banks. It would be fascinating to learn more of these metalworkers –whether captive or civil – and their techniques, some of which cannot even be guessed at.[5]

Although there is little to suggest that forgery of notes took place in the parole towns, there is more than a hint that false coins were uttered in at least one of those centres for captured officers. On the north side of the High street in the Hampshire parole town of Odiham, was an inn called 'The Tuns' which was one of the hostelries much patronised during the war. Later, when workmen were fitting a new window at the inn, a shower of 'silver' coins spilled out from behind the old frame. The landlady, Mrs Smith, explained that French officers had tried to pass the base coins on to her, but she had hidden them behind the window frame rather than be involved in trouble!

It would seem that counterfeiting was not uncommon among the convicts on the civilian hulks. It was not the practice for captains or officers – or even guards except in exceptional circumstances – to go amongst the prisoners at night; and so they depended on second-hand information and conjecture as to what went on below the battened down decks after sunset. In the Inspector of the Hulk Establishment's annual report to the Home Secretary in 1814, he included the sanguine comments of the Captain of the *Portland* hulk, moored in Langstone Harbour at Portsmouth:

'If any noise like rapping or hammering is heard after a certain hour, they are desired to go to bed, it being known that they are making money, hammering out crowns and half-crowns into sixpences, the manufacture of which he represents as having been carried on by the convicts for some years.'

The record of a counterfeiter's den, set up in the convict-hold of a vessel in the first transport fleet to Botany Bay in 1787, almost defies belief. John White, a surgeon on the transport ship, *Charlotte*, noted in his *Journal* that a convict named Thomas Barrett had started a forgers' ring, making quarter-dollars out of old buckles and pewter spoons:

'The impression, milling, character.was so inimitably executed that had their metal been a little better, the fraud I am convinced, would have passed undetected. How they could effect it at all, is a matter of the most inexpressible surprise to me; as they were never suffered to come near a fire; and a sentinel was constantly placed over their hatchway, which rendered it impossible for either fire or fused metal to be conveyed to their apartments. Besides, hardly ten minutes ever elapsed, without an officer going down among them. The adroitness, therefore, with which they must have managed, in order to complete a business that required so complicated a process, gave me a high opinion of their ingenuity cunning, caution and address.'

All of this was going on whilst the convict fleet made a break in its voyage to Australia and called into Rio de Janeiro. Whilst on shore-leave a Marine, James Baker, tried to pass one of the counterfeited quarter-dollars and the game was up. Thomas Barrett did not receive a severe punishment – although the offence may have been carefully logged and not forgotten. Shortly after he arrived in Australia he achieved a place in history by being the first convict hanged in Sydney – for stealing butter, dried peas and salt pork! The Marine who uttered the false coin was punished with two-hundred lashes. It is interesting to note that of the 736 convicts who were transported on the first ships to Botany Bay, only four had been sentenced for crimes connected with forgery of notes or documents. This was eight years before the Restriction of Cash Payments Order of 1797; after that date the numbers increased greatly.

A convicted prisoner of war who escaped sentence of death, could expect to be sent to a local gaol, but this would not be an alternative welcomed by the banks. Prosecution was an expensive business for the banks concerned. Apart from the normal legal costs, they were expected to contribute towards the subsistence of prisoners during their incarceration. (Incidentally, it makes one wonder what our prisons were like at that time, if it was considered a punishment to transfer a prisoner of war from a hulk or depot to a civil gaol.) An example of the expense involved when convicted forgers were punished short of the gallows, is the case of Nicholas Descamps and Jean Roubillard. These two, prisoners from Norman Cross Depot in Huntingdonshire, were both capitally convicted for forging £1 Bank of England notes. Their Counsel – whose fees were also charged to the Bank – pleaded that they were 'not amenable to the municipal laws of Great Britain', and they were granted a respite. They spent the next nine years in Huntingdon Gaol, until they were pardoned and repatriated when the war ended in 1814. With the expenses involved in examination and inquiries, the trial and prisoners' Counsel's costs, plus five shillings a week each towards their subsistence for nine years, the Bank of England must have cheered their departure.

There were many instances where banks tried to avoid the expense of prosecution in cases where the sentence was more likely to be civil prison than death. When I visited the Archives of the Bank of England, some years ago, Mr E. M. Kelly, who was at that time writing his book, *'Spanish Dollars and Silver Tokens'*, showed me a letter to the bank dated the 9th, June, 1812, which referred to a prisoner in Portchester Castle who was accused of counterfeiting Bank Tokens. The Governors decided that it would be useless to prosecute, as the penalty would be imprisonment, and that he could be put under additional restraint without a costly prosecution.

Quite a number of prisoners saved their accusers the cost of prosecution, by not waiting for their trial. The Edinburgh news sheets for the 21st, July, 1812, reported:

> 'Very early on Sunday morning, seven French prisoners of war, who were committed to the Tolbooth of this city on suspicion of forgery, effected their escape. They were confined to the north-west room on the third storey, and they had penetrated the wall, though very thick, till they got into the chimney of Mr Gilmore's shop (on the ground floor), into which they descended by means of ropes. As they could not force their way out of the shop they ascended a small stair to the room above, from which they took out half of the window, and descended one by one into the street and got clear off.
>
> 'In the course of the morning one of them was retaken in the Grass Market, being traced by the sooty marks of his feet. We understand that, except one, they all speak broken English. They left a note on the table of the shop, saying they had taken nothing away.'

Some time later, three were taken at Glasgow, and another got as far as Dublin before being picked up and for a while was confined to Kilmainham Jail. These four were eventually returned to the Edinburgh Tolbooth – at the expense of the banks, of course. Forgery and coining were as prevalent in Scotland as they were south of the Border but the prisoner of war convicted of those crimes was never as harshly punished as he would have been in England. So much for what was then often termed the 'savage Scot'.

Except in the Isle of Man, where forgery was not a criminal offence, and Guernsey, where possession of false money was punished by gaol and exile from the island, the law was the same in the north as it was in the south. However, no prisoner of war convicted of forgery or counterfeiting offences was ever executed in Scotland; the usual punishment was the civil prison or transfer to the hulks in England. In his specialist study of the Penicuik depots, Greenlaw, Esk Mills and Valleyfield, Ian MacDougall was more positive and said, 'no prisoner at Penicuik was ever tried for or convicted of forgery' in Scotland.[6] By this we must understand that they were never tried or convicted in civil courts – although we know that many of them spent time in tolbooths or civil jails, whilst awaiting the Transport Office decision on their fate. Which was, more often than not, transfer south to the hulks at Chatham, Portsmouth or Plymouth. It will be seen that the accused in almost all the High Court cases cited, were militiamen guards or civilian visitors to the prison markets who went there to collect and pass on prisoner-produced 'notes' or 'specie'.

'One of these trials was of Thomas Gray, a soldier stationed with the Kirkcudbrightshire Militia at Penicuik the previous December [1813] when a search had been made in the barrack room for forged notes. Gray was found to possess false notes to the value of £33 of four banks. He said he had found them in a parcel near the stockade. Despite a clever defence by his advocate, Henry Cockburn, later Lord Cockburn, Gray was found guilty and sentenced to fourteen years transportation, but soon afterward the Prince Regent reduced his sentence to six months imprisonment. Among several civilians indicted, two were not so fortunate as Gray. Nathaniel Blair, alias Sawers, a hackney carriage and horse-and-cart keeper, was found guilty of forging, uttering and selling forged notes that he had obtained from Valleyfield or Greenlaw depots, and was sentenced to be hanged at Edinburgh. While awaiting execution Blair hanged himself in the condemned cell. One who did not cheat the official hangman was James McDougall, executed in Edinburgh in August 1814 for 'vending false notes.' Ian MacDougall also quoted extracts from Edinburgh newspapers which reported other examples of forgery in the Scottish depots. The Lord Advocate's papers show that at Edmonstone near Dalkeith, John Shaw was arrested with two Bank of Scotland £1 notes on him – 'part obviously of those fabricated by French prisoners at the depot.' In January 1913 three other Aberdeen Militiamen were arrested in Glasgow on suspicion of forgery. In early April the *Edinburgh Evening Courant* reported: 'In Edinburgh of late the issuing of forged notes among the lower orders of society, has become a branch of traffic to a considerable extent and men and women frequently convicted.' In August the paper reported more forged notes in circulation. 'Counterfeit notes', the *Courant* reported on the 16th December, 'the greater part on the the Bank of Scotland and Perth Banks, are at present very prevalent in the South of Scotland.' The Procurator Fiscal for Edinburgh in 1812, noted:

> 'All the prisoners of war who had been charged with fabricating or issuing forged notes had, by order of the Board, been sent aboard the Admiral's ship at Leith [HMS *Adamant*] to be forwarded to Chatham – that the prisoners were seventeen in number, viz., nine confined in [Edinburgh] gaol, and eight brought in from Valleyfield depot.'

For a general account of the activities of forgers among the prisoners of war in Scotland, I cannot do better than employ the information contained in an article by the banker, J. Macbeth Forbes, which appeared in the *Bankers' Magazine*, Vol. LXVII. for March, 1899. I have managed to track down most of the notices and newspaper articles which he mentioned and was personally involved in the rediscovery of the so-called 'implements of forgery', 'taken red-handed from the prisoners at Valleyfield.'

Forbes wrote:

> 'Forgery is the royal road to wealth, but if it is one thing to make a note, it is a much more difficult matter to put it into circulation. Among the sentries who guarded the palisades there were always some who could be got at, especially when they were militiamen. The regular troops were at the seat of war and could not be spared for guarding the prisoners. They then made friends with worthless persons coming about the markets, whom they induced to float their notes in return for a share in the plunder.'

The first discovery of forgery by prisoners in Edinburgh Castle depot was made in 1811. The false Note was a copy of a Bank of Scotland guinea dated the 11th October, 1808. This was not, of course, the first forgery of banknotes detected in Scotland. In fact, the bank experts who had examined many examples in the past, considered that they could easily recognise French workmanship – and spelling. The first giveaway in the case of the one guinea note mentioned above was its size, it was three-quarters of an inch longer than the genuine article. The seals were only faintly embossed. and the signatures were 'ill imitated'. Nevertheless, the experts were at first uncertain as to whether or not it had been engraved. Finally, after very thorough scrutiny, they concluded that it was executed with pen and printers ink and definitely not engraved. It had been discovered on the 30th, July, 1811 and during the following weeks other guinea notes, obviously from the same source, turned up daily. Towards the end of August the engraved plate from which they had been reproduced was delivered up to a bank teller in the town. So much for the 'experts'! This set of forgeries and their plate became well-known at the time, as the 'Milldam Forgeries'. The plate had been found by a miller and his men when they were cleaning out the Mill Lade (mill-race) at Stockbridge. They were rewarded with a guinea – a genuine one – for their trouble.

In that same year, 1811, a number of Scottish banks, including the Bank of Scotland, the British Linen Company, the Leith and Aberdeen Banking Companies and Sir William Forbes & Co., got together with the Stamp Office with the idea of economising by sharing the expense of inquiries in connection with the forgery of paper money. Whilst they agreed that this would be cheaper than pursuing separate inquiries, it was decided that when it came to actual indictments and trials, each bank should pursue its own course. The Stamp Office acted for itself, because, as all Scottish Notes in those days bore an impressed Government Stamp, forgeries were thus a fraud on the Revenue as well as the banks.

As in England, the prosecutions and trials could be a costly business in Scotland. There, it was most unlikely that a convicted prisoner of war would be dealt with economically by hanging him, so the directors of the banks were often reluctant to prosecute. Civilian fakers also often got away with it on the same grounds. In a famous case which was heard on the 8th September, 1812, Alex Thomson, alias Laurie, was tried before the High Court on a charge of uttering forged notes. When he was arrested and searched, he was found to have a packet of six false one pound notes 'hidden between the sole of his foot and his stocking' – a clear case if ever there was one. At the enquiry he at first gave a most improbable account of how he came by them, but later confessed that he had a contact in the Cambridgeshire Militia, who bought the notes – which he called 'pictures' – on his instructions, from prisoner forgers in the Valleyfield Depot for two shillings each.

The interesting, and important, thing about this case was the legal stand taken by the banks. They argued that, whilst they were willing to bear the costs of precognitions and examinations, the Board of Stamps should bear the cost of the trial. The bank concerned felt that this was an opportunity for public example; that banks were public institutions, performing public functions, and as such should be protected by the law. They said that the felony of forgery was a public felony, committed against the lieges, and that it 'originated with prisoners of war, of whom there is an extraordinary number in this country'. The point was not taken and, as the bank refused to prosecute, Alex Thomson got away with it; he would not have stood a chance south of the Border, and dealing with the Bank of England. This action lent strength to the revolt against private prosecutions in criminal cases, and it is possible that the office of Public Prosecutor made its appearance in Scotland much earlier than in England, because of the attitude of the Scottish banks.

The joint agreement regarding inquiries lasted only a few months. But during its short life it was responsible for advertisements in the *Edinburgh Gazette* and the newspapers of most of the Border parole towns. These notices offered a reward of £100 for information leading to the discovery of anyone manufacturing or issuing versions of the paper currency of the banks concerned. The Bank of Scotland published similar advertisements and offered the same generous reward. Their description of the craftsmanship of the captive fakers was not very complimentary; which was, to my mind, ill-advised. It would have been wiser to have alerted people to the possibility of skilful forgeries – and these most certainly existed – than to have described only the badly produced imitations which would have fooled only fools.

ADVERTISEMENT

'Several forged Notes, in imitation of the Notes of the Governor and Company of the Bank of Scotland, have appeared chiefly in the neighbourhood of the depots of French prisoners of war. A caution is hereby, on the part of the said Governors and Company, given against receiving such forged Notes in payment.

'And whosoever shall, within three months of the date hereof, give such information as shall become sufficient, on lawful trial, to convict anyone concerned in forging or feloniously uttering any of the said Notes, shall receive a reward of a hundred pounds sterling.

'These forged Notes are executed by hand with a pen or pencil, without any engraving. In most of them the body of the note has the appearance of foreign handwriting. The names of the Bank officials are mostly illegible or ill-spelled. The ornamented characters of the figures generally ill-executed. The seals are very ill-imitated. To this mark particular attention is requested.'

Any who had taken the Bank's advertisement as a worthwhile guide, would no doubt have been fooled by the 'notes' described in the following newspaper article:

Edinburgh Evening Courant. 25 September 1811.
'On Wednesday, three French prisoners from Greenlaw were brought to town and lodged in the Jail on suspicion of having committed a forgery on some of the banks here. The notes are finely executed and it appeared on an investigation by the Sheriff, had been fabricated with a pen and pencil.'

Similar reward notices were posted up outside the depots and a version in French was displayed inside all the depots and in the *cautionnements*. These posters helped in as much as they encouraged everyone to look twice before accepting paper money, especially for small sums, as the Bank's one pound and one guinea notes, and those of the old Commercial Banking Company of Scotland, were of very simple design and most often copied.

In October 1811, a young Dutch prisoner at Valleyfield informed the Agent, Captain Moriarty, that forgery was being carried on in the Depot, enabling him to 'detect a French Prisoner concerned in the Fabrication of Forged Bank Notes.' The lad was playing a dangerous game in passing on such information to the Agent, and obviously did it in hope of reward; but his greatest reward was that his neck was saved from the vengeance of his fellow prisoners. He was sent to the Vice-Admiral's Flagship at Leith, before being sent south to Plymouth. That was probably as close as he got to Holland before the war ended. It seems that he had lodged similar information against three Plymouth prisoners, which later proved to be unfounded. 'Captain Moriarty was cautioned by the Transport Board against giving too much Credit to plausible statements of Prisoners.'

The turnkeys of all the depots were ordered to keep a strict watch on not only the prisoners but their guards and overseers. In 1811, the Deputy Governor of Edinburgh Castle, Lord Rosslyn, instructed his turnkey, John Campbell who was brother of a Bank of Scotland official, to 'observe strictly all transactions by the prisoners during the market hours, with the view of seeing if they try to pass notes'. They were still keeping diligent, but not altogether successful, watch two years later. In July, 1813, the Clerk of the Valleyfield Depot reported twenty-six forged guinea notes which the turnkey had detected as they were about to be sold in the market. And a newspaper report of November of that same year read:

'Mr. Aitken, Keeper of the Canongate Tolbooth, detected and took from the person of a private soldier in the Militia Regiment stationed over the French prisoners in Penicuik and who had come into the Canongate prison to see a friend, forged guinea and twenty-shilling notes, on two different banks in this city, and two of them in the country, amounting to nearly £70. The soldier was immediately given over to the civil power, and from thence to the regiment to which he belonged, until the matter was further investigated.'

From all this it is obvious that the manufacture of fraudulent money was no small-time enterprise, entered into by poor and desperate prisoners of war only as a last resort. Once a group of suitably talented prisoners had decided that the manufacture of false notes, or the counterfeiting of coins, should be the wartime occupation of its captive members, they set about the matter with all the industry and thoroughness displayed by those other groups who produced straw-work or carvings in bone or wood. That it was a highly organised business is shown by the fact that it had its wholesale organisations where false notes were dealt with by the packet and, perhaps an even greater proof, it had its own trade terminology or jargon. We have already heard of forged notes being referred to as 'pictures', and there were other words used to describe notes sold in bulk. Dr William Chambers, in his *Early Recollections*, remembered the trial of a Peebles man accused of uttering, where small packets of false notes were referred to as 'Small Yarn', whilst bigger packs were labelled 'Large Yarn' (so called because they were wrapped in bundles misleadingly so labelled), and as will be shown later, some imitations were known as 'Toys'.

Whilst there is no doubt that many prisoner-of-war-produced 'pictures' were fabricated in quantity from engraved plates, many, perhaps the majority, were hand-drawn, by penmen whose skills varied from the brilliant to the ham-fisted. The partially executed one guinea note on the Bank of Scotland is a remarkable relic, as it gives a clue to the penman's *modus operandi*. Macbeth Forbes was puzzled by the system of dotted lines and says, 'the forger may have feared his imitative powers were not equal to a right off reproduction. In any case, these brilliant penmen must have had some good reason for the course which they adopted'.

I believe I know that good reason. The technique of the dotted layout is probably an example of 'pouncing', which was, and is, a method used by designers, signwriters and the like, to transfer the general outline of the design to be duplicated. The forger or one of his team would have taken a genuine note and pricked through the design and lettering with some sharp-pointed instrument, probably a needle or small wheeled pouncing tool – which could have been easily obtained through the outside distributor of his work. He would then lay the genuine, and now perforated, note over his new 'banknote' paper and sprinkle it with 'pounce', a powder of charcoal, blacklead, or any other fine dark dust. Rubbing the powder through the perforations would then produce a dotted reproduction of the original note onto the paper underneath, thus providing an accurate guide for the calligrapher. This 'master note' could be used over and over again to produce any number of layouts for the penman to work to. The 'pouncing' method would have been employed by only the serious mass-producers, the one-off imitator would of course be destroying a genuine note to produce a dud!

Whilst I feel confident that the above theory explains the dots, I am less certain as to the way in which the ingenious captives employed so-called 'watermark' tools. The translucent effect of the genuine watermark is achieved during the course of paper manufacture by making it thinner where the design occurs. It could hardly be convincingly imitated by stamping, other than by crushing at a terrific pressure, far beyond that which a bone tool could withstand. However, a fairly convincing false 'watermarking' can be achieved in a number of ways: by printing or drawing the design with a clear matt varnish or with certain acids, which make the paper less opaque where

applied. All manner of unusual substances have been tried in this the most difficult of the forger's obstacles, including stamping with spermaceti wax and a drying agent and, more recently, typewriter correction fluid.

If bone plates were intended as 'watermark' tools, then it is just possible that some success may have been achieved by pressing the bone tool into false 'prison-made' paper before it was transferred from the wire, and still in a state more water than solid; but it is more likely that the tools would have been used as blocks to print a varnish image – I believe that earlier this century the stamps of New Zealand bore printed 'watermarks'. Or perhaps they were purely experimental; the unsuccessful efforts of a prisoner of war forgery-team in one of the dens in Valleyfield Depot, where they were found.

It is certain that the most convincing of prisoner of war forgeries were the result of teamwork rather than individual enterprise – and the penman, himself, was not the only important member of the team. There would have been the contact man, whose responsibility was the delicate and vital one of deciding who was likely to be bribable among the guards or civilian visitors to the depot markets. Inks, brushes and the quills for pens would have to be brought in discreetly; and paper of the right quality and substance could only have been obtained, in the main, through the assistance of outside accomplices.

I say 'in the main' for, after handling so much prisoner of war work over so many years – work which could only have been produced by brilliantly inventive adaptation of materials at hand and pains-taking effort – I would not put paper-making beyond the bounds of their ingenuity. The materials required are simple enough: a fine-wire mesh with a deep removable frame; the facilities for boiling up and beating old rags into fibre pulp; deep trays or tanks and plenty of water. And, if they got that far, the production of a 'genuine' watermark would have been simplicity itself. The design of the watermark could be made up from strips of wire and fixed to the surface of the wire mesh, so that when the frame was dipped into a tray of rag fibres suspended in water, and the framed wire lifted to allow the water to drain away, the fibres would settle less thickly over the raised portion of the design. Left to dry and held up to the light: *Voilà!* – a 'genuine' watermark.

Maybe they tried to make their own paper and watermarks, maybe not, but we know they made their own pens. Steel pen nibs had not been invented at that time, but a crow quill can be easily made into an excellent pen.

Another very important member of the den would be the carver in bone, ivory or wood – at least in Scotland. His job would have been to reproduce the Government stamp and the seals of the banks. The forger's object was to create an as good as possible general impression of the real thing, and a reasonable copy of these embossings was essential to give the 'feel of money' to the piece of paper. The seals were cut and carved from polished sheep bone, and when the penman had finished his work the necessary embossed effect would have been accomplished by placing the appropriate dies in position on the note and striking once with a hammer.

Although the prisoners of war in Scotland usually and naturally chose Scottish banks on whom to practise their deceptive art, false Bank of England Notes turned up from time to time, as did another type of false money. This latter effort to defraud could be perhaps more properly labelled trickery rather than forgery. It turned up more often in the South than the North, but a Scottish newspaper reported on the 22nd October, 1811:

> 'Several attempts have been made in Edinburgh to utter notes in imitation of notes of the Bank of England. They are of the description known as 'Fleet' notes, which, instead of bearing values of one, two, five, ten, or twenty pounds, as at first sight would be imagined, are only for so many pence – the word pence in the imitation note being substituted for pounds in the real one.'

It is thought that the 'Fleet Notes', or 'Fleet Penny Notes', originated in the Fleet Prison in London. The idea behind them was a clever one. Should a person be apprehended whilst in possession, he could argue that these were not forgeries of pound notes, and as there were no pence notes there could not be forgeries of them. There were variations on the 'Fleet Notes', where 'Pins', 'Pens' and similar words were substituted for Pounds. Clever as the idea was as a defence against the gallows, these were cynically

made to dupe the illiterate, as a literate person would have spotted the deceit immediately.

It was not long before the authorities stopped up the loophole of this and other tricky ways around the law. In 1812 a far-sweeping Act was passed in London, prohibiting plate-makers, printers and engravers from preparing plates bearing figures which could be printed in white on 'black or sable ground'. This Act was used against the 'Fleet Note' manufacturers and the products of any other similar subterfuges. A civilian, one Charles Carlisle, caught in possession of 'Fleet' notes, put up the argument that they were not paper money at all, that he only had them as 'a toy' and that 'at the Trafalgar Hosiery in the City Road they have them in the window'; but it got him nowhere, or rather, it got him to Botany Bay. It is surprising that these notes should have had any success whatsoever; but that they did, and sometimes for large sums, tells us something of the gullibility and illiteracy of their victims.

****

I will end this record of fraud and deception as practised by our foreign captives all over Britain, with the words of Dr William Chambers of Peebles. That kindly Scotsman was perfectly serious when he excused them by saying that they were:

> '...in a state of utter idleness which led, as we have seen, to criminal acts – forging bank notes, as it were, to relieve the tedium of their dismal incarceration'.

The Prisoner of War 'Implements of Forgery'.

Many years ago, whilst studying the Macbeth Forbes Papers in the Scottish Records Office in Edinburgh, I determined to try to track down the 'implements of forgery', if that were still possible. On returning south, I wrote to both the Royal Bank of Scotland and the Bank of Scotland with my query. The Royal Bank replied that there was no record in the Minutes to show that any of their notes had been forged at that time; but helpfully referred me to a page in *The History of the Bank of Scotland*, which read:

> ' ...in the years 1811 to 1815 a series of forgeries of £1 and guinea notes of several banks gave much uneasiness to them. The majority of the forged notes were traced to French prisoners of war stationed in the dungeons of Edinburgh Castle, and the camps at Greenlaw, Valleyfield and Penicuik. The Minutes record fully the steps taken to find the culprits, by the printing of placards in French and in English which were placed in the camps, announcing the frauds and offering rewards to informers. The Frenchmen concerned had fabricated the notes, it was believed, with the connivance of some English[!] militiamen who were guards at the camps. Seventeen Frenchmen were convicted and sent to the Admiralty hulks at Chatham. Those of their notes still extant display fine craftsmanship, the most curious having been executed with the aid of sheep's bones.'

The letter ended with the encouraging information that a footnote to the above stated that 'the original "matrix" is in the Head Office of the Bank of Scotland.'

I immediately wrote to the then Chief Cashier of the Bank of Scotland, Mr J. A. Winton, who regretfully replied that he had no knowledge of the whereabouts or survival of the items I had mentioned and that the archivist who may have been able to help me had retired some time ago. I decided not to give in easily and, unfairly, described the great help I had received from the Bank of England Archives department. Mr Winton replied that whilst the Bank did possess many items of historical interest, there was 'no museum as such, nor as yet any comprehensive record, with the result that the knowledge of the existence and whereabouts of particular items has presumably gone with the retiral of various officials over the years.' I replied, '…it is a great pity when historically valuable collections become separated from their documentation; and feel sure that you share my hope that one day this state of affairs will be rectified in the case of your ancient Bank.' And so our correspondence went to-and-froing for more than a year – and I must admit that the Chief Cashier showed great patience and was most conscientious in replying to my importunities. Then I had an idea. Perhaps the Bank could call on the retired archivist at my expense and assuring full acknowledgments.

After only a short silence I received the letter I had long awaited; a delighted Mr Winton informed me that the relics had been unearthed – incidentally at no charge to me – and invited me to Edinburgh to be among the first to inspect the long lost illegal artifacts. They were found in a large album-like volume, some of the pages of thick card with countersunk cutouts to take the bone 'implements'. However, that was not all; on other pages were wonderful proof specimens of notes dating back to the end of the seventeenth century! Two years later I received my last letter from Mr Winton, again inviting me to Edinburgh and telling me that 'since your visit the Bank has embarked on a thorough cataloguing of all its historical collection of items with a view to creating a small museum, and the relics in which you have a personal interest will form an important part of it.' What could be more rewarding?

Prisoner of War Paper Money?
There is a possibility that there was such a thing as 'Prisoner of War Money'; but I have seen only one example of such a Note. Spinks & Son showed it to me when they were preparing an auction catalogue a few years ago. It was handwritten on cream paper:

5 Livres, Leith. 3 Jan. 1812. Serial No.1812 (?),
at Shortbridge, Scot & Co.
and overprinted on the obverse
BANK FIVE 5 LIVRES.

Spinks conjectured that it was a 'private store note, for use with prisoners of war'. I cannot explain its purpose; but can only think its use may have been confined to paroled officers.

The Prisoner of War Forgers and Coiners.
The BANK OF ENGLAND kindly allowed me to examine Prisoner of War Forgeries which they have preserved in their Archives.

The Notes illustrated were hand-drawn by French penmen confined to the hulks. Considering the conditions under which they were produced they can only be described as brilliant examples of calligraphy. It is difficult to imagine how, on a crowded prison ship, in poor light and with makeshift materials, such penmanship was possible.

1. W.T.W. Tone ed.: *'Life of Theobald Wolfe Tone'*.

2. In April 1995, The Regional Crime Squad discovered £18,000,000 in forged Notes in an East London lock-up garage.

3. Judith Kelly's Prayer Book and Pardon are preserved in the Bank of England Printing Department. R. Thurston Hopkins: *Famous Bank Forgeries.1936.*

4. After 1821 the Bank of England one pound note was dropped from the national currency until the introduction of the one pound Treasury Note at the outbreak of World War I in 1914. The issue of Bank of England one pound notes was resumed in 1928.

5. When some sheds among the prison blocks at Stapleton Prison were demolished a few years before the end of the wars, a number of interesting discoveries were made: materials needed in the counterfeiting of coins and the forging of false banknotes – and an illicit still!

6. Ian MacDougall: *The Prisoners at Penicuik.*

Index

(Page numbers in **bold** refer to illustrations.)